THE SUPPLY
MANAGEMENT PROCESS

Alan R. Raedels, Ph.D., C.P.M.
School of Business Administration
Portland State University

Published by: National Association of Purchasing Management, Inc.
Paul Novak, C.P.M., A.P.P., Chief Executive Officer

© 2000 National Association of Purchasing Management, Inc.
P.O. Box 22160 Tempe, AZ 85285-2160 USA
www.napm.org

INTRODUCTION

Supply management professionals provide many valuable and important contributions to organizations throughout the world, whether they are public, for profit, or non-profit, and across all sectors. The field is quickly evolving and changing, reflecting the evolution of technology, the Internet, heightened professional standards, and increased collaboration between different internal departments, between suppliers, between customes, and between organizations. Supply management is affecting the bottomline more than ever before, and is "value added" for all companies and their financial success.

This new environment, however, requires all supply management professionals to stay on top of the tools, practices, policies, and knowledge relevant not only to supply management, but to the business environment as a whole. NAPM is dedicated to building the professional through education and professional development. The NAPM Supply Management Knowledge Series (previously known as the NAPM Professional Development Series) was developed to assist the supply management professional do this.

The Series has been updated to include an analysis and discussion of newly emerging trends and the new tools, practices, policies, and knowledge that have developed from these trends. Our goal in publishing the Series is to encourage and support your professional growth and contribute to the image of the profession, and to assist you with learning about and mastering these new skills . . . basically, to help you do your job the best you can.

In addition, the books are a resource for preparing for the C.P.M. and A.P.P. certification exams. The exams were also recently updated and many of the topics addressed in this four-volume series appear on these new exams.

It is my intention that NAPM will not only continue its efforts to support and build the supply management profession, but will also add to it. The NAPM Supply Management Knowledge Series is a part of these efforts.

Paul Novak, C.P.M., A.P.P.
Chief Executive Officer
NAPM
August 2000

i

NAPM – YOUR SOURCE FOR SUPPLY MANAGEMENT RESOURCES

Since 1915, the National Association of Purchasing Management (NAPM) has served thousands of supply management professionals from around the world. Domestically, NAPM works with affiliated associations across the country to continually keep its members well informed, and trained on the latest trends and developments in the field.

The information available from NAPM is extensive. One of the greatest resources is the NAPM Web site, www.napm.org. In addition to general information, this expansive site features a vast database of supply management information, much of which is available solely to members. Information includes a listing of general supply management references as well as an extensive article database, listings of products and seminars available, periodicals listing, an Online Career Center with job listings and resumes posted, contact information for NAPM affiliate organizations nationwide, and links to other related Web sites.

The monthly Manufacturing and Non-Manufacturing *NAPM Report On Business®*, including the Purchasing Managers' Index (PMI) in the manufacturing survey, continues to be one of the key economic indicators available today. NAPM members receive this valuable report in the pages of Purchasing Today® magazine, one of the many benefits of membership.

The quarterly publication *NAPM InfoEdge* is also included in membership. *NAPM InfoEdge* provides unique, how-to approaches on single supply management topics.

NAPM also publishes *The Journal of Supply Chain Management*, a one-of-a-kind publication designed especially for experienced supply management professionals. Authored exclusively by accomplished practitioners and academicians, this quarterly publication targets purchasing and supply management issues, leading-edge research, long-term strategic developments, emerging trends, and more.

Members also enjoy discounts on a wide variety of educational products and services, along with reduced enrollment fees, for educational seminars and conferences held throughout the country each year. Topics cover the entire supply management spectrum.

For executives interested in professional certification, NAPM administers the Certified Purchasing Manager (C.P.M.) and Accredited Purchasing Practitioner (A.P.P.) programs. Members receive discounts on test preparation/study materials and C.P.M./A.P.P. exam fees.

To provide a forum for educational enhancement and networking, NAPM holds the Annual International Purchasing Conference. This is a unique opportunity for members and non-members alike to learn from each other and share success strategies.

To learn more about NAPM and the many ways it can help you advance your career, or to join online, visit NAPM on the Web at www.napm.org. To apply for membership by telephone, please call NAPM customer service at 800/888-6276 or 480/752-6276, extension 401.

THE NAPM SUPPLY MANAGEMENT KNOWLEDGE SERIES

Volume 1
THE SUPPLY MANAGEMENT PROCESS
Alan R. Raedels

Volume 2
THE SUPPLY MANAGEMENT ENVIRONMENT
Stanley E. Fawcett

Volume 3
SUPPLY MANAGEMENT FOR VALUE ENHANCEMENT
Lisa M. Ellram and Thomas Y. Choi

Volume 4
THE SUPPLY MANAGEMENT LEADERSHIP PROCESS
Anna Flynn and Sam Farney

SERIES OVERVIEW

In the past decade, purchasing has moved to the center stage of the organization as it has become increasingly clear that purchasing and supply management can make a significant contribution to organizational success. Beyond simply reducing prices for purchased goods and services, purchasing can add value to organizations in many ways, including supporting organizational strategy, improving inventory management, forging closer working relationships with key suppliers, and maintaining an active awareness of supply market trends. The ability of purchasing to significantly contribute to organizational success is the core of this four-book series.

While differences exist among various types of organizations, industries, business sectors, regions of the world, and types of items purchased, these books provide an overview of current issues in purchasing and supply management. The topics covered in this series range from the basics of good purchasing practice to leading-edge, value enhancement strategies. These four books provide an excellent survey of the core principles and practices common to all sectors within the field of purchasing and supply management.

These four volumes were designed to support the National Association of Purchasing Management (NAPM) certification program leading to the Accredited Purchasing Practitioner (A.P.P.) and Certified Purchasing Manager (C.P.M.) designations. They also provide practical and current coverage of key topics in the field for those interested in enhancing their knowledge. They also can serve as useful textbooks for college courses in purchasing.

The textbooks are organized around the four modules of the C.P.M. exam as follows:

1. *The Supply Management Process* (for C.P.M.s and A.P.P.s)
2. *The Supply Management Environment* (for C.P.M.s and A.P.P.s)
3. *Supply Management for Value Enhancement Strategies* (for C.P.M.s only)
4. *The Supply Management Leadership Process* (for C.P.M.s only)

Volume 1, *The Supply Management Process*, focuses on the overall purchasing process and its major elements. It looks at the requisitioning process, sourcing, bidding, and supplier evaluation, and offers an overview of cost and contract management. This volume also examines how technology has changed procurement techniques and provides a summary of the key legal issues facing purchasers.

Volume 2, *The Supply Management Environment*, explores how the ever-changing environment in which purchasers operate is affecting their roles today and in the future. Volume 2 provides an overview of purchasing's role in strategy and looks at how globalization, just-in-time/mass customization are affecting purchasing. This volume also explores issues related to negotiations, quality, reengineering, and supply chain management. It examines the increased role and impact of information technology on purchasing, and looks at what skill sets will be required for success in purchasing in the future.

Volume 3, *Supply Management for Value Enhancement Strategies*, explores a number of traditional and leading-edge approaches for increasing purchasing's contributions to organizational success. The volume begins by looking at outsourcing and lease versus buy issues. It then delves into the many issues associated with inventory management, including inventory classification and disposal. Specific value enhancement methods, such as standardization, value analysis, early supplier involvement, and target costing, are also presented. The volume closes with a discussion of developing and using forecast data, and offers an overview of specific strategies to apply in various purchasing situations.

Volume 4, *The Supply Management Leadership Process*, provides an overview of key general management issues specifically applied to purchasing activities and purchasing's role in the organization. It begins with an overview of strategic planning and budgeting processes, and continues by presenting specific issues related to effectively recruiting, managing, and retaining good employees. Volume 4 then discusses the role of operating policies and procedures, tools to manage workflow, and performance monitoring. It ends with a presentation of how to most effectively present purchasing performance results within the organization.

It has been a privilege to edit this series for NAPM and to work with an excellent group of authors. The authors' practical and theoretical knowledge has contributed to the quality of these books. I hope you find them both useful and interesting.

Lisa M. Ellram
Series Editor

PREFACE

This book covers the purchasing process from recognition of a need through contract closeout. The purpose of this book is to provide the practitioner with an overview and grounding in the fundamentals of each of these areas. Simultaneously, the text provides information to aid the practitioner in understanding the material that is covered by *Module 1: Purchasing Process of the Certified Purchasing Manager and the Accredited Purchasing Practitioner Examination.*

All the Web addresses presented in this text were verified before publication. However, because the World Wide Web (WWW) is a dynamic entity, there is a high probability one or more of the URLs listed will no longer be valid by the time this book is in publication.

Acknowledgements

I wish to give special thanks to my friend and colleague, Lee Buddress. Without his help, insights, encouragement, and suggestions this work would not have been possible. I would also like to thank Lisa Ellram, Ph.D., C.P.M., C.P.A., C.M.A., series editor; Scott Sturzl, C.P.M., NAPM vice president of certification; and Cindy Zigmund, project coordinator, for their support, help, and patience through this process. Lastly, I would like to acknowledge the work of the authors of Module 1 of the seventh edition of the C.P.M. Study Guide: Lee Buddress, Ph.D., C.P.M.; Larry C. Giunipero, Ph.D., C.P.M.; Carolyn Gordon, C.P.M.; Mary Lu Harding, C.P.M.; Gene Keel, C.P.M.; Carla Lallatin, C.P.M., CPPO; H. Ervin Lewis, C.P.M.; Michael A. McGinnis, Ph.D., C.P.M.; Eugene W. Muller, Ed.D.; Helen M. Pohlig, Esq.; and W. J."Jack" Wagner, C.P.M. Their work provided the foundation upon which much of this book was built.

Alan R. Raedels, Ph.D., C.P.M.

To my wife, Debbie, and my daughters, Sara and Alicia.

CONTENTS

Chapter 3: Cost Analysis: How Good is the Deal?

Chapter 4: The Sourcing Process: How Do I Identify Potential Suppliers?

Chapter 5: The Competitive Bid Process: Which Type of Solicitation Should I Use?

Chapter 6: The Supplier Evaluation Process: Is This the Right Supplier?

**Chapter 7: The Legal Issues: How Do You Avoid
Going to Court?**

Chapter 8: Managing the Contract: You Want to Change What and Want It When?

Chapter 9: The Future of the Purchasing Process: Where Do We Go from Here?

CHAPTER 1

THE PURCHASING PROCESS: WHAT IS PURCHASING'S ROLE?

Chapter Objectives

- Understand what purchasing will need to do to help an organization compete.
- Delineate why purchasing is important to an organization.
- Identify the role purchasing should play in the future.
- Provide an overview of the purchasing process and its objectives.

Introduction

Organizations are currently experiencing increased competition; rapid changes in technologies; an increased emphasis on quality, total cost, long-term contracts, supplier base rationalization, and inventory reduction; increased outsourcing; and reductions in purchasing staffs. Purchasing has seen a phase-out of the traditional adversarial relationships between purchasers and suppliers and the phase-in of partnerships based upon mutual trust and respect; increased use of value analysis; increased use of single sourcing; and doing more work with fewer people.

This chapter begins by identifying what purchasing needs to do to help organizations compete in today's environment followed by a look at purchasing's importance to the organization. Next follows an overview of purchasing's new role and an overview of the purchasing process and objectives.

Competing in Tomorrow's Markets

Creating competitive advantage is what organizational strategy is all about. To compete in today's environment, organizations need to be competitive in terms of cost, quality, delivery performance, lead-time, time-to-market, and flexibility. How does this affect purchasing?

- **Purchase order price versus total cost** - The purchaser must deal with the total cost to the organization, not just the price on the purchase order. The lowest quoted price does not always equal the lowest total cost to the organization. The purchaser must evaluate the total cost of ownership (see Chapter 3).
- **Quality** - Defects result in additional work for the purchaser and additional overhead costs due to rework, production shut downs, late shipments, and lost customers. The purchaser can lessen the impact of these problems by exercising care in supplier selection and management of the quality process (see Chapters 2 and 6).
- **Reduced cycle times and leadtimes** - Purchasing can contribute to reducing cycle times and leadtimes by improving incoming quality, ensuring more frequent deliveries, ensuring early purchasing involvement and early supplier involvement in new product design and modification, reducing the supply base, and increasing usage of partnerships and alliances.
- **Paperless purchasing** - Purchasers can reduce transaction costs through the effective use of computers, electronic data interchange (EDI), procurement cards, and e-commerce.
- **Purchasing personnel** - Purchasers need to develop new skills and hone existing ones. Some organizations are hiring purchasers who have earned dual degrees (one technical and one business) and the C.P.M. designation. Exhibit 1.1 presents a summary of purchasing skill requirements for the future.
- **Outsourcing** - There is an increased movement of entire business functions to outside suppliers as companies focus on their core competencies. Purchasing must provide the analysis and understanding to aid management in making such decisions by bringing its knowledge of the supply markets to the decisionmaking process.

Purchasing has much to contribute to an organization's success. Organizations that desire to successfully compete in current and future markets must respond to the competitive issues discussed above.

EXHIBIT 1.1
Future Purchasing Skills Set Requirements

Purchasing Skills	Operational Skills
• Supply chain management • Supplier selection and evaluation • Supplier management • International sourcing experience • Knowledge of markets and industries • Competitive analysis • Familiarity with transportation issues	• Production planning • MRP/ERP • Capacity requirements planning • Knowledge of manufacturing and service process • Inventory management experience
Financial Skills	**Technical Skills**
• Familiarity with currency fluctuations • Price and cost analysis • Total cost of ownership • Activity-based costing • Knowledge of make-versus-buy issues (outsourcing) • Financial evaluation of suppliers	• Negotiations • Project management • Cycle-time analysis • Commodity expertise • Information technology

Importance of Purchasing and Supply Management

Organizations are finally beginning to understand the importance and potential impact of purchasing. Purchasing can affect an organization's cost structure, leadtimes, time-to-market, flexibility, quality, and profitability.

Cost Structure

Today's highly competitive markets have forced organizations to look for new ways to reduce total costs. Purchasing can contribute to cost reduction in several ways. One approach is to consolidate the supply base and thereby increase the organization's ability to leverage its volumes to obtain lower prices and improved service. Also, purchasing's selection of suppliers will affect a number of costs such as incoming inspection, rework, warranties, stockouts, and backorders. Purchasing can also affect transaction costs by its choice of purchasing policies regarding small orders.

Effect on Leadtime and Time-to-Market

Competition is no longer between organizations but between supply chains. The supply chain that can respond the fastest to market changes will be the winner. Purchasing plays an important role in time-based competition because of its ability to affect time-related processes and activities. Purchasing can affect material ordering cycle-time components such as communication of requirements to suppliers, the supplier's ordering and manufacturing cycle time, delivery from suppliers, and incoming receiving and inspection.

According to a survey by Trent and Monczka, the average product development cycle time declined from 3.2 years in 1990 to less than 2.5 years in 1997.[1] Organizations will continue to reduce cycle times especially in new product and service development. Organizations expect a 40 to 45 percent reduction in product development cycle times over the next several years. One way this will be accomplished is through early supplier involvement.[2]

Effect on Flexibility

Flexibility is an organization's ability to respond to changes in its environment quickly. Purchasing contributes to flexibility by selecting suppliers who are responsive to change and by promoting early purchasing and supplier involvement in the design process.

Effect on Quality

The realization that today, more and more of the cost of goods sold comes from purchased input means that purchasing has a major effect on the quality of an organization's output. The quality of a product or service begins with the specification/statement of work. Purchasing has additional input when it selects the supplier. Poor specifications and poor supplier selection increases the costs of receiving, quality control, rework, downtime, and scrap, and can result in lost market share.

Effect on Profitability

In many organizations, purchased goods and services account for a majority of the organization's cost of goods and or services sold. In some industries it is common to see 70 to 80 percent of the cost of goods sold purchased. If purchases represent 60 percent of the sales dollar, labor equals 12 percent, 18 percent is attributed to general and administrative costs, and 10 percent to profit before taxes, a 10 percent reduction in purchase costs adds six percent [(60%)(10%)=6%] to the bottomline. It would take a 50 percent reduction in labor costs [(6%)/(12%)=50%], a 33 percent reduction in general and administrative costs [(6%)/(18%)=33%], or a 60 percent increase in sales [(6%)/(10%)=60%] to have the same benefit. Clearly it is easier to reduce purchased materials and services by 10 percent than to increase sales by 60 percent or cut labor costs in half.

Role of Purchasing and Supply Management

Purchasing and supply management can contribute to an organization's success in several ways. Purchasing managers must think strategically, broaden their perspective of supply management, eliminate or automate the clerical transactions, and view themselves as service providers.

Strategic

Historically, purchasing was considered a clerical function focusing on the transaction paperwork. Purchasing evolved into a profession focusing on cost reduction. Recently, organizations have begun to realize that many of purchasing's activities are strategic in nature. What remains to be done is for purchasers to more fully embrace their strategic role.

How does purchasing become more strategic? Exhibit 1.2 lists some of the differences among the three stages of purchasing. For example, traditional purchasing focuses on the price on the purchase order while tactical purchasing looks at combining volumes through long-term contracts to obtain a lower unit price. Strategic purchasing evaluates the total cost of ownership through the life of the product or service to minimize the total cost to the organization over time. The starting point is to know your organization's mission and the strategies that have been defined to achieve the mission. The purchasing manager must then ask, "What activities are consistent with those strategies?" For example, if an organization's strategy is to be first to market, then purchasing needs to focus on early supplier involvement and purchasing policies that focus more on continuity of supply and quality and less on cost. Volume 4 presents the concept of the corporate mission and the purchasing mission in more depth.

EXHIBIT 1.2
Value-Added Assessment

Traditional (Transaction) Purchasing	Tactical ("Best Price") Purchasing	Strategic (Integrated) Purchasing
Focus is on: • Purchase on price alone • Order processing • Preparation of solicitation proposals • Number of competitive bids • Target prices • Multiple sources • Many suppliers • Contract preparation • Requirements gathering • Bid evaluation • Order follow-up • Invoice reconciliation	Focus is on: • Leverage volume for multiple to single sources • Company agreements • Goals for price, quality, and delivery • Supplier reduction programs • Supplier meetings • Intelligence gathering • Supplier cost estimating • Technical planning for negotiations • Conducting negotiations • Functional skill development	Focus is on: • Total cost • Total value • Strategic suppliers • Optimizing supply base • Supplier development • Aligning with business strategies • Developing organizational strategies to meet future needs • Developing commodity and supplier strategies • Supply performance and relationship management • Participating in long-range business planning

Supply Management

In the past, many organizations believed how they managed their suppliers had little affect on the organization's performance. Commonly, purchasers played one supplier against another, and would switch suppliers frequently and use short-term contracts. This adversarial model is giving way to a collaborative model as organizations discover that working with suppliers can lead to competitive advantage.

A result of this movement has been a reduction in the number of suppliers an organization uses. In a survey by Trent and Monczka, organizations are anticipating a 21 to 30 percent reduction in existing supply bases in the next few years.[3]

Another result is an increase in long-term contracting. The percentage of longer-term contracts has risen from 24 percent in 1990 to 36 percent in 1997 while the dollar value of those contracts has increased from 34 percent to 50 percent of total purchase dollars in the same period.[4]

Elimination and Automation of Day-to-Day Paperwork

If purchasing is to become more strategic in its outlook, organizations must continue to develop ways to reduce, eliminate, and/or automate day-to-day paperwork. Methods currently in use include procurement cards, electronic data interchange (EDI), intranets, and system contracts. Allowing the user to handle small transactions directly with the supplier frees purchasing from handling the 60 to 80 percent of transactions that account for less than 20 percent of the total purchases. The purchaser can then engage in more strategic activities such as supplier development, early supplier involvement, early purchasing involvement, supplier evaluation and certification, and supply-base reduction.

Service Providers

Purchasing provides a service to the organization. Purchasing's internal customers include management, marketing, operations, engineering, facilities, and traffic. Purchasing can serve these customers by understanding their needs, educating them on how purchasing can help meet those needs, and assisting them in meeting their goals. Some of the ways purchasing can help internal customers include:

- Searching for new products, services, and processes that further organizational goals directly or help internal customers achieve their goals.
- Suggesting materials or items to users that can improve operations.
- Standardizing where possible.
- Supplying forecast data to users.

Overiew of the Purchasing Process

Steps in the Process

Exhibit 1.3 provides an overview of the purchasing process. The process begins with a user identifying a need. The need could be a requirement for production material or a need for a professional service, spare part, or office supplies. The need instigates the requisition process, which includes development of the specifications or statement of work. Next, purchasing must identify potential sources of supply and the appropriate purchasing policy. The purchaser must then determine whether to use a competitive bid or negotiation process as the tool for working with suppliers. See Chapter 5 for a discussion of solicitation proposal techniques. The proposals and the suppliers need to be evaluated before selecting the supplier. A contract is then developed and managed to completion.

Objectives

The objectives of purchasing are to acquire materials and services of the right quality, in the right quantity, at the right price, at the right time, from the right source. What has changed is the definition of "right." As shown in Exhibit 1.2, the old definition of "right price" was the lowest unit price on the purchase order. Strategic purchasing's definition of the "right price" is the lowest total cost of ownership. "Right quality" has moved from maintaining consistency of quality to an expectation of zero defects from suppliers. "Right quantity" has changed from a traditional economic order quantity to increased frequency of delivery by improving the transportation and planning processes. "Right time" still stresses continuity of supply under both viewpoints. "Right source" has changed from developing alternate sources of supply to promoting a competitive atmosphere in performance and pricing and to developing strategic alliances with a reduced set of suppliers that are mutually beneficial. The overriding objective is to develop purchasing strategies and policies that facilitate and support the achievement of the organization's mission, strategies, and objectives.

EXHIBIT 1.3

The Purchasing Process

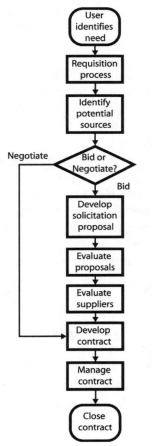

Book Overview

This book has two purposes: to help individuals prepare for Module 1 of the Certified Purchasing Manager's exam and to provide an overview of the basics of the purchasing process. The outline of the remainder of the book is as follows:

- Chapter 2 looks at the requisition process, specifications, and statements of work.
- Chapter 3 discusses cost analysis. This chapter covers cost types and costing approaches, a variety of analysis techniques, and price and cost analysis techniques.
- Chapter 4 presents the sourcing process including purchasing polices, the pros and cons of different types of sources, dealing with the small order problem, and identifying potential sources of supply.
- Chapter 5 explains the competitive bid process, solicitation proposal types, and the potential problems.
- Chapter 6 outlines the supplier evaluation process including site visits, supplier ability to perform, financial analysis, quality capability, and performance.
- Chapter 7 reviews the legal issues in purchasing including agency; warranties; rights of inspection, acceptance, and rejection; and issues regarding electronic commerce.
- Chapter 8 covers managing the contract, expediting, contract problems the purchaser may encounter, and potential ways to deal with those problems.
- Chapter 9 takes a look at the future of the purchasing process.

Key Points

1. Purchasing needs to focus on total cost, quality, reducing cycle times and leadtimes, reducing transaction costs through technology and process improvement, and improving purchasers' skills.

2. Purchasing affects an organization's cost structure, leadtimes, time-to-market, flexibility, quality, and profitability.

3. Purchasing's new role requires purchasing managers to think strategically, broaden their perspective to supply management, eliminate or automate clerical transactions, and view themselves as service providers.

4. The purchasing process includes identification of a need, the requisition process, source identification, selection of a bid versus negotiation process, solicitation proposal development, proposal and supplier evaluation, contract development, management, and closeout.

Questions for Review

1. How can purchasing help organizations compete?

2. What effects does purchasing have on an organization's cost structure?

3. How can purchasing help an organization reduce its leadtime and time-to-market?

4. What effects does purchasing have on an organization's flexibility and quality?

5. How will purchasing's role change in the future?

6. What are the steps in the purchasing process?

7. What are purchasing's objectives?

For Additional Information

Bales, W.A., W.M. Bunker, A.P. Hagstrand, S.J. Coleman, L.L. Stover, and J. Barry. "Increasing Purchasing and Supply Management's Value to the Organization," *NAPM InfoEdge*, (1:1), May 1995.

Bordon, G.G. "Is Your Staff Thinking Strategically?" *Purchasing Today®*, February 1998, p. 45.

DeFusco, R.J. and M.D.Clark. "World Class Purchasing: Your Guide to Adding Value," *NAPM InfoEdge*, (3:8), April 1998.

Moyer, M.J. "21st Century Macro Trends: Impact on Purchasing/Material," *Proceedings of the 1994 NAPM International Purchasing Conference*, NAPM, Tempe, AZ, 1994, pp. 1-4.

Trent, R.J. and R.M. Monczka. "Purchasing and Supply Management: Trends and Changes Throughout the 1990s," *International Journal of Purchasing and Materials Management*, (34:4), Fall 1998, pp. 2-11.

Endnotes

1. Trent, R.J and R.M. Monczka. "Purchasing and Supply Management: Trends and Changes Throughout the 1990s," *International Journal of Purchasing and Materials Management*, (34:4), Fall 1998, p. 4.

2. Ibid.

3. Ibid., p. 8.

4. Ibid.

CHAPTER 2

THE REQUISITION PROCESS: YOU WANT WHAT? WHEN?

Chapter Objectives

- Describe the types of requisitions.
- Identify the required information in a requisition.
- Understand the concerns the purchaser must be aware of in the requisition process.
- Understand the effects the source of funds has on the requisition process.
- Describe the priority rules for processing requisitions.
- Describe the types of specifications.
- Identify the sources of specifications.
- Describe the types of statements of work.
- Identify the components of the statement of work.

Introduction

The requisition is the start of the purchasing process. This is where the users make their needs, desires, requirements, and wants known to the purchaser. The key piece of information that must be provided with the requisition is the product specification or service statement of work. This chapter will first look at the issues involved in processing the requisition and then will discuss specifications and statements of work.

The Requisition Process

This section will look at the types of requisitions, information requirements, potential problem areas in the requisition process, budgets and sources of funds, and prioritizing systems for processing requisitions.

Requisition Types

There are several different types of requisitions. They include the standard, electronic, bill of materials, system-generated, and traveling requisition.

Standard and electronic requisitions - The basic form of requisition is the standard requisition, which is an organization's document (paper or electronic) that user departments use to communicate to purchasing (and at times to suppliers) what, when, and how many products or services they need. Purchasing relies on this information in its acquisition process. Typically, a copy of the requisition or purchase order is sent back to the original requester to show that the goods or services have been ordered.

Purchasing automation has eliminated many paper-based requisitions. Requisitioners and purchasers alike are linked by computer and requests for goods and or services and acknowledgments of action are transmitted by wire and screen. This eliminates the need for paper-based systems and it often enhances decision processes and record keeping. Intranets are often used as the mechanism to link the user and purchasing in today's information environment.

Examples - Microsoft Corporation's purchasing department employed traditional client/server solutions. A client/server application is a local area network that permits the sharing of software and information between multiple users. Each time the department created a new computer application, a setup program had to be run to install the application on each user's computer. The user then needed to learn a new user interface. Compatibility problems were common and support costs for multiple applications were high.

An intranet-based solution was developed to replace the existing client/server applications. The user interface is essentially the browser and the pages of the application — with which an Internet user is immediately familiar. Intranet solutions require no setup and extra resources —such as disk space or memory constraints — to run the application. The new requisition tool provides clear, easy-to-use Web pages for each of Microsoft's national contract partners. Contract partners supplying computers and peripherals, office supplies, books and reference materials, and food service and catering are included. In Microsoft's intranet solution, a general requisition form is also in place for items not covered under a national contract. The requisitions are then passed along electronically to the central purchasing department.[1]

Silicon Graphics, Inc. instituted an intranet-based requisition system for MRO (maintenance, repair, and operating supplies) purchases that uses passwords, as well as firewall and encryption software for security. The requester can go to the catalog system, conduct a word search, and find the desired item from multiple suppliers with existing contracts. If the requester can't find the desired item, the requester can type in the item and access the noncatalog database. If the requester orders a catalog item, an electronic requisition is generated and sent to the approver. Once the requisition is approved, the requisition is imported into an application that transforms it into a purchase order without intervention from the purchasing department. For noncatalog items, the requisition is routed to the purchasing department, which adds terms and conditions, and reroutes it through the approval system.[2]

Bill of materials - A bill of materials (BOM) is an important element in the requisition process. A BOM is a listing of all the materials and components required to produce a product or service. Like a recipe, the BOM shows each part with a description. In some organizations, purchasers acting as purchaser-planners use the BOM to generate purchase orders, or to trigger a release schedule against an existing contract.

A second application of the bill of materials concept is for projects. In this case, the purchaser is given a list of the materials and services needed for a project and instructed to purchase from the list as needed for the project.

Systems-generated requisitions - There are a variety of computer systems in use today in the production planning, consumption, supply management, and purchasing realms. Many of these systems will automatically or semi-automatically generate requisitions or direct orders with suppliers based upon previous arrangements. These are used when the information can be directly released to the supplier as in the case of systems contracts or single sourcing. For example, when an MRP system indicates it is time to order an item, the system would automatically create a purchase order. If the order met specified conditions, it would be automatically approved and sent to the supplier using EDI. The purchaser would be involved only if the order did not fall within standard parameters such as total dollar value.

Traveling requisition - In settings where high volumes of similar goods or services are being requested, a traveling requisition is often used. In a manual purchasing system, this is usually a card that has standard part/item information along with listings of past requisitions and organizations from which they have been ordered. Purchasers place the order, then insert the organization, quantity, and expected delivery date on the form and return it to be filed. With the increased computerization of the requisition process, traveling requisitions are seldom used.

Information Requirements

Organizations normally use a purchase requisition form (paper or electronic) that is designed for its own specific needs, including the information needed and the distribution of that information. The required information for a requisition varies from organization to organization, but usually includes:

- The name of the user.
- The signature (or approval code) of the person authorized to sign/approve the requisition.
- A description and use of the desired material/services.
- The quantity.
- The date needed.
- The date the requisition was generated.
- The estimated cost/budget allocation.
- Possible sources.
- The account to be charged.
- Ship to location.

An authorized signature/approval is necessary to ensure the appropriateness of the requisition. Traditionally this was an ink signature on the document. With today's electronic systems, the use of an electronic or a digital signature is required. Digital signatures ensure authenticity, integrity, and confidentiality through the use of an encryption system using public and private keys. Information encrypted using the individual's private key can only be decrypted by the corresponding public key. The purchaser would transmit the public key to the supplier through a secure method such as a diskette in the mail. Formal responsibility for appropriateness rests with the user department, not purchasing. The purchase requisition is an internal communication document and should be available to all departments requiring the information.

Special Concerns in the Requisition Process

There are several areas of concern that may affect the requisition process. They include unauthorized purchasing, the approval process, authority limits, and socioeconomic goals such as use of historically underused businesses and environmental issues.

Unauthorized purchasing - In most organizations, the only legally authorized purchasing agent is the purchasing department. When a non-agent in an organization makes a direct commitment with a supplier without contacting an authorized agent, this is known as unauthorized purchasing. Usually this is the result of backdoor selling by a supplier's representative. The sales representative avoids dealing with purchasing, tries to get the user to sign the order, and then ships the goods. If the organization pays for the goods, the unauthorized purchaser's actions are ratified. The best ways to prevent such actions are to notify all suppliers of the names of the authorized purchasers and, when unauthorized purchases occur, immediately notify the supplier that the user is not an authorized agent and in the future, orders from that individual will not be accepted. The names of the authorized agents should then be supplied

Problems that can arise from unauthorized purchasing include:

- Circumventing the proper budgeting systems, thereby resulting in lack of expenditure control.

- Committing the organization's funds to less-than-qualified suppliers.
- Circumventing the approval procedures for purchases.
- Loss of volume from authorized contracts issued by purchasing.
- Making commitments with "sham" or boiler-room suppliers, creating unnecessary expenditures of funds.

While there are problems with unauthorized buying, purchasing should not be the sole organizational contact with suppliers. Many purchasing systems allow users to make direct releases to suppliers on contracts or agreements established by the purchasing department. These direct-release systems include the use of systems contracts, blanket orders, and credit card purchasing. In situations where supplier partnership arrangements exist, it is common for users to contact suppliers directly for technical and product advice. Furthermore, users often perform the tasks involved in contract administration. When coordinated through purchasing, such arrangements provide users with a quick response to their needs.

Appropriate approvals - Usually the director of purchasing, delegated individuals, and organization teams are responsible for the commitment of funds to acquire materials, equipment, and services. The establishment of organization-wide contracts typically requires approval from the chief purchasing officer for the organization.

If there is an emergency or other situation where it may prove advantageous to the organization to do so, competitive bidding may be waived through management documentation of such actions. (Note: This may be more restrictive in the public sector, which has less flexible policies for the procurement process than the private sector, often requiring more extensive use of formal advertising and competitive bidding.) In most cases, purchasers are required to justify purchases from single or sole sources. For standard materials in common and repetitive use, most purchasing managers have some latitude to exercise judgment in purchasing for stock in advance of specific requirements.

Authority limits - Internal purchase requisitions must be approved by signature or electronically ratified by individuals having the proper dollar-authority levels. Reasons for obtaining proper requisitioner approvals include maintaining control over spending and spotting potential internal fraud. In some organizations, the finance or accounting department is in charge of maintaining lists of authorized internal requisitioners and their respective dollar approval limits. While requisitioners are responsible for obtaining correct approvals on purchase requisitions, purchasers must verify this prior to placing orders. Requisitions not following guidelines are returned to the orig-inating department. Often, blanket approval is given by management for direct material items used in production and requested by inven-tory/production control.

Requisitions and other requests from internal customers affect specific purchasing personnel in terms of their "authority" to acquire the items. When individual purchasers, purchasing agents, and man-agers are given specific dollar limits, this is termed "limits of author-ity." Thus, a purchaser may be able to authorize an individual pur-chase order up to $50,000, while a senior purchaser may have author-ity up to $100,000. An order over this amount requires the signature of the purchasing manager, and in certain cases, a higher-level pur-chasing executive. Contracts for continuing needs, such as blanket orders or open-end orders where the dollar expenditure level exceeds the individual's authority, should contain the manager's signature. This is true even though individual order releases will be less than the purchaser's authority limit.

Socioeconomic goals - The continued development of an under-utilized business procurement program is a common practice in many organizations. The competitive benefits that organizations realize from such sources are not unlike those experienced when developing new suppliers. Requisitions should be reviewed for consideration for placement with this type of supplier.

Executive Order 95-507, which dates back to the early 1980s, extended the requirement that government contractors, and not just the government per se, had to increasingly use minority-owned business enterprises (MBEs). Some time later women-owned business enter-prises and other organizations such as handicapped workshops were added to this directive. Purchasers should be aware of the legal chal-lenges that are currently proceeding through the judicial and legislative systems. In June of 1995, the Supreme Court ruled that federal contract awards based on minority status must show compelling governmental interest and must be narrowly tailored to further that interest.[3] Many organizations believe diversifying the supplier base to include women and minority business development is a sound business decision.

Green purchasing - Green purchasing involves making environmentally conscious decisions throughout the purchasing process beginning with product and process design through product disposal. This decision is cost- and strategy-driven, economically sound, and integrated throughout the purchasing process. Green purchasing begins in the requisition process when users request a new material. For example, an automotive company requires that if a requisitioner proposes a new indirect material such as a paint or solvent, the Material Safety Data Sheet (MSDS) must be presented to the facilities environmental engineer and approved by a hazardous materials review committee. The purpose of the process is to ensure that the facility's emission standards are not violated, workers are not affected, and the effects on the environment are known.[4] Exhibit 2.1 presents a list of questions purchasers can ask when reviewing the requisition that will help them select products and suppliers that are environmentally friendly. In order to encourage users to pursue "green" strategies, purchasing should emphasize teamwork structures such as early purchasing involvement and early supplier involvement that bring together suppliers, manufacturing, design engineers, marketing, and purchasing.

EXHIBIT 2.1
Identifying Environmentally Friendly Requisitions

<u>**COST**</u>
- How does the cost compare with "environmentally friendly" products?
- What are the long-term disposal costs and potential problems with the item?

<u>**QUALITY**</u>
- What is the proposed item's content and are any of the components harmful to the environment?
- How does the quality compare with recycled or remanufactured products?

<u>**LEADTIME**</u>
- How long will the material take to decompose?
- Are recycled items available?
- How does the availability compare with the original item?

<u>**FLEXIBILITY**</u>
- Can the item be replaced with an item that is more environmentally friendly?
- Does the organization have the required safety program in place?
- Are products that use recycled materials available?
- Does the supplier have a reverse logistics service?

Budgets and Sources of Funds

In most operations, a purchase order should not be executed unless the expenditure is first authorized in the requisitioner's or organization's budget. Large variances should be brought to the attention of the requisitioner prior to placement. Non-budget acquisitions normally require greater scrutiny and authorization prior to execution. The purchaser should have a clear understanding of the budgeted appropriation and proceed with the procurement of the goods or services in a cost-effective manner.

Funds for purchases in organizations are typically made available through one of the following five types of budgets:

- **Materials budget** - A materials budget covers an organization's need for production materials and components.
- **Capital budget** - The capital budget covers the acquisition of equipment and construction that is capitalized as a depreciable asset on an organization's balance sheet.
- **Maintenance, repair, and operating supplies (MRO) budget** - The MRO budget covers items needed for the operation of a facility, but are not part of the finished product.
- **Administrative budget** - This type of budget covers office operations and includes office furnishings and office equipment.
- **Open-to-purchase budget** - The open-to-purchase budget, often used in the retail sector, is similar to a cash flow budget. Open-to-purchase budgets link cash requirements and expenditures during a budgeting period with funds availability during the budgeting period. In retail, marketing strategies are often divided into separate programs that are measured by return on investment. The open-to-purchase budget allocates funds based on the planned investment by budgeting period. Those funds are then used for inventory replenishment. When a requisitioner makes a request to purchase, it may be limited by the availability of funds for that program and budgeting period. Limited funds may also affect the purchaser's ability to obtain volume discounts.[5]

Most public sector entities require that funding for the requisition be pre-encumbered or set aside at the time of requesting. This pre-encumbered dollar amount is adjusted, if necessary, by the "encumbrance" at the time the purchase order or contract is issued.

Some contracts allow the supplier to be reimbursed for its costs. These contracts would specifically identify which costs are allowable and the requirements for documentation. The purchaser must exercise careful judgment in reimbursing expenditures in an effort to control costs. In government contracting, unallowable costs are identified in the Federal Acquisition Regulations (FAR).

Processing Requisitions

In many organizations, a prioritization process exists for processing requisitions. The activity may be formal or informal. In formal systems, a supervisor may receive and review all requisitions as they are submitted. Assignments may be based on urgency and workload of individual purchasers. In informal prioritization, users may bring urgent requisitions direct to the appropriate commodity purchaser. Routine requisitions are deposited in a central location to be collected and prioritized by individual purchasers.

- **First come, first served** - This approach ignores how important or critical a request is in favor of the concept of fairness to all requistioners.
- **Arrangement by need date** - Process by need date improves the delivery performance as measured against the requestor's need date but ignores the issue of supplier leadtime. Thus, orders with longer leadtimes may get processed after orders which are needed sooner but are ahead of the leadtime. For example, item "A" has a leadtime of 20 weeks and item "B" has a leadtime of three weeks. The need date for item "A" is 18 weeks in the future and the need date for item"B" is five weeks in the future. If the requests for both items arrived at purchasing at the same time, item "B" would be ordered first because it has the earliest need date even though the leadtime is only three weeks while item "A" would be ordered second even though it is inside the normal leadtime.
- **Rush orders/emergencies** - Rush or emergency requisitions are the top priority of any purchasing organization. They may occur for a variety of reasons, each of which requires immediate attention by purchasers. This urgency requires purchasers to put aside other tasks, address the rush requirement, and then return to the previous activity. In addition, suppliers are often selected for

proximity rather than least total cost, and premium freight charges are incurred. Because of the additional costs related to rush orders, many organizations require supervisory concurrence to expedite a rush requirement. This initial prioritization balances individual urgency against organizational needs.

- **Order of importance/impact** - With this approach, requests are prioritized using a variety of criteria. Relevant measures could include the difference between the need date and estimated lead-time, the magnitude of dollar expenditure, the critical nature of product or service, and the complexity of the purchase.
- **Seasonal** - This approach prioritizes purchasing requests based upon purchasing seasonal items first because they may not be available at a later point in time.
- **Longest leadtime** - Another important determination of requisition priority is the leadtime required for delivery of the item. Often, items with the longest leadtimes are ordered ahead of short leadtime items, all other things being equal.

Specifications

Specifications are the major means users have of communicating requirements to both purchasing and the potential supplier. Specifications can take the form of description by brand, physical or chemical characteristics, material, performance, or method of manufacture; engineering drawings; or market grade.

Specifications are a description of the technical requirements for a material, product, or service that includes the criteria for determining whether these requirements are met. A specification may describe the performance parameters that a supplier has to meet, or it may provide a complete design disclosure of the work or job to be done.

Specifications define what constitutes an acceptable product or service. They are required before a purchase takes place to ensure that both purchaser and supplier have the same understanding of what is being purchased. After delivery, the specifications become the standard for determining whether or not the product or service is satisfactory.

To purchase a product or service with poorly defined or nonexistent specifications is to invite problems. If the purchasing organization is not clear about what it wants, how can the supplier be expected to deliver a "good" product or the "right" service? Purchasing has the ability to require its internal customers to focus clearly on what they want and what attributes matter. They can insist that no quotation activity will occur until the specifications are clearly defined.

Specifications are the primary method of communicating in specific terms to potential suppliers what is being sought. Suppliers need to have specifications before they can prepare quotations or enter into negotiations. Specifications help suppliers decide whether they can provide the product or service at all, and if they can, at what cost. When multiple suppliers quote from the same set of specifications, the results provide an "apples-to-apples" comparison. Good specifications also ensure that the resulting product or service meets the needs of the organization and provides grounds for rejection if it does not.

Types of Specifications

There are a number of different ways to specify a product including:

- **Blueprints or drawings** - A common form of specification is the engineering drawing or blueprint. This form of specification is particularly useful for machined, cast, forged, or stamped parts; construction; and electronic circuits and assemblies.
- **Brand or trade names** - The use of brand or trade names may be required when the product or service is protected by patent or trade secret, the quantity required is too small to develop a specification, or when users express clear preference for a particular brand. The difficulties associated with brand names include overpriced products or services, restricted sourcing opportunities, or discontinued products or services. For example, a utility company issued a request for quotation (RFQ) for a tractor for mowing grounds at various locations. The specification listed the current brand, model, and options on the current tractor model. The purchaser received numerous questions from the suppliers regarding the various features. Perhaps most important was the issue of the cutting width. Should it be the standard 37 inches or could it be 36 or 38 inches? However, the specification had to be redeveloped when the dealer of the current brand could not provide the equivalent piece of equipment. One way to reduce these prob-

lems is to include a wide range of brand names, any one of which could fulfill the user's needs. To determine which brands are equal, list the salient or mandatory characteristics of the item; determine which products satisfy particular requirements; and identify differences such as minor variations in size, weight, speed, and capacity.[6]

- **Chemical or physical specifications** - Specifications by chemical or physical characteristics define the properties of materials the purchaser desires to purchase. This form of specification leaves the method of manufacture up to the supplier. (A service example of a physical specification is advertisement sizes for a magazine.) See Exhibit 2.2 for additional examples.

EXHIBIT 2.2
Example Specifications

Physical Specification – Cold Formed Sections of Road Crush Barriers

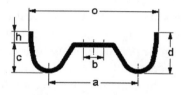

(a) mm	Tolerance mm	(b) mm	Tolerance mm	(c) mm	(d) mm	(h) mm	(o) mm	Thickness t
194	±2	30	±2	54	80	26	30	63

Source: Egyptian Iron and Steel Company, HADISOLB at www.steel-eg.com/road-bar.htm.

Chemical Specification - Fuel Ethanol

Ethanol, %v/v	92.1 min.
Methanol, %v/v	0.5 max. (5,000 ppm)
Water, %v/v	1.0 max. (10,000 ppm)
Solvent-washed gum, mg/ 100 ml	5 max. (50 ppm)
Chloride ion, mg/L	40 max. (40 ppm)
Copper content, mg/kg	0.1 max. (0.1 ppm)
Acidity as acetic acid, %w/w	0.007 max. (70 ppm)
Appearance	Visibly free of suspended or precipitated contaminants (clear and bright).
Denaturant	A minimum of 1.96% v/v and a maximum of 4.76% v/v of natural gasoline, gasoline components, or unleaded gasoline.

Source: The Online Distillery Network, www.distill.com/specs/US-1.html.

- **Commercial standards** - Commercial standards describe the quality of materials and workmanship, dimensions, chemical composition, methods for testing, and so on. Example products include nuts, bolts, pipes, fasteners, and electrical components. Commercial standard items should be used whenever possible, as they help to reduce costs by simplifying product design, giving the purchaser a wider range of potential suppliers from which to source, and reducing inventory requirements.

- **Design standards** - Design specifications provide a complete description of what the product or service must look like and often defines the process by which a product will be made and the materials that will be used. Design standards may include step-by-step instructions to carry out a service. Design specifications give the buying organization maximum control over the end result, and the purchaser assumes the risk for proper performance of the product.

- **Market grades** - Market grades only apply to a select number of products. Examples include lumber, agricultural products, and meat and dairy products. The major problems with market grades are the variability of the product quality over time and rating consistency by the graders. All food and feed product grades are established by the U.S. Department of Agriculture.

- **Material and method-of-manufacture specifications** - Material and method-of-manufacture specifications tell the supplier exactly what materials to use and how to manufacture the product. Because the purchaser is telling the supplier how to complete the work, the supplier is relieved from the implied warranty of fitness for a particular purpose.

- **Performance specifications** - Performance specifications define what the product or service must do. They are used to define the acceptability of capital equipment and many types of services. The purchaser is interested in the final result. Typically the details of how the performance will be achieved are not specified and rest with the supplier. When performance specifications are used, the supplier has maximum latitude to determine how to go about satisfying the requirement and also assumes the risk for proper performance of the end product.

- **Qualified products list** - Some organizations may provide a list of qualified products that have been approved for use in the organization.
- **Samples** - A physical sample can be used as a specification. When the sample meets the purchaser's needs, the specification will reference the sample and state that any others should be produced just like it.
- **Combination** - A purchaser could use a combination of the above methods as no one method is best for all situations.

Sources of Specifications

If specifications do not exist, they must be developed. If they already exist, they should be reviewed prior to use to make sure that they are complete and current. Inputs may come from both internal and external sources.

Internal sources - Some organizations, especially manufacturing companies, have formalized procedures for specification generation. Specifications for technical products are often generated by technical experts such as research and development or quality. For complex purchases, such as equipment, systems, or software, a team may be formed with representatives from each affected function. Organizations that have many specifications on file may have a department, often called document control, tasked with maintaining specifications.

If there is no formal process for generating specifications, then the obligation rests with the requisitioner to clearly define what he or she wants. Purchasing has the responsibility to see that the requisitioner does this before the solicitation process begins. Exhibit 2.3 presents a checklist for developing specifications.

External inputs - If the supplier is already working with the buying organization in a trusted relationship, then its inputs to the specification can be very valuable in ensuring that the product or service is deliverable and that all attributes have been clearly defined. This also ensures that when the product or service is produced, both organizations have a complete understanding of how it will be used and what constitutes acceptable quality.

EXHIBIT 2.3
Specification Development Checklist

Purpose

Attributes
- Quantity
- Size
- Color
- Maximum and minimum
  dimensions
- Quality
- Documents/drawings required

Performance
- Methods of acceptance, testing,
  and inspection
- Response times
- Guaranteed up-time
- Site inspection process

Legal Issues
- Warranties
- Guarantees
- Limits of liability
- Liquidated damages
- Bonds
- Other remedies
- Dispute clause or procedure
  for handling complaints/errors

Service
- Logs of visits and repairs
- Preventive maintenance schedules
- Operating manuals
- Training
- Storage of materials, equipment, or
  spare parts

Terms and Conditions
- Location or method of delivery
- Methods of invoicing and payments
- Length of contract
- Renewal options
- Method of adjusting prices for
  long- term agreements

Environmental
- Wasted supplies
- Work site clean-up
- Equipment and disposal of
  packaging and boxes
- Trade-ins and disposal of old
  equipment
- Recycle items or efforts

Miscellaneous
- Retrofit or bring up to standards
- Labor and material outside of contract not
  the responsibility of contractor
- Utilities
- Work security
- New versus used parts or equipment

Source: Woods, D.L., Coaching Users to Develop Great Specifications, *Proceedings of the 1996 NAPM International Purchasing Conference*, NAPM, Tempe, AZ, 1996, pp. 86-91.

If the expertise needed to properly define specifications does not exist within the organization, consultants who possess such expertise may be hired to assist in generating the specifications.

Industry standards exist for many commodities. If applicable, they can be used as specifications. This saves time and effort and ensures that both the supplier and the buying organization are using the same definition. Examples of industry standards are fasteners, wire thickness, bar codes, and wood grades.

If consistency across organizations is useful (for example, with EDI), then peers in different organizations may collectively define standards. The National Association of Purchasing Management (NAPM) also provides sample specifications for a variety of situations (see www.napm.org). When specifications require special knowledge or expertise, organizations may hire consultants to aid in developing the specifications.

Standardization within an industry, such as the railroad or petroleum industries, can lead to the use of a competitor's specification for a "standard" item, such as a pump. In other industries, differentiation is crucial and specifications may be generated to provide a brand-specific look and feel.

Problems with Specifications

If specifications are not appropriate for the intended applications, the organization may not receive the desired products, may incur extra costs, and possibly delay a customer's shipment. Some causes of poor specifications are:

- **Lack of standardization** - In order to keep inventories at a minimum, specifications should be developed to meet as wide a range of applications as possible. Developing unique specifications for every application leads to a proliferation of part numbers and inventories.
- **Over-specification** - Over-specification means that the developers of the specification have made its provisions stricter than what is necessary or appropriate. A typical result of this practice is higher purchase costs and/or exclusion of viable suppliers because they cannot meet the too-tight specification. A common over-specification is surface finish, which is caused by a failure to review drawing standard specifications. The drawing's standard finish specifications may require additional machining on

surfaces that are not visible or functional. This increases the cost to the customer but does not increase the value.

- **Under-specification** - Under-specification means that the developers of the specification have omitted key details or have put limits on key parameters that render them inadequate. A typical result of these errors and/or omissions is continuous quality problems. Items delivered from the supplier meet the specifications but do not work in the desired application.

- **Slanting specifications** - Specifications can be written to favor a specific product or supplier. Typical results include artificially limited competition, higher purchase prices (because the supplier knows that it has a lock on the specifications), and the likelihood of using only that supplier in the future (with the promise of future problems).

- **Non-use of generic specifications** - Specifying a brand name when a generic product will suffice limits competition and generally results in higher prices. Generic equivalents are often less costly, such as pharmaceuticals.

- **Obsolete/outdated specifications** - Because suppliers will use the specifications to quote prices and provide guidelines for production of the product or delivery of the service, obsolete specifications will result in all subsequent work being invalid and potentially very costly.

- **International standards differences** – It is important that both the purchaser and supplier operate within the same standards conventions. Issues as simple as the use of metric versus U.S. measurements can create problems if the supplier operates with one system and the purchaser with another.

Statements of Work

When purchasing services, specifications are usually defined in the form of a statement of work (SOW). Exhibit 2.4 presents a list of acquisitions that typically require a SOW. Each SOW is unique as it describes the specific requirements applicable to a particular item or service. The SOW provides potential suppliers with a clear description of the work to be performed, including inspections, testing and acceptance, quality, support services, documentation, maintenance, results to be achieved, and other requirements. Many disputes between the purchaser and supplier after services are performed are the result of a difference of understanding regarding what was desired.

EXHIBIT 2.4
Acquisitions Typically Requiring a Statement of Work (SOW)

	Performance	Functional Design	Level of Effort
Arts and entertainment services		X	
Benefits administration	X		
Capital equipment installation or dismantling			X
Construction			X
Consultant services		X	
Contract manufacturing	X		
Design work		X	
Environmental, health, and safety services	X		
Experiment/development			X
Facilities management	X		
Fleet rental and maintenance services	X		
Groundskeeping services		X	
Inspection and test services	X		
Janitorial services	X		
Lab services	X		
Level-of-effort or support services			X
Maintenance services		X	X
Outsourcing			X
Publications and advertising		X	
Repairs			X
Software development		X	
Studies			X
Telecommunication services	X		
Temporary employee services			X
Trade shows and exhibitions	X		
Travel services		X	

Source: Sickinger, J. "Writing a Complete and Effective Statement of Work," *NAPM InfoEdge*, (3:3), November 1997, p. 5.

A simple SOW defines the work to be done, the boundaries of that work including the timeframe, the expected end product or result, and criteria for evaluating performance and quality. All important attributes should be defined. As the services become more complex, so does the statement of work. For lengthy and/or very expensive projects, a properly detailed SOW provides the mechanism to manage the project throughout its duration.

The SOW may include a description of the work that is divided into segments. Each segment can then be managed as a separate subproject. The overall project can also be quoted and managed using the work breakdown as a form of project management chart, such as PERT, to sequence the activities.

When the SOW is divided into segments, it may be advisable to condition continuation upon the successful completion of each segment. As each segment is completed, a quality assessment can take place to ensure that the specifications of the SOW are met to this point and that specific approval has been granted before work continues. This safeguards against the project going too far awry before the deviation is discovered.

Poorly written statements of work may lead to the following problems:

- Poor quality products or services.
- Wasted time and money.
- Unfavorable pricing.
- Contractual disputes and lawsuits.
- Uninvited scrutiny by protesters, attorneys, and, in some instances, government officials.
- Lost sales.
- Customer dissatisfaction.

Well-written statements of work lead to:

- Effective internal planning and communications.
- Solicitation of high-quality, competitive proposals.
- Minimization of ambiguities.
- Clear description of who will do what.

- Clear indication of the standards of measurement that will be used.
- Satisfied customers.

Types of Statements of Work

Like product specifications, there are several formats for statements of work including the following:

- **Performance SOW** - The performance statement of work is similar to the performance specification. The purchaser describes the performance attributes of the end product while leaving the design up to the supplier. For example, a "mopped floor" is defined as free of any dirt, debris, streaks, standing water, or splash marks or spots on the baseboards.[7] Progress is measured by testing whether the performance attributes have been obtained (see Appendix 2-A for an example performance SOW).
- **Functional SOW** - In the functional SOW the purchaser describes the problem to be solved and leaves the method and design to the supplier. Progress is measured by whether the problem has been solved (see Appendix 2-A for an example functional SOW).
- **Design SOW** - The design statement of work, used mainly in construction, the manufacture of goods, or equipment projects, is the most detailed form of the SOW. In this statement of work, the purchaser describes both the methods and design but does not specify the performance attributes. Progress is evaluated by comparing the product against the design.
- **Level-of-effort SOW** - The level-of-effort SOW is a special form of performance statement of work that is generally used in research and development or studies contracts. The purchaser describes the performance attributes of a means-to-an-end product and may specify the method and design. Progress is evaluated by peer review.
- **Hybrid SOW** - The hybrid SOW uses any combination of the four forms listed above.

SOW Outline

Like the specification, the key to developing a SOW is to follow a standard outline to ensure nothing is forgotten.

- **Project objectives** - The project objectives will be reflected in the type of statement of work chosen. For example, the performance SOW would have as its objectives the desired deliverables. A functional SOW would have as its objective the problem to be solved.
- **Background information** - The background information would present information about the history of the problem, why the problem needs to be solved, possible limitations, and any other information of which the supplier might need to be aware of.
- **Project/work scope requirements** - This section defines the project itself; scope of work; requirements; technical considerations; references; documents; tasks; test, acceptance, and performance criteria; and purchaser and supplier responsibilities.
- **Schedule** - The schedule section presents the timetable of when particular phases need to be accomplished and what the measurable outcomes are at each milestone.
- **Deliverables** - This section describes what is to be delivered, the review cycle, criteria, and the information to be gathered.
- **Progress report deadlines** - Progress report deadlines cover the information to be included in the progress reports.
- **Performance evaluation factors** - Every SOW should clearly state all performance and quality criteria and how they will be measured. When the supplier's performance is evaluated, the results should be clear to both parties.

Sample SOWs can be found at the following Internet sites:

- www.airtime.co.uk/users/wywywig/sow_mt.htm
- www.acq-ref.navy.mil/turbo/arp34.htm
- www.diamond.spawar.navy.mil/specs/wise/manual/manual.html
- www.napm.org

Key Points

1. The four types of requisitions are standard/electronic, bill of materials, system-generated, and traveling.
2. The required information in a requisition includes user, authorization signature, description of the desired product or service, quantity, date required, estimated cost, possible sources, account information, and delivery location.
3. Purchaser concerns in the requisition process include unauthorized purchasing, appropriate approvals, authority limits, socioeconomic goals, and green purchasing.
4. Sources of funds include materials, capital, MRO, and administrative budgets.
5. Priority rules for processing requisitions may include first come, first served; need date; rush orders; order of importance; seasonal; or leadtime.
6. Types of specifications include description by brand, specification of physical or chemical characteristics, specification of material to be used, specification of performance, specification of method of manufacture, engineering drawings, or market grade.
7. Sources of specifications can be developed from internal and external sources.
8. Types of statements of work are performance, functional, design, and level-of-effort.
9. The components of the statement of work are the project objectives, background information, project requirements, schedule, deliverables, progress report information, and evaluation factors.

Questions for Review

1. What are the types of requisitions?
2. What concerns does the purchaser need to be aware of in the purchasing process?
3. What effects does the source of funds have on the requisition?
4. Why does purchasing have different priorities for processing requisitions?

5. What are the different types of specifications and when is each useful?
6. What are the sources for developing new specifications?
7. When should the purchaser use the various types of statements of work?

For Additional Information

Brusman, C. "The Statement of Work Primer," *NAPM Insights*, p. 49.

Hearn, S.R. "Inside vs. Outside... And How Much? " *NAPM Insights*, June 1995, p. 14.

Handfield, R.B. and S.A. Melnyk. "GreenSpeak," *Purchasing Today®*, July 1998, pp. 32, 34-38.

Nachmann, J.O. "How High is Your EQ?" *Purchasing Today®*, July 1996, p. 4.

Karoway, C. "The Intranet — Your Own Company-wide Web," *Purchasing Today®*, August 1996, p. 28.

Lallatin, C.S. "Sweet'n Low or Equal?," *NAPM Insights*, April 1994, pp. 54-55.

Lallatin, C.S. "How Can I Categorize My Service Purchases?," *Purchasing Today®*, November 1997, p. 8.

Murphee, J. "They're Staying the Course," *NAPM Insights*, August 1995, p. 44

Sickinger, J. "Writing a Complete and Effective Statement of Work," *NAPM InfoEdge*, (3:3) November 1997.

Taylor, M. "Intranets in Action," *Purchasing Today®*, April 1998, p. 31.

Weiss, B.D. "Click and Contract," *Purchasing Today®*, June 1998, p. 4.

Woods, D.L. "Coaching Users to Develop Great Specifications," *Proceedings of the 1996 NAPM International Purchasing Conference*, NAPM, Tempe, AZ, 1996, pp. 86-91.

Wright, B. "Sign (Electronically) on the Dotted Line," *Purchasing Today®*, August 1997, p. 18.

Yates, R. "Open To Buy: Managing Cash and Inventories," *Purchasing Today®*, July 1998, p. 42.

Endnotes

1. Karoway, C. "The Internet — Your Own Companywide Web," *Purchasing Today®*, August 1996, p.28.
2. Karoway, C., p. 28.
3. Murphree, J. "They're Staying the Course," *NAPM Insights*, August 1995, p. 44.
4. Handfield, R.B and S.A. Melnyk. "GreenSpeak," *Purchasing Today®*, July 1998, p. 32.
5. Yates, R.A. "Open To Buy: Managing Cash and Inventories," *Purchasing Today®*, July 1998, p. 42.
6. Lallatin, C.S. "Sweet'n Low or Equal?," *NAPM Insights*, April 1994, p. 55.
7. Lallatin, C.S. "How Can I Categorize My Service Purchases?," *Purchasing Today®*, November 1997, p. 8.

APPENDIX 2-A

EXAMPLE STATEMENTS OF WORK

Example Functional Statement of Work

1. **Scope** - Include a statement about what the SOW covers. In some cases, background information may be helpful to clarify the needs of the procurement.

    1.1.Background – Do not discuss work tasks in the scope section of the SOW.

2. **Applicable documents** - All documents invoked in the requirements section of the SOW must be listed by document number and title. These documents may include standards, specifications, and other reference documents needed to identify and clarify the work task or deliverable product. However, instructions are promulgated to control in-house work efforts and will not be invoked in the SOW to control contractor efforts. Also, any document listed in this section must be invoked and selectively tailored to meet the minimal needs of the planned procurement in the requirements section.

    2.1. Specifications.

    2.2. Standards.

    2.3. Other Documents.

3. **Requirements** - The arrangement of technical tasks and subtasks within the requirements section will be dictated by program requirements. It may be helpful to have a general task to orient the planning and use of the subsequent subtasks. The following outline is a generalization and in no way reflects the ultimate SOW arrangement or requirements.

    3.1 General.

    3.2 Detail Tasks.

    3.2.1 System Engineering.

    a) Technical studies (including life-cycle costs).
    b) System effectiveness planning (i.e., reliability, maintainability, and human factors).

3.2.2 Design-to-Cost Goal.

3.2.3 Configuration Management Program.

3.2.4 Safety and Hazard Engineering.

3.2.5 Quality Program.

3.2.6 Integrated Logistics Support Program - Requirements including logistics support analysis (LSA).

3.2.7 Design, Fabricate, and Testing.

Example Performance Statement of Work

1. **Scope** - A statement defining what the SOW covers is always required in this section. However, in most research procurement, it is necessary to provide information on the background and alternate approaches that have been investigated. Because the results required are expressed as objectives or goal attainments in this type of SOW, extra care must be exercised to ensure that work tasking and deliverable products are not discussed in this paragraph. Discuss only what the SOW covers and possibly some ways this particular approach can be expressed as an introduction, a background, or both.

2. **Applicable documents** - All documents invoked in the requirements section of the SOW must be listed by document number and title. These documents may include standards, specifications, and other reference documents needed to identify and clarify the work task or deliverable product. However, instructions are promulgated to control in-house work efforts and will not be invoked in the SOW to control contractor efforts. Also, any document listed in this section must be invoked and selectively tailored to meet the minimal needs of the planned procurement.

3. **Requirements** - Various approaches are used in defining tasks in the SOW to meet particular program needs for creative efforts. Task breakout or task phasing methods are used to simplify completion and control of the effort in complex acquisitions. Requirements may be segregated into general tasks that have application to the overall program requirements.

    3.1. General - General task statements may be included in the SOW to satisfy overall creative program requirements and for planning the use of the results of the acquisition.

3.2. Detail - The contractor will perform the following tasks:
   a. Develop
   b. Organize
   c. Accomplish milestone and cost planning

Source: Sickinger, J. "Writing a Complete and Effective Statement of Work," *NAPM InfoEdge*, (3:3), November 1997 pp. 14-15.

CHAPTER 3

COST ANALYSIS: HOW GOOD IS THE DEAL?

Chapter Objectives

- Develop an understanding of types of costs and costing approaches.
- Apply breakeven analysis, learning curves, life-cycle costing, and total cost of ownership where appropriate.
- Understand the three components of pricing from the supplier's point of view.
- Understand price analysis techniques and when each is applicable.
- Describe the common types of discounts.
- Determine when the various costing techniques are appropriate.

Introduction

A fundamental goal of the purchasing function is to lower material and service costs while maintaining and improving quality, delivery, and service from suppliers. This chapter provides the tools for analyzing the costs of materials and services. We will first review the basic components of the cost structure and how costs are allocated to products and services. Next, we will present several models for evaluating costs followed by a comprehensive cost analysis example. However, not all prices given by suppliers are solely based on cost. Market structure and perceived value to the customer may also influence pricing. A number of pricing models and analysis techniques are then reviewed. The chapter ends with a model for evaluating which technique to use based on the supplier relationship and the nature of the purchase.

Understanding the Cost Structure

Cost analysis takes more time and costs more to do than price analysis, but it yields much more information. Cost analysis is most appropriate for high-volume custom products and services and as a negotiation tool. This section first describes the components and types of costs, then discusses activity-based costing.

Components of Cost

Many factors determine the total cost of a product or service. They include the following:

- **Material** - Materials directly used in the production of the good or service such as raw materials, components, and subassemblies which are purchased.
- **Labor** - Labor includes the direct labor costs associated with the production of the good or service.
- **Overhead** - Overhead includes both labor and material costs that cannot be directly attributed to a product or service but are necessary costs of doing business. Examples include production supplies, maintenance supplies, material handling labor, and first-line supervision.
- **Tooling** - The cost of tooling incurred for a specific product. This item is typically expensed.
- **General and administrative** - This component includes management, marketing, accounting expenses, and any other expenses that cannot be directly associated with producing the product or service.
- **Profit** - Profit is an expected part of doing business. An organization that does not make a profit will not stay in business long. Profit is a reward for risk-taking and efficiency on the part of the supplier. Also, suppliers should be allowed higher profit margins on smaller orders to compensate for the higher overhead costs associated with handling those orders. Likewise, the supplier's profit margin should decline as order size increases. Profit can

also serve as a means to reward suppliers for reliability and service over time.

Types of Cost

Costs can be categorized along several different dimensions. Those dimensions include direct versus indirect costs, fixed versus variable costs, and common versus joint costs.

Direct versus indirect costs - Direct costs are costs that can be directly associated with the production of one unit or providing a service to one customer. Examples include direct labor and materials. Indirect costs are incurred in the production of a good or service but cannot be attributed to one unit. Examples include rent, property taxes, depreciation, utilities, supervision, and production and maintenance supplies.

Fixed versus variable costs - A fixed cost is constant throughout an entire range of output, activity, or time period (usually at least one year). Examples include facility costs, equipment costs, and management costs. A variable cost changes in direct proportion to activity or volume. Examples include direct labor and materials.

Common and joint costs - Common costs are costs necessary for the production of two or more products or services that cannot rationally be allocated to either. Corporate overhead is a good example. It is necessary but standard overhead allocation bases (e.g., revenue, labor hours, material costs, space, or investment) have no relationship to the actual costs and, therefore, result in arbitrary cost allocations. Joint costs are costs of an activity that unavoidably produces two or more different products. For example, cracking petroleum produces a number of products including gas, diesel, and naphtha. What should be the basis for allocating cost?

Activity-based Costing

Traditional costing systems allocate overhead costs based on direct labor or materials. Activity-based costing (ABC) assigns costs to products or services based on the special activities associated with production of a particular product or service. A careful analysis of costs assigned to a particular product might, for example, disclose that the supplier's engineering overhead is being applied to a mature product for which engineering is not required.

ABC is relevant to purchasing for a number of reasons including the following:

- **As a tool for analyzing supplier prices** - John Deere and Company's Horicon Works plant used ABC to evaluate its supplier costs. An ABC analysis of a powder metal component identified a number of misallocated or inappropriate costs. The analysis led to process and specification changes that lowered the component cost from $2.73 to $1.27 on a volume of more than 200,000 units per year.[1]
- **To support the analysis of the cost of doing business with a particular supplier** - Tycos, a manufacturer of blood pressure gauges and stethoscopes, was considering the use of a less expensive raw material to reduce product cost. When the true costs of adding a new supplier were considered such as additional design costs, engineering support, receiving additional shipments from a new supplier, and adding a new supplier to the system, the proposed new material was determined to cost more than the current material.[2]
- **To identify problem suppliers**
- **To improve purchasing systems and processes** - John Deere and Company applied ABC to its purchasing department costs. The study identified five categories of purchasing activities: productive materials, tooling management, general operations, research and development, and manufacturing support. Previously purchasing costs were allocated as a flat percentage of overhead.[3]

There are four basic components of an ABC system: activities, cost drivers, cost objects, and bills of activities.

- **Activity** - An activity is a process or procedure that causes work and thereby consumes resources. An example of activity is telephoning a supplier to place an order.
- **Cost driver** - A cost driver is the direct cause of the work. A cost driver reflects the demands placed on activities by products or other cost objects. For example, if the activity were the paying of invoices, the cost driver would be the number of invoices to be

paid. A cost driver should be relevant and easy to measure. Relevancy relates to whether the activity affects your cost of doing business. Ease of measurement means being able to easily measure how much the activity costs and the product or service's use of the activity. Common drivers of purchasing activities include the number of requisitions, number of part numbers, number of schedule changes, number of suppliers, and number of late deliveries.[4]

- **Cost object** - An entity that requires the performance of an activity. Examples are products, customers, markets, distribution channels, and projects.
- **Bill of activities** - A listing of the activities and associated cost required by a product or other cost object.

In Exhibit 3.1, there are two products, "L" and "S". Product L has a production volume of 1,500 units and Product S, 150 units. Each product requires two production changeovers at an estimated cost of $900 per change. Two dollars of direct material is required to produce one unit of Product L and $3 for Product S.

EXHIBIT 3.1
ABC Example 1

	Product L	Product S	Total
Production volume	1,500	150	1,650
Number of changeovers	2	2	4
Cost per changeover	$900	$900	$3,600
Materials cost/unit	$2.00	$3.00	$3,450
Conventional overhead/unit	$2.08	$3.13	
ABC overhead/unit	$1.20	$12.00	

Using conventional costing methods the total cost of the production changeovers of $3,600 [($900)(4 changes)=$3,600] would be allocated using the total direct material costs of $3,450 [($2/unit)(1,500 units) + ($3/unit)(150 units)=$3,450] yielding an allocation of $1.04 per dollar of material used [($3,600)/($3,450)]. The overhead allocation is $2.08 for Product L and $3.12 for Product S. With this approach Product L is bearing the burden of Product S's changes as Product L will absorb $3,120 [(1,500 units)($2.08/unit)] of the production changeover costs even though it was only responsible for $1,800 of changeover costs.

An activity-based costing approach recognizes the cost driver is the number of production changeovers and uses that to allocate the costs to each unit. For Product L, the allocation would be $1.20 [(2 changes)($900/change)/(1,500 units)] while for Product S the allocation would be $12.00 per unit [(2 changes)($900/change)/(150 units)]. Now the costs associated with each product's production have been properly allocated.

Exhibit 3.2 presents a second costing scenario. Both Product L and S have estimated volumes of 1,500 units, but Product L requires only two production changeovers while Product S requires 10 production changeovers. Product L uses two dollars of direct material while Product S uses three dollars of direct material. Using conventional costing, the total cost of the product changes, $10,800 [(12)($900)], would be allocated across the total direct materials costs of $4,500 [(($2/unit of L)(1,500 units of L)+($3/unit of S)(1,500 units of S))]. The resulting allocations are $2.88 per unit of L [($2 of material/unit)($1.44/$ of material)] and $4.32 per unit of S [($3/ unit)($1.44/$ of material)]. Again Product L absorbs more than its share, $7,200 out of the $12,000, while it only incurred $2,000 of engineering change costs. Using activity-based costing, Product L's allocation would be two dollars per unit [(2 changes) ($900/change) /(1,500 units)] while Product S's allocation would rise to six dollars per unit [(10 changes)($900/change)/(1,500 units)]. Thus, if your supplier is not using ABC techniques your product costs may be higher or lower than necessary as you are absorbing costs not associated with your product.

EXHIBIT 3.2
ABC Example 2

	Product L	Product S	Total
Production volume	1,500	1,500	1,650
Number of changeovers	2	10	12
Cost per changeover	$900	$900	$10,800
Materials cost/unit	$2.00	$3.00	$7,500
Conventional overhead/unit	$2.88	$4.32	
ABC overhead/unit	$1.20	$6.00	

Evaluating Costs

In this section, several tools for evaluating costs are presented, including breakeven analysis, learning curves, life-cycle costing, and total cost of ownership.

Breakeven Analysis

Breakeven analysis is a technique for comparing two alternatives to determine the point at which the purchaser is indifferent between the alternatives. The traditional formula for determining the breakeven volume given unit revenue, unit variable cost, and total fixed costs is as follows:

Total revenue = Total fixed cost + Total variable cost

or

(Revenue/unit)(# of units) = Total fixed cost + (variable cost/unit)(# of units)

The equation can be solved if three of the four values (revenue per unit, number of units, total fixed cost, or variable cost per unit) are known. The examples below illustrate the application of breakeven analysis to a make or buy decision and an equipment replacement decision.

Example - A small manufacturing company has been purchasing a casting in its final, machined form. The company is now considering purchasing the rough casting and performing its own machining. The purchase price of the machined part is $4.25 per unit. The price of the unmachined casting is $1.30 per unit, but it requires $1.80 per unit in labor if the company does its own machining. If the company machines the castings, fixed costs will increase by $48,000 per year. At what annual volume is the total cost to purchase equal to the total cost to make?

The breakeven formula is as follows:

(Total annual cost to purchase) = (Total annual cost to manufacture)
($4.25/unit)(# of units) = ($48,000/year) + ($1.30/unit + $1.80/unit)(# of units)
($4.25/unit)(# of units) - ($3.10/unit)(# of units) = $48,000/year
($1.15/unit)(# of units) = $48,000/year
# of units = ($48,000/year)/($1.15/unit) = 41,739 units

If the company's expected annual volume exceeds 41,739 units, it will be advantageous for the company to do its own machining. Below that volume it is less expensive to purchase finish-machined castings.

Example - A supplier approaches you with a proposal to replace your current copy machine with a new, improved model that allows two-sided copying. Your current volume is 100,000 copies per year at a cost of $0.03 per page for copier expenses such as toner, maintenance, and $0.01 per sheet of paper. The new machine, which costs $1,250, will lower the cost per copy to $0.025 per side and you estimate that 50 percent of your copies could be two-sided. How long would it take to pay for the new copy machine?

Although the information is not expressed in normal breakeven terms, the problem is one of determining the breakeven point in terms of the number of copies between the old copier and the proposed new copier. That is:

Total cost of old copier = Total cost of new copier

The total cost to operate the old copier is $0.04 per copy ($0.03 per copy + $0.01 per sheet of paper) times the number of copies, X. The total cost to operate the new copier is a little more difficult to determine. With the new copier, 50 percent of the copies made will be one-sided and cost $0.035 per copy ($0.025 per copy + $0.01 per sheet of paper). The other 50 percent will be two-sided copies at a cost of $0.03 per copy [(($0.025 per copy)(2 copies/sheet) + ($0.01 per sheet))/(2 copies/sheet)]. The fixed cost is the cost of the new copier, $1,250. The resulting formula is as follows:

($0.04/copy)(X copies) = $1,250 + [($0.035/copy)(0.5X copies) + ($0.030/copy)(0.5X copies)]

Solving the above for X yields a solution of 166,667 copies. At an annual usage rate of 100,000 copies per, 166,667 copies is equivalent to 1.67 years or one year, eight months. In other words, comparing the old machine to the new machine, the additional costs of the new machine will be recovered through its lower per-copy costs in 20 months. The recovery will occur sooner if copy volume rises, later if volume falls.

Learning Curves

The concept of learning curves was first observed by Curtis in the manufacture of airplanes in the 1930s. The observed phenomenon was that every time the total number of units produced doubled, the direct labor hours decreased by a constant percentage. The application for purchasers is that price should go down with volume, especially for short production runs. If the supplier is pricing the hundredth unit at the same price as the first, the purchaser is paying too much.

The formula for calculating the time required to produce unit number "x" at a given learning curve is:

$$Yx = (K)(xn)$$

where

Yx = the time for unit x,
K = the time required to produce the first unit,
x = the unit number, and
n = log b/log 2 where b is the learning percentage.

For example, an 80 percent learning curve and the time required to produce the first unit, is 43 minutes, the time required to produce the fifth unit will be:

$$Y5 = (43 \text{ minutes})(5(\log 0.8/\log 2)) = 25.6 \text{ minutes}$$

The same result could be obtained by using the improvement factor for unit five for an 80 percent learning curve in Exhibit 3.3 (0.5956) and multiplying by the time required to produce the first unit (43 minutes).

All repetitive tasks will show the effects of learning as the number of repetitions increases. The more complex the task, the larger the percentage decrease in cost; the less complex the task, the lower the decrease in costs.

Example - As the contract negotiator for your organization, you have been asked to purchase three additional units of a machine that is custom manufactured for you. The supplier for the first three units experienced a 90 percent learning curve. The first unit took 2,000 labor hours. How many labor hours should the supplier require for the units four through six?

Using Exhibit 3.3 the time for units four through six would be:

Unit 4 = (2,000 hours for unit 1)(0.8100) = 1,620 hours
Unit 5 = (2,000 hours for unit 1)(0.7830) = 1,566 hours
Unit 6 = (2,000 hours for unit 1)(0.7616) = 1,524 hours
Total = 4,710 hours

EXHIBIT 3.3
Learning Curve Improvement Ratios

Unit	90% Learning Curve Improvement Ratio	80% Learning Curve Improvement Ratio	70% Learning Curve Improvement Ratio
1	1.0000	1.0000	1.0000
2	0.9000	0.8000	0.7000
3	0.8462	0.7021	0.5682
4	0.8100	0.6400	0.4900
5	0.7830	0.5956	0.4368
6	0.7616	0.5617	0.3977
7	0.7439	0.5345	0.3674
8	0.7290	0.5120	0.3430
9	0.7161	0.4929	0.3228
10	0.7047	0.4765	0.3058
11	0.6946	0.4621	0.2912
12	0.6854	0.4493	0.2784
13	0.6771	0.4379	0.2672
14	0.6696	0.4276	0.2572
15	0.6626	0.4182	0.2482
16	0.6561	0.4096	0.2401
17	0.6501	0.4017	0.2327
18	0.6445	0.3944	0.2260
19	0.6392	0.3876	0.2198
20	0.6342	0.3812	0.2141

Life-cycle Costing

Life-cycle costing, sometimes called total cost of ownership, evaluates the costs associated with a product, supplier, or piece of capital equipment over the life of the item or relationship. Life-cycle costing is primarily used in evaluating the purchase of capital equipment, though it could be applied to selection of one supplier versus another. Costs considered include the following:

- Maintenance costs
- Training costs
- Repair part costs
- Energy use
- Cost of scrap and by-products
- Operating costs (labor and materials)
- Installation costs (including layout changes)

Life-cycle costing also takes into consideration salvage value or disposal costs at the end of the useful life of the equipment. Alternatively, costs associated with changing suppliers would be considered at the end of a relationship.

The following steps are suggested when performing a life-cycle cost analysis:

1. Determine operating cycle, types of operation, routine maintenance, overhaul, and actions (costs incurred) required.
2. Identify and quantify factors that affect costs such as power consumption, labor requirements, material usage, maintenance costs, failure rates, and downtime costs.
3. Project costs through the life of the equipment, including salvage value.
4. Discount costs to obtain present values and sum to obtain total life-cycle cost.

Example - The example shown in Exhibit 3.4 compares two different machines. Machine "A" has a projected five-year life with an initial cost of $80,000. Engineering and installation will cost $10,000 each, and training will cost $4,500. The first-year labor cost to operate the machine is forecast at $40,000 and the first-year energy use is estimated at $50,000. The percentage of downtime is estimated to be four percent for Machine A resulting in an estimated first-year cost of $12,000.

Machine "B" also has a five-year life, but costs more, $100,000. Engineering and installation will again cost $10,000 each and training is slightly more expensive at an estimated cost of $5,000. The first-year labor cost to operate the machine is forecast higher than Machine A at $50,000, but the first-year energy cost is estimated to be lower, at $40,000. The percentage of downtime is estimated to be two percent for Machine B, resulting in an estimated first-year cost of $5,000.

Both machines' costs are forecasted to increase yearly, with labor increasing by five percent per year, energy costs by 10 percent per year, and downtime costs by eight percent per year.

In Exhibit 3.4, the "Total" row for each machine presents the total costs for each year. The "PVF" row gives the present value factors using a 12 percent interest rate for each year. The "Present Value" row gives the present value of the column total. For example, the column total for Machine A for year one is $102,000 and the present value factor is 0.893. Multiplying the two together yields a present value of $91,086. Comparing the total present values shows that Machine A (which had the lower initial investment of $104,500) costs $527,387 to operate over its five-year life while Machine B (which cost $125,000 initially) costs only $514,112 over the five-year period. Therefore, Machine B has the lower life-cycle cost and is the better purchase.

A life-cycle cost analysis focuses on the total cost of ownership, use, and disposal of a piece of equipment, not just its purchase price.

EXHIBIT 3.4
Life-Cycle Costing Example

Machine A
(5 year life, 4% downtime)
YEAR

COST	0	1	2	3	4	5
Purchase	$ 80,000					
Engineering	$ 10,000					
Installation	$ 10,000					
Training	$ 4,500					
Labor		$ 40,000	$ 42,000	$ 44,100	$ 46,305	$ 48,620
Energy		$ 50,000	$ 55,000	$ 60,500	$ 66,550	$ 73,205
Downtime		$ 12,000	$ 12,960	$ 13,997	$ 15,117	$ 16,326
Total	$104,500	$102,000	$109,960	$118,597	$127,972	$138,151
PVF @ 12%	1.000	0.893	0.797	0.712	0.636	0.567
Present value	$104,500	$ 91,086	$ 87,638	$ 84,441	$ 81,390	$ 78,332

Total Present Value = $527,387

Machine B
(5 year life, 2% downtime)
YEAR

COST	0	1	2	3	4	5
Purchase	$100,000					
Engineering	$ 10,000					
Installation	$ 10,000					
Training	$ 5,000					
Labor		$ 50,000	$ 52,500	$ 55,125	$ 57,881	$ 60,775
Energy		$ 40,000	$ 44,000	$ 48,400	$ 53,240	$ 58,564
Downtime	————	$ 5,000	$ 5,400	$ 5,832	$ 6,299	$ 6,802
Total	$125,000	$ 95,000	$101,900	$109,357	$117,420	$126,141
PVF @ 12%	1.000	0.893	0.797	0.712	0.636	0.567
Present value	$125,000	$ 84,835	$ 81,214	$ 76,862	$ 74,679	$ 71,522

Total Present Value = $514,112

Total Cost of Ownership

Total cost of ownership (TCO) is a costing method similar to life-cycle costing. Total cost of ownership looks not only at the price paid for an item or service but also includes costs of acquisition, possession, use, and disposal.

Today's quality emphasis has caused managers to realize that product/service quality cannot exceed the quality of input from suppliers. Total cost of ownership looks at the total cost of the purchase including use, warranty, and returns. Total cost of ownership can help determine which suppliers to retain by examining the relationship costs, such as supply chain costs and value. The increase in global competitiveness has made organizations aware of the need to manage total cost not only on a purchasing basis but for the total product as well.

Approaches for determining TCO - There are two fundamental approaches to determining the total cost of ownership. The first approach, called dollar-based, gathers and allocates actual costs for the relevant total cost elements. There are two dollar-based approaches: direct cost methods and formula-based methods. Direct cost methods are based on the actual cost and are predicated upon the ability to trace where costs actually originated. This requires an ABC system to understand the cost drivers involved. Good applications for direct cost methods include supplier selection, supply-base reduction, make versus buy/outsourcing, and process improvement. The major advantages of direct cost models are the ability to tailor the factors considered to the specific decision situations, their flexibility, the ability to manage the level of complexity to the decision, and their usefulness in identifying critical issues. The disadvantages to these models include the length of time it takes to create them, they are not very useful for repetitive decisions, and they are not cost-effective for low dollar value purchases.

The formula-based methods use formulas to allocate the actual costs. These formulas are based on the effort or resource level required to support a given activity. Because they are generalized, they are good for repetitive decisions. Appropriate applications include supplier volume allocations, supply-base reductions, ongoing supplier evaluation, and process improvement. Formula method models are easy to use once created and are effective for use in repetitive decisions. Their disadvantages include the length of time it takes to create the model, the need to periodically review the formulas, the fact that each type of decision will require a new model, and that they only consider a limited set of factors.

The second approach, called value-based, combines quantitative data with qualitative data. These models are very similar to the cost-ratio supplier evaluation models (see Chapter 5) but include other factors. The primary applications of value-based approaches are supplier selection, make versus buy/outsourcing, and process improvements. The advantages of value-based models are their ability to incorporate issues where cost cannot be determined, their use of weights to indicate the importance of various factors, and their easy use for repetitive decisions. On the other hand, these models are time-consuming to develop, only useful for important and/or repetitive decisions, and make it difficult to determine factor weights.

Standard versus unique TCO models - An alternate classification system for total cost of ownership models is the unique versus standard models. Unique models are appropriate when the purchases to be evaluated vary greatly, no one set of factors captures the critical issues in the various situations, and there is a desire for flexibility in modeling. Standard models are more appropriate when the issues are the same across the various purchases, there is a need for a user-friendly model, there is a desire to automate or computerize the systems, and there is a need to analyze repetitive purchases.

Although many costs can be included in total cost of ownership models, the most common are price; delivery; service; supplier's EDI capabilities; acquisition costs; and quality costs including inspection; cost of nonconformance; and quality programs.

Example - Exhibit 3.5 presents a standard TCO analysis for capital equipment purchases. The standard assumptions data is given as used in the analysis. The capitalized costs are given for two suppliers "A" and "B." The only major cost differences are in the purchase prices and the option costs. The capitalized cost per year is the sum of the capitalized costs divided by the number of years in the useful life in this case four. The expensed costs for the first year are then estimated for each supplier. The total for each supplier indicates that Supplier A's equipment is lower in cost than Supplier B.

EXHIBIT 3.5
Example of Stand TCO Model for Capital Purchases

Standard Assumptions

Fully Burdened Labor Rates		Facilities Standards	
Exempt: Manager	$36.00	Space valuation per foot	$2,650
Exempt: Engineer, etc.	$36.00	No. of weeks operating/year	52
Programmer	$24.00	Financial Standards	
SNE: Technician	$40.00	Useful life	4 years
Hourly: Operator	$12.00	Cost of funds	12.8%
SNE: Administrative	$15.00	Tax rate	38.0%

Equipment Costs

Capitalized costs

	Supplier A	Supplier B
Purchase price	$657,059	$746,785
Options and upgrades	$ 2,915	$ 479
Service contract	$ 14,815	$ 14,815
Installation	$229,630	$229,630
Freight/duty	$ 70,000	$ 70,000
Packing	$ 14,815	$ 14,815
Other	—	—
Amortization period	4 years	4 years
Capitalized costs/year	$247,309	$269,131

Expended Costs - First Year

	Supplier A	Supplier B
Engineering expense	—	—
Spares cost	$ 8,400	$ 48,000
Purchase-off costs $ 39,000		$ 39,000
Training	—	—
Travel	$ 20,000	$ 20,000
Other	—	—
Equipment expense		
First year	$ 67,400	$107,000
Total Cost of Ownership	$317,709	$376,131

Barriers to TCO implementation - There are a number of barriers to the use of total cost of ownership models. The major categories include availability of data, complexity of models, resistance by users, and organizational culture. Even though an organization may desire to use the total cost of ownership model, it may not be able to obtain the necessary data or even determine what it is needed. Because of the model complexity, the time investment to develop a model is high, it is difficult to develop easy-to-use models, the relevant factors are constantly changing, and there is a general lack of user expertise. User resistance takes the form of resistance to standard models (every situation is unique), fear of loss of control, and fear the model will be too theoretical. Organizational cultures are difficult to change. The price only mentality is still alive and well. Overcoming this resistance requires that purchasers receive new skills and communication across the organizations.

Comprehensive Cost Analysis Example

The following problem illustrates many of the concepts discussed above.

The Situation

Purchaser Smith, C.P.M. has to purchase 10 special electronic modules that have been purchased twice before. The part history record shows that the first purchase was for five items at $1,500 each and the second purchase was for five items at $1,350 each. Smith asked the supplier to substantiate the price for the new order and received the following breakdown:

Direct labor:18hours/unit @ $14.50/hr	$261
Manufacturing overhead @ 100 percent of direct labor $261	
Material	$385
General and administrative expenses @10 percent of cost of goods sold	$ 90
Profit	$100
Total unit price	$1,097

The supplier indicated that the original estimate for five units was projected on a 90 percent learning curve. The 90 percent curve was used because labor studies showed that this rate of improvement could be realistically maintained throughout production. The actual hours required to produce the first five units, 20 hours for engineering and planning and 96 hours for production, had been in line with the original estimate. When asked for the number of hours required to produce the second five units, the supplier said the information was not available because the lot was still being made.

The direct labor rate was based on the average rate of $20 per hour for engineering and planning personnel, $11 per hour for skilled shop personnel, and $8.54 per hour for unskilled shop personnel, and a 10 percent estimate for wage increases.

The bill of materials was as follows:

Quantity/unit	Description	Unit price
10	Resistor	$ 12
1	Integrated circuit	$ 15
5	Capacitor	$ 20
5	Diode	$110
1	Transformer	$150.
1	Casing	$ 40
Various	Miscellaneous items	$ 3
10% scrap allowance		$ 35
Total		$385

The indirect rates, overhead and general and administrative costs, are revised by the supplier's accounting department every six months and are based on recent experience. The scrap rate was based on experience for all production jobs.

The engineering and planning effort was applicable to the first order. There was little, if any, need for additional engineering and planning. The purchaser's personnel department indicated that a six percent yearly wage increase was reasonable for the type of labor involved.

Purchasing records indicated that the transformer supplier was currently quoting the following unit prices:

Quantity	Unit Price
1-5	$200
6-10	$150
11-25	$120

Is the supplier's price appropriate and if not, what would you counteroffer to begin negotiating with the supplier?

Direct Labor Analysis

Cost - Because engineering and planning are not required for this order, it is appropriate to recalculate the labor rate based on only the skilled and unskilled shop labor, then apply a six percent labor cost increase.

Supplier's proposed labor rate $= [(\$20.00/\text{hr} + \$11.00/\text{hr} + \$8.54/\text{hr})/3][1.1]$
$= \$14.50/\text{hr}$
Purchaser's proposed labor rate $= [(\$11.00/\text{hr} + \$8.54/\text{hr})/2][1.06]$
$= \$10.36/\text{hr}$

Time - The supplier used an estimate of 18 labor hours per unit for units 11 through 20. Using the learning curve concept and assuming the supplier's estimate of a 90 percent learning curve is appropriate, the total time to produce the first five units relative to the time to produce the first unit would be the sum of the improvement factors for units one to five. Using the 90 percent learning curve improvement factors from Exhibit 3.3 the total is 4.3392. Therefore, because production used 96 total labor hours, dividing by 4.3392 gives a first unit time of 22.1 hours. If the 90 percent learning curve holds, the total time relative to the first unit to produce units 11 through 20 would be the sum of 90 percent learning curve improvement factors for units 11 through 20 in Exhibit 3.3 that is 6.6134. The total labor hours to produce units 11 through 20 would be:

(6.6134)(22.1 hrs) = 146.2 total hours or 14.6 hrs/unit average

Total labor cost - The estimated labor cost per unit would then be the average labor hours per unit of 14.6 hours per unit times the purchaser's proposed labor rate of $10.36 per hour yielding an estimated labor cost of $151.26 per unit.

Material Cost Analysis

The cost for material other than the transformer totals $200. With the addition of a 10 percent scrap factor the total becomes $220 per unit. The supplier could take advantage of the quantity discount available on transformers and provide for a 10 percent scrap factor at the same time. The total cost to purchase 10 transformers is $1,500 while the total cost of 11 units is $1,320 Therefore, the transformer cost including scrap is $132 per unit. The total material cost is then:

$220 + $132= $352.

New Price Estimate

Using the new labor and material estimates the new cost estimate is as follows:

Direct labor	$ 151.26
Manufacturing overhead	$ 151.26
Material	$ 352.00
General and administrative	$ 65.45
Profit	$ 100.00
Total	$ 819.97

This is still generous in that the supplier's profit has been left untouched. If the supplier's profit is calculated as a percent of cost, the markup is 11.3 percent which, when applied to the new cost estimate, would yield a total price of $801.33.

Marketing Perspectives on Pricing

There are different perspectives on how to set the price of a product or service. The supplier defines a fair price as either a price that covers the full cost to produce the product or service, including overhead costs plus a reasonable profit, or as a price which compensates the supplier based on the value of the product or service to the purchaser and that covers all the relevant costs. A "reasonable" profit is defined as a profit that rewards the supplier for the risk involved. The purchaser defines a "fair" price as the lowest price required to get the desired product or service. The purchaser's perspective is normally focused on the cost of the product or service.

Three dimensions come together to determine price from the supplier's point of view: market structure affects on price, cost-based pricing models, and value-based pricing. Each is discussed below.

Market Structure

One factor that clearly affects price is the level of competition. The various types or degrees of competition range from one seller with many buyers (i.e., a monopoly) to many sellers with one buyer (i.e., a monopsony) as explained below:

- **Monopoly** - One seller with many buyers. In the United States most monopolies are regulated (e.g., public utilities) to keep prices reasonable. With no competition, the seller could set any price it desired.
- **Monopolistic competition** - Few sellers and many buyers. The few sellers create the illusion of many sellers through product differentiation. An example is the breakfast cereal industry, in which a few companies control the market but offer a wide variety of products that compete for market share not only with other companies but also with the organization's own brands.
- **Oligopolistic** - Few sellers and many buyers. Price is controlled by either an industry leader or a cartel. The steel industry was traditionally an oligopoly, i.e., one company would propose a price

and the rest of the industry would often quickly adopt that price. An example of a cartel is the petroleum industry where OPEC establishes the price for all its members.

- **Perfect competition** - Many buyers and sellers. In a perfect market, all buyers and sellers have equal importance. Most markets are not perfect but function effectively like a perfectly competitive market. Price is established based on supply and demand.
- **Oligopsonistic** - Many sellers with few buyers. In this market, buyers have a major effect on pricing because all the sellers compete for their business. An example is the meat-packing industry.
- **Monopsony** - Several sellers and one buyer. This is the reverse situation of a monopoly where the buyer controls the pricing. An example would be the market for military fighter aircraft where the United States government controls the sale of the product by domestic producers.

Cost-based Pricing

Cost-based pricing models start with an estimate of the unit cost of goods sold, which includes direct labor, materials, and overhead. Three common approaches to pricing are straight markup, rate of return, and variable, as explained below.

Straight markup - In the straight markup model, price is calculated by multiplying the unit cost times a markup fraction to cover the contribution to overhead and profit, then adding the unit cost. Mathematically, the formula is as follows:

Price = Unit Cost + (Unit Cost)(Markup Fraction)

For example, if the unit cost is $80 per unit and the markup rate is 20 percent the price would be $96.

Price = $80/unit + ($80/unit)(0.2) = $96/unit

The questions the purchaser should ask include the following:

- **What costs are included in the unit cost?** The purchaser is concerned about costs not related to the product/service being included such as product/service development costs for another product/service or fully depreciated tooling. The purchaser should also ask what material and labor costs are keeping costs high.

- **Is the supplier marking up both direct costs and overhead?** Overhead may already include a contribution to profit, thus the supplier is making a profit on profit.
- **Is the markup appropriate given the supplier's cost structure?** A supplier may be proposing a higher markup than normal without a commensurate increase in risk.

Rate of return - The rate of return model is based on recovering all costs plus a return on the required investment. This model could be used when a supplier must invest substantial funds in tooling or equipment. The model's five steps are as follows:

1. **Determine the desired rate of return (ROR) on the investment** - The desired ROR is equal to or greater than the organization's required investment return rate. For example, a 15 percent rate of return would be expressed as 1.15; thus the investment should return the original investment plus 15 percent.
2. **Estimate required investment** - This could include tooling, equipment, and additional materials.
3. **Estimate sales quantity** - The estimated volume of units to be produced by the investment.
4. **Estimate unit cost** - The unit cost should be a fully absorbed cost including contribution to overhead and profit.
5. **Calculate the price** - The price is calculated using the following formula:

Price = [(ROR)(Investment)/(Sales quantity)] + unit cost

Example - Your supplier is quoting you a price on a new part it would like to produce for you. If the supplier's desired rate of return is 15 percent, the required investment $150,000, the estimated sales quantity 5,000 units, and the unit cost $80, the price would be:

Price = [(1.15)($150,000)/(5,000 units)] + $80/unit
       = [$34.50/unit] + $80/unit
       = $114.50/unit

This, then, is an all inclusive price from the supplier, which includes product costs, product markup, tooling investment, and a return on the tooling investment. In this case, the purchaser would want to verify that the desired rate of return is reasonable, that the investment costs are appropriate, and the estimated sales quantity is realistic. Also, the makeup of the unit cost is subject to investigation. It may help clarify costs if the purchaser asks for separate quotes for the product and tooling.

Variable pricing - In some cases, suppliers will temporarily price products and/or services based only on their variable costs. Their reasons for doing so may include the following:

- Keeping their work force employed during lean times to retain skilled labor
- The product is a by-product of a process and the overhead is already covered
- The item is a loss leader meaning, its purpose is to get customers to purchase other items)
- Suppliers are trying to purchase the business (i.e., get a foot in the door) and plan to raise prices in the future
- A purchaser needs to understand a supplier's rationale for such pricing; suppliers cannot absorb the losses caused by variable pricing in the long run

Value-based Pricing

Many factors affect a purchaser's perception of value as it relates to price. Value can refer to the total benefits or satisfaction such as a utility that a customer receives from the product or service. Another concept of value is the exchange value or economic value to the customer. This value is based on what the customer's perceived alternatives are. Among the factors that affect a purchaser's perception of value are the following:

- **Perceived substitutes** - The greater the availability of potential substitute products or services, the lower the purchaser's perceived value. Purchasers are more price sensitive the higher the product's or service's price relative to the prices of perceived substitutes. A supplier's ability to raise price is influenced by the

alternatives of which the purchasers are aware and the extent they
know the prices of substitutes. The supplier may increase perceived value by how it positions its product's/service's image.
Associating the desired product and/or service with a higher
priced alternative enables the supplier to charge a higher price.

- **Unique value** - Purchasers are less sensitive to a product' and/or
  service's price the more they value any unique attributes or features that differentiate the product and/or service from the competition.

- **Switching cost** - Purchasers are less sensitive to the price of a
  product and/or service the greater the added cost, (both monetary
  and non-monetary, of switching suppliers. The extent to which
  purchasers have both monetary and psychological investments in
  a supplier affects their perceptions of the importance of price.

- **Difficulty of comparison** - Purchasers are less sensitive to the
  price of a known and proven product and/or service supplier
  when they have difficulty comparing alternatives. Purchasers
  face this problem often when considering "or equals". The more
  difficult it is to determine if a substitute product and/or service is
  equivalent the more likely it is that a purchaser will be willing to
  pay more for a known, proven product and/or service than accept
  a less expensive substitute.

- **Price-quality** - Purchasers are less sensitive to a product's and/or
  service's price if a higher price indicates better quality. If a pres-
  tigious image is an important product and/or service attribute and
  it is difficult to evaluate product and/or service quality before
  purchase, the lower the purchaser's sensitivity to price.

- **Expenditure size** - Purchasers are more price sensitive the larger the expenditure. The more significant the expenditure is to the
  purchaser, the greater the purchaser's price sensitivity.

- **End benefit** - Purchasers are more price sensitive when the purchaser's finished products or services are being sold in a highly
  competitive market. Because material cost is a major determinant
  of a product's price, the more price competitive the market the
  greater the purchaser's concern about material cost.

- **Shared cost** - The smaller a purchaser's portion of the purchase
  price, the lower the price sensitivity. Thus, if a patient makes only
  a $10 co-payment for a doctor's visit, he or she is probably not

concerned much about the entire cost of the visit, most of which is paid by his or her medical insurance.

- **Fairness** - Purchasers are more sensitive to price when it is outside the range they perceive as "fair" based on previous price, competitor's price, and necessity. For example, a request for a 15 percent price increase when market demand is lower, raw material and labor costs are stable, and the average inflation rate is three percent, would not be considered fair.

- **Inventory** - A purchaser's ability to hold inventory for later use substantially increases the purchaser's sensitivity to temporary price deviations from expected long-term price levels. The greater a purchaser's ability to maintain large inventories of an item, the lower the purchaser's need to react to what are perceived as temporary price changes.

- **Location or time** - Purchasers are often willing to pay more if a supplier's goods are located near the purchaser's needs. Thus, an industrial purchaser often purchases from a local distributor, usually at a higher price, rather than order from a distant manufacturer.

- **Supplier's reputation, service, and relationship** - The perceived reputation, prior service performance, and current relationship will affect the purchaser's perception of value. If these factors are generally positive, the purchaser will often be willing to pay more rather than switch to an unknown supplier.

Price Analysis Techniques

Several methods can be used for analyzing price quotations from suppliers including competitive proposals from other suppliers, comparison with published prices, historical comparisons, and internal cost estimates. These methods are relatively fast and inexpensive. They work best when acquiring industry-standard materials and components. Each method is explained in detail below.

Competitive Proposals

Competitive proposals are used in a competitive market to ensure that prices quoted by suppliers fairly reflect cost, value, and risk. This is often the situation for industry standard products where many companies offer interchangeable products. For the price analysis to work, the following conditions for a competitive bid must be met:

- Clear and adequate specifications are provided.
- Adequate time exists for the bidding process.
- An adequate number of suppliers exist.
- Suppliers actively compete for the business.
- A sufficient volume of business to interest suppliers.
- Special tooling or setup costs do not constitute a major portion of the cost.

Competitive proposals may cause problems, however, when the following situations exist:

- The existing contract holder has a competitive advantage due to access to costs and volumes.
- The specifications are slanted in favor of one supplier.
- There is a lack of competition such as when demand exceeds supply the prices may become unreasonable.
- The use of performance specifications may result in solution proposals that differ significantly making cost comparisons difficult, if not impossible.

Comparison with Published Prices

Publicly available price quotes may exist for some items. One source is regulated prices, such as utility and transportation prices. A second source of information may be the market price established by the transactions between a number of purchasers and suppliers. Advertisements may be another source of information. A fourth source is published catalogs that list supplier's initial asking price.

Historical Comparisons

Another way to evaluate prices is by comparison with past prices. There are several caveats a purchaser must consider when using historical prices, including the following:

- The past does not determine the future. Market conditions change, sources of supply change, and economic conditions change.

- Purchase quantities may change over time, which can also lead to different prices (smaller orders, for example, generally lead to a higher unit price).
- The pricing in the past may have been based on one order or on total purchases over a specified period of time.
- If the item was purchased using competitive bidding, the prices would differ from the prices charged if the item was purchased from a sole supplier. Single or multiple sourcing differences may also cause price variation. Startup costs associated with the previous pricing, such as tooling or equipment investments that have been recovered.
- Historical comparisons of prices also require the availability of price indexes.

Internal Cost Estimates

Cost estimates are often needed for new items. Purchasers have three methods for obtaining an internal cost estimate: roundtables, comparisons with similar products and/or services, and detailed estimation.

Roundtables - In a roundtable, representatives from engineering, manufacturing, purchasing, and finance (accounting) are brought together to develop an estimate based on their experience, product and/or service knowledge, and market knowledge. Although roundtables are quick and relatively inexpensive, the results are extremely subjective. This technique works best when a quick estimate is needed and the organization has experience with similar products and/or services.

Comparison with similar products and/or services - If an organization has experience with similar products, services, or components, the purchaser may be able to use that information in pricing a new product and/or service. The technique can be done at the cost-element level or at the total price level. Cost-estimating relationships are developed from observations of historical costs and parameters such as weight, speed, area, volume, and density. Purchasers can develop mathematical models (such as multiple regression) to estimate the new cost.

The advantages of this approach are that it establishes a baseline for future estimating, it is relatively time efficient, and it is economical. On the negative side, a purchaser must be concerned about comparability of the data used in developing the cost relationships. The technique projects past inefficiencies, requires complex mathematical models, and assumes no major changes in quality or technology.

Detailed analysis - If adequate time exists, a cost estimate can be derived through a thorough review of all components, processes, and assemblies. This bottom-up approach takes advantage of the fact that small items can be estimated more accurately than large ones and that errors in estimating individual elements tend to cancel each other out. Data requirements include specifications, delivery quantities and rates, bills of materials, purchased component and material prices, drawings, understanding of the manufacturing process, quality requirements, time standards, overhead, and profit estimates.

Detailed analysis is potentially the most accurate method for estimating the production costs for an item. This analysis can also provide a historical base for future estimates. However, detailed analysis is time-consuming, expensive, requires the efforts of many people, and requires detailed specifications. Nonetheless, it yields the best, most complete information for use in negotiating important purchases.

Discounts

Discounts also affect pricing. Common discounts are quantity, trade, cash, and seasonal. Each is described below.

Quantity discounts - Quantity discounts are price reductions offered in recognition of the lower unit costs associated with larger orders. These reductions may result from manufacturing economies of scale such as distributing setup costs over a longer production run. Other cost reductions may be administrative. An invoice, for example, costs the same to process whether it is for $10 or $10,000. Quantity discounts are often reflected as "price breaks" on suppliers' price sheets depending on the quantity ordered.

Quantity discounts can be applied in several ways. One approach is to apply the discount only to a specific quantity purchased at one time. The purchaser may want to investigate the feasibility of purchasing the next larger amount to obtain a price break in order to achieve a lower total cost. This concept is often useful when purchasing transportation where a lower cost can be obtained by shipping goods in the next higher weight category at a lower rate per pound.

Example - An order to be shipped from Portland to Seattle weighs 3,800 pounds. The published rate is $2.75 per hundred pounds (cwt.) for loads between 3,500 and 3,900 pounds. If shipped as 3,800 pounds at $2.75 per cwt., the total cost would be $104.50. The published rate for 4,000 pounds, however, is $2.50 per cwt. If the 3,800-pound order were shipped as 4,000 pounds, the cost would be 4,000 pounds times $2.50 per cwt., which equals $100.

Quantity discounts can also be based on the total dollar value of an order, regardless of the number and quantity of items purchased. Thus, the discount is taken as a percent of the total value of the order.

A third approach to quantity discounting is to base the discount on the total dollars spent with a supplier over a specified time period. This type of discounting can be used with blanket orders or systems contracts. A caution here is that the discounts should be immediately payable when earned. Occasionally a supplier will propose payment of discounts months after they are earned. This can cause a loss of discounts if the purchaser changes suppliers.

Trade discounts - Trade discounts are reductions from a list price that are allowed to various classes of purchasers and distributors to compensate them for performing certain marketing functions. Trade discounts are stated in the form "25-10-5" which translates to the retailer receiving a 25 percent discount off the list price, the wholesaler receiving a 10 percent discount off the retailer's purchase price, and the manufacturer's price is five percent below the wholesaler's purchase price.

Example - A series discount of 25-10-5 based on a $100 retail price would yield the following:

Retailer:	Discount is ($100 x 0.25)=$25.00, so the purchase price is $75.00.
Wholesaler:	Discount is ($75 x 0.10)= $7.50, so the purchase price is $67.50.
Manufacturer:	Discount is ($67.5 x 0.05)= $3.38, so the manufacturer's selling price is $64.12.

Cash discounts - Cash discounts are offered by suppliers to encourage payment within a specified time period. For example, terms of "2-10/net 30", mean that a two percent discount is allowed if an invoice is paid within 10 days; otherwise, the full invoice amount is due within 30 days. Cash discounts can provide substantial savings. For example, a "2-10/net 30" discount is equivalent to a 36.5 percent annual interest rate [((365 days/yr)/(20 days))*0.02=0.365]. The term "2/10 EOM" means the purchaser receives a two percent discount if the invoice is paid within 10 days after the end of month in which order is shipped. The purchaser may also be able to get a price discount for prepayment.

Seasonal discounts - Seasonal discounts are offered to induce purchasers to purchase items during the off-season for which there is a seasonal demand pattern. The purchaser must determine whether the discount received offsets the increased inventory carrying costs. One way to avoid higher inventory carrying costs is to order the goods in the off-season, but not take delivery until a later date.

A variation of this discount occurs when the buying organization takes delivery of the goods during the off-season but does not pay for them until much later. Here, although price is not discounted, the delayed payment terms are equivalent to discounts. In either case, these seasonal incentives are effective mechanisms for sharing inventory-carrying costs.

Selecting a Cost/Price Analysis Technique

This chapter examined a number of cost analysis techniques including life-cycle costing, learning curves, target costing, and total cost of ownership. Price analysis techniques such as competitive bidding, comparisons with published prices, historical comparisons, and cost estimates were also discussed. The question which naturally arises is, "Which technique to use?" Dr. Lisa Ellram, C.P.M., suggests considering the nature of the purchase (one-time versus ongoing) and the relationship desired with the supplier (arm's-length to strategic).[5] The resulting matrix can be divided into four quadrants. Labeled leverage, strategic, low-impact, and critical (see exhibit 3.6).

EXHIBIT 3.6
Cost/Price Analysis Techniques

Ongoing	**Leverage**	**Strategic**
	Cost analysis focus	Continuous improvement focus
	• Estimating cost relationships	• Target cost analysis
	• Analysis of supplier cost breakdown	• Total cost of ownership
	• Internal cost estimates	
Nature of Purchase	• Total cost modeling	
	Low impact	**Critical**
	Price analysis focus	Life-cycle cost focus
	• Competitive bids	• Total cost analysis
	• Comparison of price list/catalog	• Life-cycle costing
	• Comparison to established market	
	• Historical comparison	
Onetime	• Price indexes	

Arm's length   Strategic alliance

Type of relationship sought with supplier

Source: Ellram, L.M. "What Tool to Use When?," *NAPM Insights*, September 1996, pp. 6-7.

Low-impact Purchases

Low-impact purchases are one-time or infrequent purchases that have little affect on the organization's success, because these types of products or services use fast, low-cost price analysis techniques such as historical costs, comparison to published prices, or competitive bidding.

Leverage Purchases

Leverage purchases are ongoing purchases that are performed on an arm's-length basis. Because these items are relatively important, the purchaser's focus is on cost analysis. Relevant tools include estimating cost relationships, total cost of ownership, and internal cost estimates.

Critical Purchases

Critical purchases are often large, one-time or infrequent acquisitions that are critical for the success of the organization. Examples could be capital equipment or computer systems. The most appropriate costing technique is total cost of ownership.

Strategic Purchases

Strategic purchases are important ongoing acquisitions where the purchaser desires a strong relationship with the supplier. An example might be production materials. Appropriate tools are total cost of ownership, historical comparisons, and internal cost estimates.

Key Points

1. Activity-based costing is a useful tool for analyzing supplier costs to identify misallocated or inappropriate costs.
2. Breakeven analysis, learning curves, life-cycle costing, and total cost of ownership models are valuable tools for analyzing costs.
3. From the supplier's point of view, price is a function of market structure, cost, and value.
4. Cost-based pricing models include straight markup, rate of return, and variable models.
5. Price analysis techniques include competitive proposals, comparisons with published prices, historical comparisons, and internal cost estimates.
6. Common discounts are quantity, trade, cash, and seasonal.

Questions for Review

1. What are the components of cost?
2. How does activity-based costing help the purchaser to obtain lower prices?
3. When should the purchaser use the various models for evaluating costs?
4. Why use total cost of ownership models?
5. What is the supplier's perspective on pricing?
6. How does cost-based pricing differ from value-based pricing?

7. What are the standard price analysis techniques?
8. What are the common discount types?

For Additional Information

Ellram, L.M. and S.P. Siferd. "Purchasing: The Cornerstone of the Total Cost Concept," *Journal of Business Logistics*, (14:1), 1993, pp. 163-184.

Ellram, L.M. "A Taxonomy of Total Cost of Ownership Models," *Journal of Business Logistics*, (15:1), 1994, pp. 171-191.

Ellram, L.M. "ABC and ABM: New Tools for Managing Purchasing Costs," *NAPM Insights*, May 1994, pp. 65-67.

Ellram, L.M. *"Total Cost Modeling in Purchasing,"* Center for Advanced Purchasing Studies, Tempe, AZ, 1994.

Ellram, L.M. "After ABC: Is It Working?," *NAPM Insights*, February 1995, p. 8.

Ellram, L.M. "What Tool to Use When?," *NAPM Insights*, September 1996, pp. 6-7.

Ellram, L.M. "The ABCs of 'Fair' Costing," *Purchasing Today®*, March 1999, p. 39.

Garcia, H.F., "Assignment of Overhead Costs in a Service Organization Using Activity-Based Costing," *Proceedings of the 1995 NAPM International Purchasing Conference*, NAPM, Tempe, AZ, 1995, pp. 21-26.

Harding, M.L. "The ABCs of Activities and Drivers," *NAPM Insights*, November 1994, p. 6.

Landeros, R., R.F. Reck, and F.T. Griggs. "Evaluating Suppliers' Overhead Allocations," *International Journal of Purchasing and Materials Management*, (30:2), Spring 1994, pp. 40-50.

Mathers, M. "Learning the Learning Curve," *Purchasing Today®*, July 1998, p. 14.

Mathers, M. "Finding the Best Lifetime Price," *Purchasing Today®*, July 1998, pp. 22-23.

Polzin, D. and N. Skjerseth. "ABC Results," *NAPM Insights*, March 1995, p. 8.

Porter, A.M. "Purchasing Pros Insist They Buy on Far More Than Price," *Purchasing*, May 1, 1997, pp. 18-19.

Endnotes

1. Polzin, D. and N. Skjerseth. "ABC Results," *NAPM Insights*, March 1995, p. 8.
2. Ellram, L.M. "After ABC: Is It Working?," *NAPM Insights*, February 1995, p. 8.
3. Ellram, L.M. "ABC and ABM: New Tools for Managing Purchasing Costs," *NAPM Insights*, May 1994, pp. 65-67.
4. Harding, M.L. "The ABCs of Activities and Drivers," *NAPM Insights*, November 1994, p. 6.
5. Ellram, L.M. "What Tool to Use When?," *NAPM Insights*, September 1996, pp. 6-7.

CHAPTER 4

THE SOURCING PROCESS: HOW DO I IDENTIFY POTENTIAL SUPPLIERS?

Chapter Objectives

- Understand the internal, external, and product factors that affect sourcing.
- Identify the different purchasing policies available to purchasers.
- Understand the benefits and disadvantages of sole, single, and multiple sourcing.
- Evaluate the choices between different types of sources.
- Identify the alternatives for dealing with the small-order problem.
- Identify the resources available for identifying potential suppliers.
- Understand the tradeoffs between current and new sources of supply.

Introduction

Finding and selecting suppliers is perhaps the most important part of the purchasing process. Given today's trend toward outsourcing and that in many manufacturing companies purchased materials and components account for 60 to 90 percent of the cost of goods sold, the organization's ability to compete can be greatly affected by the choice of suppliers. Continuity of supply, the most important purchasing responsibility, is largely a function of how well the supplier selection process has been performed.

This chapter first looks at the factors affecting the choice of a sourcing strategy. Next, is a discussion of the variety of decisions the purchaser must make regarding buying policy, number of sources, type of source, and supplier relationship. The third area covered is the small-order sourcing problem followed by resources for identifying potential sources. The chapter concludes with a comparison of using current versus new sources of supply.

Understanding Sourcing Strategies

Every class of product or service an organization purchases should have a defined sourcing strategy. A strategy is a long-term action plan that defines what needs to be done to attain a stated goal. A strategy should enable the organization to establish or maintain a competitive advantage and must support the business unit and organization's goals. The presence of a strategy gives the purchaser guidance in finding and selecting suppliers that will help support and improve the organization's competitive position.

There are several internal and external factors that will affect the development of a sourcing strategy for a particular commodity or class of products as well as the product itself.

Internal Factors

Internal factors are factors within the buying organization that affect the choice of sourcing strategy. The greater the strategic importance of purchasing in terms of the value-added by product line, the more important the strategy. For example, at Apple Computer purchased items account for 92 percent of the cost of goods sold. Therefore, Apple's sourcing strategies needed to focus on continuity of supply and the cost of items. The sourcing strategy for office supplies would be completely different given their low value and abundant supply. One way to measure the importance of purchasing is to measure the percentage of total product and/or service costs represented by purchased materials, components, and services. Other factors include quality, the need for materials control, cost containment objectives, and costs associated with switching suppliers.

External Factors

Factors outside the buying organization will also affect the sourcing strategy. The complexity of the supply market as measured by the size of the supply base is one factor. Another is the amount of vertical integration within the industry. Other factors include the scarcity of supply; the technology involved; barriers to entry such as patents or investment levels; the logistics of the product (for example, prefabricated concrete panels are obtained locally due to the high cost of transportation); the need and desire to develop new suppliers; the availability of domestic suppliers; availability of substitute materials; importance of volume to the supplier; general economic conditions; countertrade obligations; trade quotas; and the structure of the market (see Chapter 3 for a discussion of market types).

Product Factors

Spanning both internal and external factors in terms of sourcing strategy formulation is the question of whether the product is made to an industry standard or custom-made. An industry standard product is one that is essentially made to the same specifications by all organizations in the marketplace. Examples of industry standard products include fasteners, light switches, pipe elbows, and bearings. The interchangeability of standard product offerings and the number of standard suppliers compared to available custom suppliers may dictate very different sourcing strategies.

Sourcing Strategy Components

The components that make up the sourcing strategy include the organization's purchasing policy, sourcing policy (including number of sources and type of source), and supplier relationship. These are summarized in Exhibit 4.1.

EXHIBIT 4.1
Sourcing Strategy Components

Buying Policy	Number of Sources	Type of Source	Supplier Relationship
Subsistence Forward Speculative Volume Purchase Agreement Life-of-Product Supply Consignment	Sole Single Multiple	Proprietary Information Directed Manufacturer vs. Distributor Large vs. Small Local vs. National Minority International vs. Domestic Cooperative/Leveraged Joint Venture Integrated Supply	Transactional Ongoing

Buying Policy

There are a number of buying policies available to the purchaser. A buying policy deals with how the goods are acquired. Common buying policies include subsistence buying, forward buying, speculative buying, volume purchase agreements, life-of-product supply, and consignment. Each of these is discussed below.

Subsistence buying - Subsistence buying, also called hand-to-mouth buying, is purchasing today only what needs to be purchased today. The actual product leadtime could be anywhere from one day to nine months. The subsistence buying policy does not consider whether the purchase is economical but operates on the rationale that if the order is not placed today production will be delayed.

Forward buying - Forward buying is the purchase of planned or anticipated requirements. This may be done to obtain a lower price through quantity discounts; to obtain lower transportation costs through the use of truckload, containerload, or carload quantities; in anticipation of supply shortages; or to avoid anticipated or announced price increases. The danger is that the costs incurred by having the extra inventory may offset the anticipated benefits of having the extra inventory. A good rule of thumb is the anticipated savings or cost avoidance from forward buying should exceed three percent for each month of extra inventory purchased. For example, if a six-month supply is purchased, the expected savings from the larger purchase should exceed 18 percent of the cost to purchase one month's supply.

Speculative buying - Speculative buying is purchasing materials beyond the organization's current and anticipated requirements in anticipation of a price increase or shortage so that the organization may sell the materials at a later date for a profit. Normally, this is not part of purchasing's responsibility. This may be undertaken if a major price increase is predicted or a significant shortage of material is anticipated. The purchaser is hoping that the value of the inventory will increase by more than the cost of carrying it.

Volume purchase agreements - One way to obtain the anticipated benefits of forward buying, without the inventory carrying cost, is to negotiate purchase agreements with suppliers based on the total dollars to be spent with the supplier over a designated time period. The agreements may be step-based where the purchaser pays a lower price as total volume increases or may be volume-based where the pricing is based on a total volume over a predetermined time period. For example, an organization might agree to purchase all of its requirements for copier paper from a single supplier in return for pricing based not on individual order size, but on total annual consumption.

Life-of-product supply - A life-of-product contract is a means to interest suppliers in providing materials at attractive prices in the case of lower volumes by guaranteeing the supplier as the single source of supply throughout the entire life of the product. For example, a automobile manufacturer might contract with a supplier to purchase bumpers for a particular model for as many years as that model remains in production.

Consignment - An increasingly common purchasing strategy is for the supplier to provide and maintain an inventory at the purchaser's site that is owned by the supplier and for which the purchaser pays only when the product is withdrawn from inventory. For example, a bearing supplier might, as part of a long-term contract, agree to maintain a bearing inventory at a remote mine site. The mining company would pay for the bearings only as they are used.

Number of Suppliers

Beyond the buying policy, the purchaser must also consider the sourcing policies regarding the number of suppliers. There are three primary sourcing policies: sole, single, and multiple sourcing.

Sole sourcing - Sole sourcing occurs when a supplier is the only provider of a product or service. An example could be a patented product. The purchaser's options are severely restricted and even large companies may have little clout with a sole source supplier. The purchaser's alternatives are to work with the designer or requisitioner to change the specifications to increase the sourcing options or to work with other suppliers to develop an alternate source of supply. While negotiation on product price may be limited, it may be possible to obtain special packaging, delivery, or payment terms for the standard price.

Single sourcing - Single sourcing is the conscious choice by the purchaser to use only one source of supply even though several more may exist. For example, an organization may choose to purchase all of its office products from one supplier even though many office products suppliers exist. The benefits of single sourcing include the following:

- Increases purchasing's leverage when negotiating price and delivery terms.
- Lowers administration costs including identification and tracking of quality problems, accounts payable, receiving, and ordering.
- Increases quality and reduces variability by selection of high quality suppliers.
- Creates stable supply base that allows the supplier to be included in product design and easier coordination of production schedules.
- Minimize the number of tool sets in which the purchaser must invest if tooling is required.
- Allows the purchasing organization to build a competitive advantage from the supply base by selecting the best sources.

The major arguments against single sourcing are the following risks:

- Supply interruption by natural disaster, strike, or late delivery.
- Price increases by the supplier.
- Supplier's dependence on purchaser for survival.
- Overwhelming supplier's capacity and financial resources.

There continues to be strong debate over the advisability of using single sourcing. Many of the risks still exist even if multiple sourcing is used. If an item is dual sourced, the assignment of the business is normally not equal between the two suppliers. If the major supplier was to experience an interruption by natural disaster, there is little likelihood that the secondary supplier could absorb all of the first supplier's business. Thus, multiple sourcing provides the appearance of peace of mind, but in reality it may be an expensive insurance policy with minimal benefit. Many of the risks named can be reduced or avoided through prior planning with the supplier to develop policies and action plans to deal with those issues should they arise. These risks are largely mitigated for industry standard products because many additional suppliers of those same products are readily available. Single sourcing is most effectively used when using systems contracts, the item supplied is a critical component of a product where cost and quality must be tightly controlled, the purchaser desires early supplier involvement in the design and development process, or the quantity purchased is small.

Multiple sourcing - A multiple sourcing policy has been favored, where the orders are distributed among several different suppliers. The advantages of this approach are seen to include:

- Reducing supplier dependence on the purchaser by making the purchaser's business a smaller proportion of the supplier's business.
- Reducing the risk of a major supply interruption. This advantage is largely neutralized for industry standard products.
- A competitive price because suppliers are constantly competing with each other to obtain the dominant share of the purchaser's business.

The arguments against this practice include:

- The purchaser may be giving up price clout by purchasing smaller volumes from each supplier.
- The supplier's competitive price, when it knows it has to constantly compete for the business, may not be the lowest price the supplier is willing to charge. A supplier will bid a higher price knowing it must cover all its fixed costs in one order as opposed to being able to cover them over an extended period of time.
- Supplier administration costs such as supplier visits, material tracking, expediting, and defective material returns are higher than with single sourcing. Other increased administration costs include multiple ordering, receiving, and accounts payable activities.

Multiple sourcing is preferred when the total requirements are too great for one supplier to handle or they would create an undesired supplier dependence on the purchasing organization for the supplier's continued existence. The dependence of a supplier upon one major customer may create a social responsibility that the purchasing organization would rather not deal with if it finds it must end the relationship. Other situations where multiple sources may be desirable include market conditions where the availability of material is limited by industry production capacity or is scarce in nature, there are no price advantages to be gained by purchasing larger volumes from a supplier, or there is a need for both domestic and international sources.

Type of Source

There are several other considerations, which affect the choice of sole, single, or multiple sourcing as a policy.

Proprietary information - The use of single sourcing may be indicated if the information that the supplier needs is confidential in nature such as trade secrets or national security information. The fewer suppliers who have access to this information, the lower the likelihood of its disclosure.

Directed sourcing - An organization may specify the suppliers to be used through company policy (use other divisions or sister organizations first), a government contract that sets conditions suppliers must meet (minority suppliers, set asides, security), or to meet countertrade requirements with a particular country.

Manufacturer versus distributor - One tradeoff the purchaser must consider is the choice between purchasing directly from the manufacturer or using a distributor. Purchasing directly from the manufacturer may afford the opportunity to obtain a lower a price by bypassing a local distributor. However, the manufacturer is likely to require purchase quantities to be much larger than those from a distributor and may be in excess of the organization's requirements. Some manufacturers refuse to sell direct in order to maintain the support and loyalty of the distribution channel.

Distributors provide the ability to purchase in smaller quantities. They may able to provide a variety of products and perform value-adding activities such as kitting, custom packaging, and light custom manufacturing or assembly. A growing trend in the MRO area is integrating distribution where a number of distributors work together to present a single point of contact with the customer but provide a wide variety of products and services.

Large versus small supplier - Large suppliers generally have more facilities and resources at their disposal to apply to the resolution of problems. However, their size may result in slower response time and a lack of personal touch. Also, the purchaser's business may be such a small proportion of the large supplier's business that it is difficult to get the supplier's attention.

Small suppliers may provide specialized expertise and put greater value on the customer. The larger purchaser does run the potential risk of becoming too large a proportion of the supplier's business or may have requirements that will overload the supplier.

Local versus national supplier - The advantages of using a local supplier include easier communication, ability to quickly meet demand, presence of local inventory, and building local goodwill.

National suppliers generally have more resources, and may have greater capability. They may be able to provide materials to multiple locations more easily, and because of their size, diminish the impacts of material shortages.

Minority supplier - Should the purchaser use minority, small businesses, and/or women-owned businesses as suppliers? The use of minority suppliers may be mandated if an organization provides products to federal, state, or local governments. Otherwise, it may be part of the organization's social responsibility policy or community involvement activities to purchase from these suppliers. For example, the City of Florence in South Carolina, based on a request by the city council, obtains a list from the Governor's Office of Small and Minority Business Assistance of certified minority- and women-owned businesses for each project. These firms are sent an invitation to bid. The city also requires general contractors to make a good faith effort to solicit minority- and women-owned firms.[1]

International versus domestic suppliers - The use of domestic suppliers generally is easier than dealing with international suppliers as the purchaser will have fewer problems due to cultural, communication, monetary, or international logistics issues. International suppliers may be preferred when there is small or reduced domestic supply or significant price-quality advantages, or to meet countertrade obligations.

There are several ways to approach international sourcing. These include the following:

- Domestic sales representatives of international suppliers.
- Domestic third-party global sourcing company.
- Overseas sourcing representatives.
- International purchasing office.

- Direct to supplier.[2]

Determining which approach to use is based on numerous criteria including volume, commitment, and internal resources. Issues of concern to the purchaser include culture, government, monetary, and transportation.

Cultural issues that arise when using an international source include negotiation tactics and processes, the perceived function of a contract, the legal system, response to authority, meaning of time, and paperwork requirements. For example, to develop a joint venture in Korea requires 312 documents, 162 administrative procedures, and a time investment of two years and nine months; in Japan, 325 documents and 46 administrative procedures; and in the United States, 23 documents and nine administrative procedures.[3]

In international purchasing, the governments of both the purchasers' and suppliers' countries have laws that will affect the transactions and that can complicate the flow of goods across borders. Governments, for instance, place various types of restrictions on imports, including import licenses, customs duties, and quotas. Governments also typically require complex sets of documents including export licenses, import declarations, certificates of origin, commercial invoices, customs invoices, insurance policies, and bills of lading. In addition, The Convention on Contracts for the International Sale of Goods (CISG) has produced a relatively new body of law that brings some uniformity to the rules governing international sales. The CISG is likely to have a significant affect on international purchasers and suppliers.

Monetary problems associated with using international suppliers include currency exchange rate fluctuations; the presence of import duties, tariffs, and/or quotas; and payment mechanisms. When purchasing overseas, the purchaser needs to consider the rate of exchange, which refers to the price at which one currency can be bought with another currency or gold. The relative position of the exchange rate between two nations affects the price level of traded purchases and sales between them creating either an advantage or a disadvantage for the purchaser. The problem is that currency levels are often unpredictable and therefore constitute a true risk in conducting business overseas.

There are two major forms of payment for international purchases. The most frequently used is a letter of credit. A letter of credit involves a specific line of credit granted by the importer's bank. A second form is a bill of exchange or draft, which is a document issued by the seller instructing the purchaser to make payment in full at a specified point in time. A bill of exchange is similar to a check that instructs a bank to pay on a depositor's behalf. It becomes a negotiable instrument if and when the buying organization acknowledges its obligations by signing, upon which it becomes a trade acceptance. In general, international procurement can be expected to result in the tying up of capital for longer periods of time versus domestic transactions.

Increasingly, trade occurs between affiliates or subsidiaries of the same corporation. This method simplifies the foreign purchase process and reduces overhead costs. Rather than purchasing with a letter of credit, a U.S. purchaser working with a German supplier would have its German subsidiary execute a domestic German purchase transaction. The subsidiary would then sell to the U.S. firm on open account. Recent surveys have concluded that over one-third of all international trade is now conducted in this manner, and the trend seems to be growing.

Duties are taxes levied by governments on the importation, exportation, or use of goods. Most goods entering into U.S. markets have duties assessed on them. There are three major types of duties:

- Specific duties - These are charged as a specified rate per unit (for example, $15 for each crate).
- Ad valorem duties - These are duties charged as a percentage of the appraised value (e.g., three-percent ad valorem). This is the type of duty most often applied.
- Compound duties - These are duties that combine specific and ad valorem rates (for example, $2.15 per gallon plus eight-percent ad valorem).

The benefits of international procurement must be weighed against the costs of longer transportation links. Shipments into the U.S. from Canada and Mexico can be transported overland via truck and rail, but overseas shipments must be made by air or ship. Air transport involves relatively high freight charges, yet is the preferred method for overseas shipments of sensitive items like electronic equipment, or perishables like food. The United States can be reached by air within 48 hours from nearly all points in the world. Overseas shipping services offer lower costs for the transportation of goods, but at much slower speeds. Water transportation is typically used for large volume purchases and the transport of raw materials. The logistics of international shipping and the time involved increases the risk of a late delivery. Having a price or quality advantage is of little value if your material is in a container which is jettisoned or lost at sea or if the carrier's ship has been impounded in another port because of an accident.

The following steps will help you determine which products to consider for international procurement:

Step 1. After performing an ABC analysis, select only those "A" items with annual volumes of at least $100,000 (or other value as appropriate).

Step 2. Group the selected parts by manufacturing process.

Step 3. Evaluate the parts for stability, difficulty to manufacture, and longevity. Do not consider parts that are proprietary, subject to frequent design changes, or have manufacturing, quality, or design problems.

Step 4. Rank the remaining parts by potential savings of using international sources. Confirm that domestic prices used for comparisons are the best possible so that savings are measured from the best domestic price.

Step 5. Select the top one or two candidates for each process group to solicit RFQs.

Step 6. Identify any information not included in the specifications that is treated as common knowledge for inclusion in the RFQ.[4]

Example - Based on an ABC analysis,[5] a Midwestern manufacturer identified 174 "A" parts with an annual activity of $56 million as possible candidates for international sourcing. A preliminary analysis indicated potential savings of up to 28 percent. If a third-party was used, the overseas purchase price could be expected to be

5 to 20 percent higher, which would increase costs $4 to $11 million per year. The added cost to deal directly with the suppliers would only amount to $300,000 to $400,000. The company selected the direct approach to gain the advantages of greater control, to develop internal capabilities, to avoid the country preferences of third parties, and to obtain lower total material costs.[6]

Cooperative/leveraged buying - Cooperative buying is typically used by purchasers to increase their purchasing effectiveness. This type of buying involves joining two or more groups or organizations together for the purpose of preparing specifications and proposals, collectively receiving bids, and making awards to the lowest responsible bidders. Thereafter, each organization issues its own contract and is responsible for administering the remainder of the procurement function, including its own payments. This type of buying arrangement enables smaller organizations to secure price and other advantages associated with large-volume purchasing. The normal savings are in the range of five to 15 percent. Additional advantages include reduced paperwork and increased opportunities for networking. Disadvantages include communication problems members who bypass the consortium and contact suppliers directly.   Examples - An example consortium is TOMCOM, comprised of Bell Atlantic, NYNEX, USWest, New Vector Group, and AirTouch Communications. The consortium purchases cellular telephone equipment as well as hardware, software, and technology consulting services. Although the organizations offer the same services, they are in different areas of the country and do not compete. The consortium members have experienced 5 to 10 percent savings.[7]

On the service side is the Kansas City Regional Council for Higher Education which consists of 15 campuses and 215 educational, not-for-profit, and social service organizations. The consortium purchases janitorial services and supplies, professional services such as career counseling, and office equipment and supplies. The consortium's savings have been in the 28 to 32 percent range.[8]

Joint venture - A joint venture is a venture or investment undertaken by two or more organizations. For example, two automobile manufacturers may pursue a joint venture to produce a new model vehicle. Joint ventures enable the partners to share costs, technology, and know-how; reduce financial, technical, and political risks; and achieve economies of scale that would not be possible individually. The risks of joint ventures may include providing technical knowledge to partners that enable them to become competitors, less control over the project, and conflicts among the partners.

Integrated supply - Integrated supply is a special type of partnering arrangement, usually developed between a purchaser and a distributor on an intermediate or long-term basis. The objective of an integrated supply relationship is to optimize, for both purchaser and supplier, the labor and expense involved in the acquisition and possession of MRO products — items that are repetitive, generic, high-transaction, and have a low unit cost. Integrated supply can take various forms ranging from blanket contracts to outsourcing a total activity, such as supply room activities. Integrated supply offers a wider range of products for which the distributor takes responsibility than in a normal systems contract. All integrated supply agreements shift some of the responsibilities normally performed by purchasing to the supplier.

Products and services that are non-value added or have low strategic value are excellent candidates for integrated supply relationships. Examples of items included in integrated supply agreements in manufacturing firms include maintenance parts, equipment repair and overhaul, safety equipment, and equipment rental. Examples in not-for-profit and government organizations include janitorial services, office equipment, temporary labor, and office supplies.

Competition in integrated supply occurs during supplier identification, qualification, selection, and contract formation. After the arrangement is finalized, competition is limited by the terms of the contract and the switching costs associated with changing suppliers.

Example - Witco Corporation, a producer of specialty chemicals, consolidated its purchases of less-than-truckload chemicals from 200 different distributors to one, Brenntag, Inc. Witco then took a step beyond consolidating suppliers by working with Brenntag to negotiate bulk pricing supplied to Brenntag with major materials manufacturers. Brenntag purchases from the manufacturer at the bulk price and adds a charge for packaging. The program has resulted in significant savings.[9]

Supplier Relationship

A fourth component of the sourcing strategy is based on the type of supplier relationship the purchaser wishes to maintain. The relationship could be transactional or ongoing.

Transactional relationship - A transactional relationship is focused on the current transaction with little or no concern about future transactions. The transactional relationship makes sense for infrequent or one-time-only purchases where there is little expected or required continuing service support. Non-repetitive requirements do not require relationships sustainable beyond the transaction itself, but this is not to imply that the relationship is unimportant. Many one-time purchases, such as construction projects, span long time periods during which the supplier relationship is critical.

Ongoing relationship - Among the most misunderstood terms in purchasing today are "purchaser-supplier partnerships" or "purchaser-supplier alliances." The problem is that a single term is used to describe what in reality is a range of relationships. Ellram has developed four classifications to describe the range of relationships possible over time between the purchaser and supplier. They are as follows:

- **Contractual relationship** - The purchase order or contract is the basis for the arrangement. There is very little sharing of information and usually that which is shared is usually on an "as needed" basis. This is essentially an arm's-length relationship. There is no commitment to the relationship beyond the life of the contract.

- **Operational relationship** - There is some mutual trust beginning to develop based on personal interactions around transactions. There is some sharing of ideas and people when dealing with joint problem solving.

- **Business relationship** - An increased recognition of mutual dependence is beginning to develop between purchaser and supplier. The purchasing organization has reduced its supply base and is working with the remaining suppliers. There is limited concurrent engineering and joint technology development.

- **Strategic relationship** - The business relationship has progressed to include the sharing of long-term strategies, early supplier involvement, and ongoing joint teams.[10]

The choice of relationship is based on the criticality of the item(s) to the organization's competitiveness. For example, there is little value to developing a strategic relationship with an office products supplier. On the other hand, it would be appropriate when the supplier's technology is your basis for competitive advantage. The other factor which affects the type of relationship is the willingness of both supplier and purchaser to enter into a particular relationship. Moving from a contractual to a strategic relationship takes time, commitment, the development of personal relationships, and trust.

The Small-Order Problem

A common sourcing problem for purchasers is dealing with small orders. It is estimated that as much as 90 percent of items purchased are relatively insignificant in total dollar value and up to 80 percent of purchases are made for expenditures of less than $250.[11] Various approaches are used to deal with small orders such as central stores, systems contracts, telephone orders, electronic commerce, petty cash, procurement cards, and purchase order drafts. Exhibit 4.2 shows how the small order problem can overtake purchasers. The objectives of all these approaches are to minimize small-dollar orders and to obtain the maximum value relative to total cost. To accomplish these objectives, the purchaser needs to understand the requirements of other functions and have a clear working relationship with end-users. By understanding the requirements of other functions, the purchaser can better select the approaches that will meet the end-users needs most effectively.

EXHIBIT 4.2
How to Waste Time and Let Low-Dollar Purchases Overtake You

- Don't manage supply relations.
- Don't consolidate supply.
- Have no strategy.
- Don't bother to forecast.
- Change your priorities often.
- Ignore the team approach.

- Ignore the customer and/or end-user.
- Keep inventories high.
- Don't concern yourself with delivery problems.
- Don't study the process.
- Don't review process documentation.
- Don't communicate objectives and expectations.
- Be reactive, not proactive.

Source: Griffiths, D. and L.M. Ellram. "Managing Small-Dollar Purchases,"
   NAPM InfoEdge, (1:7), January 1996, p. 5.

Central Stores

A common approach for dealing with small orders is to establish a stores area where the goods ordered in quantity are stored and then disbursed to the requisitioners as requested. This requires carrying inventories, incurring carrying costs, and assigning personnel to monitor and control the inventory. Central stores are useful when the need for the item is immediate and unpredictable. An example is spare parts for equipment repair. Many organizations are moving to other methods such as systems contracts and procurement cards.

Systems Contracts

Systems contracts are long-term contracts where the supplier and purchaser agree on a set of products and/or services that are covered by the agreement. The user orders the items and/or services directly from the supplier who delivers the items or performs the services directly to the user. Purchasing does not get involved in the individual transactions but does focus on negotiating prices, terms, and delivery.

Example - Aetna's internal customers were purchasing telephone headsets from more than six suppliers. A contract has been developed with one supplier that allows the users to select the items they want from their desktop workstations. Upon approval, the orders are transmitted to the supplier by EDI. The supplier ships directly to the user who generally receives the product within two to three days. The benefits to Aetna include cost savings, less purchasing paperwork, and better records of equipment purchased and repair information. cost savings.[12]

Telephone

Many organizations place small orders directly with suppliers using the telephone without generating a purchase order. An example is a large electronics firm that places 60 percent of all orders annually by telephone. The suppliers send no invoices because the purchaser negotiates a firm fixed price that is paid upon receipt of the goods.[13]

Electronic

Electronic approaches can take several forms. The first is the use of a fax to transmit the order to the supplier. Use of a fax immediately provides the supplier with a hard copy of the order. The second electronic approach is the use of electronic mail to transmit the order to the supplier. Again the supplier receives the information quickly but both fax and e-mail require reentry of the order information, which increases the potential for data entry errors. The most recent approach is the use of the Internet/World Wide Web to find items and place orders directly with suppliers. With the development of online catalogs, organizations are using the Internet and intranets for ordering items from integrated supply or systems contracts. Combined with procurement cards, systems contracts, or blanket orders, the transaction costs can be lowered and much of the activity can be transferred to the user freeing purchasing from low-value, non-strategic activities.

Petty Cash and C.O.D.

Petty cash is one way to deal with small, infrequent purchases when the need is immediate. Many organizations are moving away from the use of petty cash because of security concerns and making sure there is an adequate balance on hand. Procurement cards are steadily replacing the use of petty cash.

Ordering goods C.O.D. (cash on delivery) is generally reserved for emergency purchases and for those instances when there is no other way to get the product or service in time. Procurement cards are replacing the use of C.O.D. as well.

Procurement Cards

Procurement card systems have distinct features, capabilities, and controls tailored to procurement operations. The supplier accepts the card as payment and is then paid by the credit card issuer. The advantage to the purchasing organization is that it makes one payment for all the transactions made by all its credit cardholders. Purchasing cards are generally used for low value, non-repetitive, non-inventory items.

Purchasing cards add value to the organization in the following ways:

- Reduces the number of low value transactions in purchasing and accounts receivable.
- Reduces acquisition cycle time.
- Increases user satisfaction.
- Reduces total cost of acquisition.

The estimated cost to process a purchase order through accounts receivable ranges from $80 to $150 per transaction. The estimated transaction cost using a purchase card is $5 to $10.

Purchase Order Draft

A purchase order draft, also called a check with purchase order, is used with small orders and one-time purchases. The supplier fills in the check for the appropriate amount including cash discounts and transportation and does not invoice the purchasing organization. The canceled check is the purchasing organization's receipt.

Selecting an Approach

How does a purchaser determine which of the techniques discussed above to use? Exhibit 4.3 presents a process for evaluating which technique to use. The vertical axis is the frequency of the requirement. It asks how often the demand takes place. The low end is best served with purchase order drafts, petty cash, and C.O.D. orders, all of which are good candidates for replacement by a procurement card program. As the demand grows in frequency, blanket orders are a more desirable approach. As the frequency grows, integrated supply contracts and systems contracts are better approaches. Stores are used when demand is frequent and the need for the item is immediate.

EXHIBIT 4.3
Selecting the Appropriate Approach to the Small-Order Problem

Frequency of Requirement	High	Systems contracts Integrated supply contracts Online catalogs Central stores Blanket orders Procurement card Internet Purchase order draft Petty cash
	Low	Telephone

Resources for Identifying Potential Suppliers

Buying in the industrial or public setting is not the same as purchasing a consumer good. Knowledge of sources is a prime consideration for efficient purchasing. There is a myriad of potential sources of information for identifying potential suppliers. A few are discussed below.

Buyers' Guides

Buyers' guides are lists of manufacturers. These guides provide relevant information such as addresses, phone numbers, and products. They may be indexed by commodities, company names, geographic regions, and trade names, or trademarks. Examples include *McRAE's Blue Book and Thomas Register of American Manufacturers* (accessible on the Internet at www.thomasregister.com).

Business and Telephone Directories

Business directories are lists of businesses in a geographic area or in a specific industry. They are often published by local chambers of commerce or economic development agencies.

The yellow pages of telephone directories are a potential source of suppliers. They give little information about the company but may serve as a starting point because they are usually well indexed by product or service. There are regional yellow pages available as well.

Traditionally, a purchaser would have to go to a public library to obtain the yellow pages for other areas. Today, many yellow pages or their equivalents are available on the Internet. For example, NYNEX has its yellow pages for the areas it serves in the northeast. Another directory is BigYellow (www.bigyellow.com), which lists over 16 million companies nationwide and is searchable by state, city, and street.

Trade Associations and Trade Exhibits

Trade associations are potential sources of information through references, advertisements in trade publications, and association-sponsored trade shows. Industry and association-sponsored trade shows can be very cost effective means to identify a large number of potential suppliers and gather information on their offerings. For example, the Industrial Distribution Association will provide a list of its members in a particular region. See Appendix 4-A for a list of several trade associations available on the Internet as well as other helpful sourcing information.

Colleagues

Personal networks may be established through professional associations such as the National Association of Purchasing Management (NAPM), the American Production and Inventory Control Society (APICS), the National Institute of Governmental Purchasers (NIGP), the National Contract Management Association (NCMA), or through personal acquaintances. The experiences of colleagues can be invaluable to the purchaser seeking a recommendation to or for further information about a particular supplier.

Mail

Advertising materials received by mail can be used to identify potential suppliers. The difficulty is in maintaining an organized system of such information for access at a later time.

Sales Personnel

Besides supplying information on their organization's products and services, sales personnel may be able to suggest other sources such as other customers or even competitors when they do not carry the product in question.

Government

There are many sources of information regarding potential suppliers within the federal government such as the International Trade Administration, the U.S. Department of Commerce, the U.S. Customs Service, and the Federal Supply Service. Other countries' governments may provide information on international sources through embassies, consulates, trade missions, and commercial attachés.

Minority Suppliers

Sources of information about minority suppliers include the Small Business Administration, minority business directories, and minority purchasing councils.

Internet/World Wide Web (WWW)

The World Wide Web (WWW) has a wealth of information about suppliers. Not only are there company-specific Web sites, but a number of directories for finding new suppliers. The Web offers business directories such as *Thomas Register of American Manufacturers*; trade and industry information such as PCB Europe that provides information about European printed circuit board manufacturers, service providers, electronic design, associations, news/magazines, and Web services; and material exchanges such as *Recycler's World* that provides access to and allows searches of 23 categories of available and wanted items including scrap and precious metals, chemicals, computer components, textiles, and electronic goods. Appendix

4-A lists a number of sources of information to help purchasers identify potential suppliers available on the Internet. These sources are categorized by trade associations, domestic sources, international sources, and material exchanges.

Current Versus New Sources of Supply

The decision to continue using existing sources or to try new sources depends on a number of factors and situations. Each alternative may have both advantages and disadvantages. The major considerations include market conditions, product complexity, supplier characteristics, and supply continuity.

Market Conditions

If a purchaser works with only one supplier, it would be advisable to maintain surveillance of market conditions to be sure that the supplier remains competitive. By seeking new sources for the product in demand, the purchaser can guard against unreasonable increases in price by the current supplier.

New suppliers represent opportunities for expanded supply options. They can help a purchaser alleviate a sole source situation and may offer technical services not available from current sources. A disadvantage may be that new suppliers may bid low only to have a purchaser gain dependency on them and then return the following year with higher contract prices based on new costs. This tactic is best avoided by not depending too strongly on any one supplier, thoroughly evaluating new suppliers, preparing thorough specifications (for tangible items) and statements of work (for services), negotiating adjustment clauses when negotiating prices, and carefully evaluating supplier cost data before purchasing from a new supplier.

Product Complexity/Technology Changes

An existing supplier may be the sole owner of a certain patent or process, precluding the possibility of using other sources. If the product involves costly tool, die, mold, or set-up charges, the expense of duplicating this equipment will also discourage the use of new suppliers. On the other hand, remaining with existing suppliers may result in a purchaser's loss in terms of new technology that could be offered by a new supplier's product or service.

An existing supplier may be so outstanding in the quality and service it provides that purchasing elsewhere may not be a serious consideration. On the other hand, if a current supplier's quality or service has been marginal, a new supplier may be a prudent alternative. A new source may be eager to gain new business and might apply special efforts to provide superior service.

Supplier Characteristics

How does the supplier produce and distribute the product? To what extent does the supplier outsource? What are its processes for acquiring, producing, and maintaining the goods and services?

Though the immediate key goal is price, it is also critical that purchasers look at suppliers in the long-term with regard to innovation, maintaining quality and service, product and process technical innovation, responsiveness to changing requirements, and the ability to satisfactorily resolve problems.

Prior commitments, a successful past relationship, or an ongoing long-term contract with a preferred supplier might preclude even the possibility of using a new source. Supplier goodwill is promoted by granting more business as a reward for good service. Though shopping around for better opportunities has its merits, this can come at the cost of uniformity and continuity of supply. High turnover among suppliers can also create an image of the purchaser as an opportunistic customer. Sound purchasing programs (like sound business programs) are based on long-term considerations.

The identification of potential suppliers and development of new sources is important to maintaining a continuous supply of products and services. In spite of precautions in the supplier selection process, there will always be sources that perform less than satisfactorily. Such suppliers should be put on notice and given an opportunity to correct poor performance before being dropped. There are times, however, when replacing suppliers who continue to perform below expectations with new suppliers is the only feasible course of action.

If an existing supplier undergoes a major upheaval, such as the retirement of key personnel, a merger, or a takeover, the likelihood of interruptions in supply or quality may increase. When one dominant individual manages a firm, and that firm grows too large for the individual to handle, smooth operations may be disrupted. Such circumstances may warrant seeking new suppliers.

Supply Continuity

Supply disruption is an important consideration when deciding whether to use existing sources or purchase from a new source. Disruptions of supply with existing suppliers may be due to strike, fire, act of nature, capacity constraints, quality or production problems, problems with suppliers' sources, financial problems, and changes in ownership. Supply continuity with existing suppliers can be enhanced if realistic disaster contingency plans exist, multiple production facilities are available, effective production and quality control systems are in place, and succession plans for management have been developed. Supply disruption with new sources may result from an inability to provide promised price, quality, and service due a number of factors. Those factors may include poor communication of requirements to the supplier, inability of the supplier to meet requirements, capacity limitations, and an unexpectedly quick phase-out of the previous supplier. In some instances, supply continuity problems with an existing supplier may not be solved by seeking a new source. In this instance, working with the existing supplier may be the best alternative.

The establishment of a new supplier will inevitably involve time, expense, and training. If the product is needed immediately, the use of a new source may not be practical.

By seeking new sources of supply, a purchaser works to protect the organization's supply lines in case one of the existing suppliers is unable to perform as promised. However, remaining with existing suppliers is advantageous if such companies have proved that they can and will meet standards of quality, service, and delivery at competitive prices over the long-term. Proven suppliers can be better in the long run, simply because of past performance, and may be good candidates for some type of partnering arrangement.

Key Points

1. Sourcing strategies are affected by internal factors, external factors, and product factors.
2. Components of the sourcing strategy include buying policy, number of suppliers, type of supplier, and supplier relationship.
3. Common approaches for dealing with the small-order sourcing problem include central stores, systems contracts, blanket orders, telephone orders, electronic ordering, petty cash, C.O.D., procurement cards, and purchase order drafts.
4. There are a variety of resources for identifying potential sources of supply.
5. Considerations for deciding between using a current supplier or a new supplier include market conditions, product complexity, supplier characteristics, and supply continuity.

Questions for Review

1. What are some of the internal, external, and product factors that affect sourcing strategies?
2. What is the difference between subsistence, forward, and speculative buying policies?
3. What are the advantages and disadvantages of single sourcing relative to multiple sourcing?
4. What are the relative advantages of a manufacturer versus distributor? Local versus national source? International versus domestic source?
5. What is the difference between a transactional and an ongoing supplier relationship?
6. What are three common approaches for dealing with small-order sourcing?
7. What factors must the purchaser consider when choosing between a current or a new supplier?

For Additional Information

Anderson, R. and K. Macie. "Using Cooperative and Consortium Buying for Better Purchasing," *NAPM InfoEdge*, (2:4), December 1996.

Bendorf, R.H. "Going About It Globally," *Purchasing Today®*, September 1998, pp. 34-39.

Bills, A. and K. Snow. "The Basics of Purchasing Cards," *NAPM InfoEdge*, (1:12), July 1995.

Birou, L. and S.E. Fawcett. "International Purchasing: Benefits, Requirements, and Challenges," *International Journal of Purchasing and Materials Management*, (29:2), Spring 1993, pp. 28-37.

Cohen, M. "It's in the Cards" *Purchasing Today®*, February 1997, pp. 50-51.

Curtis, D. and J.D. Etheridge. "Integrated Supply Strategies," *NAPM InfoEdge*, (4:4), December 1998.

Duross, N. "Procurement Card Dos & Don'ts," *Purchasing Today®*, May 1996, pp. 42-44.

Griffiths, D. and L.M. Ellram. "Managing Small-Dollar Purchases," *NAPM InfoEdge*, (1:7), January 1996.

Guetter, P. "Dispelling Common Myths," *Purchasing Today®*, May 1996, p. 4.

Johnstone, J.M. "The Consortium: Basic Antitrust Principles," *Purchasing Today®*, May 1996, pp. 18-19.

Miller, J. "They Lead by Example," *NAPM Insights*, January 1995, pp. 45-47.

Motlok, T. "Sourcing Aids," *NAPM Insights*, July 1995, pp. 50-51.

Snow, K. "Procurement Cards 101," *Purchasing Today®*, September 1996, p. 10.

Vanatasky, R.M. "International Political Risk and Sourcing Policy," *Proceedings of the 1996 NAPM International Purchasing Conference*, NAPM, Tempe, AZ, 1996, pp. 229-234.

Endnotes

1. Miller, J. "They Lead by Example," *NAPM Insights*, January 1995, p. 46.
2. Bendorf, R.H. "Global Sourcing Approaches and Implementation Issues," *Proceedings of the 1999 NAPM International Purchasing Conference*, NAPM, Tempe, AZ, 1999, p. 128.
3. De Mente, B. *Korean Etiquette & Ethics in Business*, NTC Business Books, Lincoln, IL, 1988, p. 44
4. Bendorf, pp. 130-131.
5. "A" items are high-value and/or high-volume items, "B" items are moderate-value and moderate-volume items, and "C" items are low-value and/or low-volume items.
6. Bendorf, p. 130.
7. Pye, C. "Coming Together to Cut Costs," *Purchasing Today®*, May 1996, pp. 32-33.
8. Pye, p. 33.
9. Reilly, C., "Witco Moves Toward Globally Integrated Supply," *Purchasing*, July 15, 1999, CPI edition supplement.
10. Ellram, L.M. and L.M. Birou. *Purchasing for Bottom Line Impact*, Irwin Professional Publishing, Burr Ridge, IL, 1995, p. 106.
11. Griffiths, D. and L.M. Ellram. "Managing Small-Dollar Purchases", *NAPM InfoEdge*, (1:7), January 1996 p. 6.
12. Cooper, T., B. Isikoff, and T. Mercado-Perez. "Single-Source Situations That Work," *Purchasing Today®*, May 1997, p. 38.
13. Griffiths and Ellram, p. 8.

APPENDIX 4-A

INTERNET SOURCES OF SUPPLIER INFORMATION

Trade Associations

Organization	Web Address	Description
Electronic Design Automation Consortium	www.edac.org	International association of companies engaged in the development, manufacture, and sale of design tools to the electronic engineering community. Site provides a forum for discussion of industry-wide problems and concerns.
Electronic Industries Alliance	www.eia.org	This site contains information on the association and its activities, and links to other related groups, divisions, and associations.
Industrial Distribution Association	www.ida-assoc.org	Provides information regarding theassociation's activities, members, and educational programs in industrial distribution
Industrial Fasteners Institute	www.industrial fasteners.org	Provides information about the institute, technical information, trade show information, and a list of available publications.
Material Handling Industry of America	www.mhi.org	Provides information on trade shows and conferences, upcoming events, literature, and MHI publications.

Organization	Web Address	Description
Metal Treating Institute	www.metaltreat.com	Includes a metal treating buyers' guide, industry information, and lists of available educational materials.
Precision Metalforming Association	www.pma.org	Provides buyers' guides and organization information including publications and seminar information.
SEMATECH	www.sematech.org	Features acronyms and abbreviations, SEMATECH dictionary, information about SEMATECH, programs and divisions, job opportunities, and technology transfer information.
SemiOnline	www.semi.org	Features electronics industry information such as news, business outlook, market statistics, newsletters, standards, and trade show information.
Steel Manufacturers Association	www.steelnet.org	Information on sources of steel products and steel-making equipment and links to related sites.
Telecommunications Industry Association	www.tiaonline.org	This site provides information about the TIA, trade shows, standards, publications, and links to other sites.

Domestic Sourcing Information

Organization	Web Address	Description
CompaniesOnline	www.companies-online.com	Directory of businesses with Web sites. It provides information on over 60,000 companies at no charge.
Electronics Engineering Network	www.eenet.com	Online directory for the electronics industry with over 11,000 links.
ElectroBase	www.electrobase.com	A comprehensive listing of distributors, representatives, services, and component manufacturers of interest to the electronics industry.
Electronet	www.stknet.com	A subscription service that provides an electronic parts locator database that lists current inventories of franchised dealers.
EBN's Interactive	www.ebnonline.com	Sourcing directory provided by distributors and manufacturers of components that can be searched by product category.
Electronics Purchasing Guide to Distribution	www.theepgd.com	A directory of component distributors searchable by region, manufacturer, and distributor.
FAST Electronic Broker	www.fastparts.com	A computer network broker for electronic parts, components, products, test instruments, and laboratory equipment.
LogLink	www.loglink.com/logistics/	Contains URLs relating to logitics, logistic references, trucking, and other logistics topics.

Organization	Web Address	Description
Manufacturers Information Net	www.mfginfo.com	Provides information on suppliers, manufacturers, professional services, and other resources.
MASSnet Packaging Mall	www.massnet.com/ package.htm	Contains links to various suppliers and manufacturers of packaging equipment and supplies.
Metal Suppliers Online	www.suppliersonline.com	A database of metals suppliers.
Minority Business and Professional Yellow Pages	www.minority business. com/.htm homepage	Magazine-style directory of minority and women-owned businesses.
The Nell Register	www.nell.com	Online listing service of industrial equipment and supplies. The database is global and can be searched by product or company.
Oil-link	www.oillink.com/	Sourcing directory for oil and gas.
PartNET	www.part.net	Component information system which allows searching for electro-mechanical, electronic, and mechanical parts from a number of suppliers simultaneously.
Professionals Online	www.prosonline.com	Site containing links to a variety of online resources for business users.
QuestLink Technology, Inc.	www.questlink.com	QuestNet IC Cross Reference and Index for semiconductor information.
SemiWeb	www.semiweb.com	Provides information on companies, employment opportunities, research, and related Web sites for semiconductor-related resources.

Organization	Web Address	Description
SMTnet	www.smtnet.com	Reference center for surface mount technology and electronics manufacturing. Features a technical library and lists electronics manufacturing suppliers, contract manufacturers, component manufacturers, service providers, distributors, and OEMs.
Thomas Register	www.thomasregister.com	Online search ability of Thomas Register's database and "How to Buy It" tutorials.

International Sourcing Information

Organization	Web Address	Description
AsiaOne	www.asia1.com	Provides links to a variety of resources about Asia, lists of companies in Singapore, and other information.
Asian Sources Online	www.asiansources.com	Includes product, supplier, and country searches as well as information on trade shows, travel services, and trade services.
China External Trade Development Council	www.tptaiwan.org.tw	How to use CETRA's resources, tips on doing business in Taiwan, and trade show information.
All Business	www.comfind.com/	A global directory with millions of listings and links to over 100,000 Web sites in 150 countries.
IMEX Exchange	www.imex.com	Provides international business information including a worldwide database of products and services.
Netsource Asia	www.netsourceasia.com	Provides information on Asian suppliers, manufacturers, and traders, and links to other Asia-related trade sources.

Organization	Web Address	Description
PCB Europe	www.pcbeurope.com	Offers information about service providers, manufacturers, electronic design, associations, news/magazines, and Web services.
Sweden Online	www.swedentrade.com	Offers links to business news, trade, inquiries, and a searchable directory of companies with interests related to Swedish-American business.
World Access NetworkDirect (WAND®)	www.wand.com/	An international directory of global import/export trade. Search for products and materials using harmonized codes.

Materials Exchange Information

Recycler's World	www.recycle.net/ recycle/index.html	Provides access to and allows searches of 23 categories of available and wanted items including scrap and precious metals, chemicals, computer components, textiles, and electronic goods.
Tecnet	www.tecnet.com	An online database for buyers of pre-owned technical equipment.
United Computer Exchange Online	www.uce.com	An interactive trading and electronic auction system for buying and selling of computer equipment. Includes United Used Computer Price Index that provides statistical data on average used street prices, new prices, introduction dates, and discontinued dates.

CHAPTER 5

THE COMPETITIVE BID PROCESS: WHICH TYPE OF SOLICITATION SHOULD I USE?

Chapter Objectives

- Understand the differences between the request for information, request for quote, request for proposal, and request or invitation for bid.
- Identify when it is most appropriate to use competitive bidding versus negotiation as a procurement approach.
- Identify the information necessary in the solicitation proposal.
- Understand what makes a good solicitation proposal.
- Identify potential problems in the bidding process.
- Identify additional terms and conditions required in the bidding process.

Introduction

For decades the mainstay of purchasing has been the competitive bid. In this age of single sourcing, competitive bidding is not going away. What is changing is how technology is being used to manage the process in both the public and private sectors. This chapter will first discuss the criteria for deciding between when to use formal competitive bidding and when to use negotiations. Next, methods for obtaining price and product and/or service information from suppliers are presented. The bid process and its elements are then presented and the chapter ends with bid terms and conditions.

Solicitation Methods

What is the proper solicitation method? The answer is depends upon the purchaser's objective. There are four basic methods of obtaining information from suppliers. They are the request for information (RFI), request for quote (RFQ), request for proposal (RFP), and request or invitation for bid (IFB). Each method is discussed below and also is summarized in Exhibit 5.1.

Request for Information

The request for information (RFI) is used to obtain information about products, services, or suppliers. The RFI is informal and non-binding on both the purchaser and the supplier. The outcome of the process is information usually in the form of catalogs, price lists, and brochures. The RFI is a quick way to obtain information from suppliers and is usually followed by a RFQ, RFP, or IFB to actually obtain the good or service.

Request for Quote

The request for quote (RFQ) is used to obtain commitments for designated items or services. The quote can include price, delivery, quantity, service, and quality. The strength of the RFQ is that it responds to specific requirements without obligating the purchaser. The purchaser is free to negotiate but the supplier is bound by the quote. The use of an RFQ only ensures that the purchaser pays the lowest price among the bidders, not the lowest possible price.

Request for Proposal

The request for proposal (RFP) is used when the purchaser asks the suppliers to recommend solutions to a problem. This allows the purchaser to gather information and negotiate without committing his or her organization to a purchase until the best source is discovered.

There are a few caveats in using the RFP. First, information given to one supplier must be given to all suppliers. If a supplier is allowed to modify its proposal, all suppliers must be given equal opportunity to modify their proposals. The purchaser can negotiate with one or all suppliers on any points not clear in the proposal. The purchaser may consider paying for the proposal to compensate all suppliers for their time and ideas. This avoids the problem of one supplier proposing a good solution and a second supplier then underbidding the first supplier.

EXHIBIT 5.1
Comparison of RFI, RFQ, RFP, and IFB

Solicitation Type	Purpose	When Used	Flexibility	Result	Pros	Cons
Request for Information (RFI)	To obtain information about products, services, and suppliers.	Prior to specific requisitions.	Informal, not binding.	Catalogs, price lists, and brochures.	Easy, fast.	Not targeted. Still requires RFQ or IFB
Request for Quote (RFQ)	To obtain supplier commitment for specific items or services.	Specific desired items or services are known.	Formal, addresses specific requirements.	Specific offers that can be compared between suppliers.	Purchaser can negotiate all aspects while supplier is bound to quote.	If request not well prepared, bids may not be comparable.
Request for Proposal (RFP)	To have suppliers suggest the best solution to a requirement.	Suppliers perform evaluation or when purchaser is uncertain of processes, quality, services, standards, or other elements.	Allows for negotiating and information gathering without committing to the purchase until best source is determined.	A variety of potential solutions from which to choose.	Purchaser can negotiate with one or all suppliers on any points of proposals.	If one supplier is allowed to revise a proposal, all bidders must be allowed to modify proposals.
Request or Invitation for Bid (IFB)	Provide equal opportunity for all suppliers to make their best offer.	For higher-priced items or when there must be proof of lowest price.	Binding on both supplier and purchaser.	Best and final offers.	Formal process provides for comparability between bids and process documentation.	Preferable to use other methods as they give more flexibility to purchaser.

Request for or Invitation for Bid

The request for or invitation for bid (IFB) gives all suppliers an equal opportunity to make their best offer. Because the bid process commits both the purchaser and supplier, the IFB should only be used if the specifications or statement of work (SOW) are well defined, the dollar value is significant, it is required by statute, and one of the previous methods is not adequate. Because the formal bid process is costly for both purchaser and supplier, the IFB should not be used when one of the other methods can provide the necessary information.

To Bid Or Not To Bid

The decision whether to use bids or to negotiate with a supplier is based on a number of considerations. Factors to consider include whether the criteria for using bidding are met, the size of the purchase, the urgency of the request, and the capabilities of the existing supply base.

Criteria for Bidding

There are several requirements that should be met in order to use competitive bidding. They are as follows:

- **Sufficient dollar volume** - The amount of business at stake should be substantive enough to warrant the supplier spending the time necessary to develop a formal quotation.
- **Clear specifications** - The specifications need to be carefully defined to ensure comparability between quotations. The evaluation of quotations for products or services which vary significantly in quality, reliability, or capacity is difficult if not impossible.
- **Adequate number of suppliers (3-10)** - Without adequate competition, the supplier has little incentive to develop a proposal which aggressively seeks the purchaser's business. A selection of 3 to 10 suppliers should be adequate.
- **Active suppliers** - Even if there are an adequate number of suppliers, they must also be interested in obtaining the business. A common reason for a lack of supplier interest is a large backlog. If a supplier's capacity is already taxed, a higher quotation may

result. This may be caused by either higher margins or higher costs associated with full capacity operations. Increased costs could result from overtime pay, use of subcontractors for all or part of the process, and use of higher cost materials.

- **Enough time** - The time required for the normal competitive bid process can easily take three to four weeks at a minimum just to award the contract. More time would be required for larger, more complicated proposals. Today's electronic tools can shorten the time requirements needed to issue and receive a bid. For example, an electronics company reduced its sourcing and procurement cycle time from 13 weeks to 4 weeks after installing an Internet-based sourcing and procurement system. The comparisons before and after are as follows:

Process	Original Time Requirement	New Time Requirement
Supplier identification	5 weeks	2 weeks
Managing supplier list	Did not exist	1 day
RFP/RFQ development	1 week	1 day
RFP/RFQ dissemination and response	4 weeks	1 day
RFQ change creation, dissemination, and response	1 week	1 day
RFP/RFQ response analysis	2 weeks	1 day
Total Time Required	13 weeks	4 weeks[1]

- **Tooling or setup costs are relatively low** - If the purchase requires little or no special tooling, all suppliers have equal opportunity. If significant special tooling and/or setup are required, a previous supplier may have an unfair advantage if it already owns the tooling. This situation may form the basis for the argument that because the purchaser eventually pays for special tooling, it may be advantageous to purchase and pay for the tooling separately to retain ownership and flexibility.

Criteria for Negotiation

If the criteria for bidding are not met, the purchaser may choose to use negotiation as an approach to selecting a supplier. However, there are conditions when negotiation is the first choice as a course of action. Those conditions include the following:

- **Substantial amounts of money** - The time and effort involved in a formal negotiation process imply that the size and, therefore, the potential for savings warrant the increased cost of the negotiation process compared to bidding.

- **"Making" is an option** - If the purchasing organization has the option of producing the product internally, then the purchaser has better cost information for evaluating a supplier's proposal. The purchaser has the ability to walk away from the negotiation, if necessary, because the purchasing organization is not dependent on an outside source.

- **Prices quoted are very similar** - When there is little differentiation between quotations, as may be the case with generic or commodity items, the purchaser may use negotiation as a tool to obtain additional benefits such as special packaging, delivery conditions, or payment terms.

- **Unique and/or little experience** - If the product or service is new to the purchaser and/or supplier, negotiation may be a more appropriate way to approach the issues as they arise because the ability to anticipate future problems or issues is limited. For example, if a supplier is asked to develop a new technology, the process may not be known so the supplier would be unlikely or unable to offer a bid or fixed price.

- **No satisfactory bids** - If none of the bids received is satisfactory, the purchaser may elect to reject all bids and negotiate with one or two of the bidding suppliers.

- **Need to change contract or design** - In the case of research and development or new product design, there are usually numerous changes which will affect cost and delivery. These issues are best handled through negotiation because they vary on a case-by-case basis.

- **Purchasing capacity** - When developing long-term contracts with a supplier, the exact mix of products and/or services required in the future may be unknown. Therefore, the purchaser may purchase a portion of the supplier's capacity with the exact product and/or service mix to be determined at a future point. The important issues to the purchaser may be leadtime, notification requirements, and flexibility rather than cost.

- **High risk of technical products** - If the viability of the proposed product or project is in question or the required investment by the supplier is high, negotiation is often used to balance the risk between purchaser and supplier.

Generating the Solicitation Proposal

Once a sourcing strategy has been determined, the purchaser must determine whether to simply place the order with a supplier or develop a solicitation proposal. There is no single best way to write a solicitation proposal. The structure, content, and method of managing the information before, during, and after submission of the bid by the supplier should be guided by the principles of ethical and fair purchasing practice and organizational policy. The purchaser should also understand the business culture in the applicable country and/or industry. Some forms of bidding may not be appropriate in all places. In some forms of solicitations, such as IFBs, alternate proposals may not be allowed and may disqualify the bid. This should be specifically pointed out in the bid document. Alternate proposals are generally accepted in RFPs.

The steps in generating a solicitation proposal are to determine the type of bidding process, establish a cross functional team, define the objectives of the process, develop an evaluation matrix and weighting scheme, develop the document, conduct a supplier information session, and evaluate the proposals.

Types of Bids

More complex or large-dollar transactions often involve a formal bidding process. Here, the specifications, transaction, and bidding requirements are communicated to potential suppliers usually by mail, but perhaps by fax or e-mail. The purchaser may also choose to request bids by advertising in trade publications, newspapers, or on the Internet. These transactions often involve voluminous bid packages and require extensive analysis and comparison. This formal bidding process usually involves sealed bids due at a specific date and time.

Less complex or costly transactions may be accomplished in a less formal manner. Here, telephone or fax quotes/bids from suppliers may be sufficient and comparison and contract/order award is comparatively simple.

An alternative to the normal bidding process is the two-step process. In the two-step process the proposals are first evaluated on technical merit only and price is not a consideration. Each proposal is evaluated and scored against a predetermined scale representing the purchaser's technical requirements. Only those proposals that meet the minimum technical requirements in step one are considered in step two when the costs are included. The advantage of a two-step process is that each proposal is evaluated solely on its technical merits. The problem with the two-step approach is that the proposals that make the second round may exceed the funds available for the purchase resulting in the specifications being modified and a repeat of the entire process.

The question is often asked, is purchasing services different? The answer is not clear-cut. Research has shown the following:

- The complexity of purchases of materials primarily depends on the clarity and specificity of the material specification or SOW.
- Material specifications are generally much more complete than a service statement of work.
- Cost analysis and negotiations are much more difficult for services than for materials.[2]

The intangible nature of services makes them more difficult to specify and evaluate. The process is the same whether the purchaser is purchasing materials or services. For example, Thompson lists the process used at Canadian National to contract for an employee assistance plan and medical services.[3] Exhibit 5.2 presents the process used at Canadian National.

Exhibit 5.2
Canadian National's Outsourcing Process

- Establish procurement team with representation from all stakeholder areas.
- Define the project.
- Identify potential suppliers.
- Develop an initial set of evaluation criteria.
- Prepare the requests for proposal.
- Conduct supplier information session.
- Evaluate the proposals.
- Issue requests for quotation.
- Evaluate the quotations.
- Negotiate with the selected finalists.
- Draft the contract after selection of the successful supplier.
- Plan the transition and execution of the project.
- Follow through and manage the relationship.

Source: Thompson, G.I. "Outsourcing Services — The Steps to Success," *Proceedings of the 1997 NAPM International Purchasing Conference*, NAPM, Tempe, AZ, 1997, pp. 302-303.

Creating the Team

For large or complex acquisitions, it is useful to create a cross-functional team to oversee the process. The team should consist of the purchaser, contract manager, and representatives from engineering, quality assurance, operations, and any others with a stake in the acquisition. The first task of the team is to define the objectives of the acquisition process and then develop the specifications.

Development of Specifications

The next phase of the acquisition process is the preparation of specifications and other relevant materials. The development of specifications is discussed in Chapter 2. The purchaser is obligated to avoid specifications that are slanted in favor of a particular supplier. In addition to the product specifications or statement of work, the solicitation proposal should include information on the following:

- **Quantity** - The number of units required which may be expressed as a fixed quantity or a minimum quantity. Quantity may also be expressed as a percentage of a supplier's capacity.

- **Conditions and timing of deliveries** - A definition of "on-time delivery" should be included. For example, one organization defines on-time delivery as the range between three days early to zero days late. If the delivery is to be spread out over time, the proposal should indicate the proposed quantities and corresponding delivery dates.

- **End use** - If a performance specification is used because the purchaser is relying on the supplier's expertise, it is essential to indicate the planned usage of the item. Indicating end use is necessary to invoke the warranty of fitness for particular purpose granted under the Uniform Commercial Code (UCC).

- **Bid terms and conditions** - Requirements regarding warranties, performance guarantees, price adjustment processes, payment terms, bid bonds, performance bonds, and pre-bid conferences should be included.

- **Bid evaluation criteria** - These are factors that will be considered in selecting the winning bid/proposal. Relevant factors may include delivery date, technical support, price, quality, supplier performance history, service, and technology.

- **Quality definition** - The required quality may be defined in terms of market grades, brand or trade names, commercial standards, chemical or physical specifications, performance specifications, material and method-of-manufacture specifications, blueprints or drawings, samples, qualified products lists or a combination of the above. It is also useful to indicate the methodology that will be used to evaluate supplier quality, whether incoming or performed at the supplier's facility.

- **Deadline** - This is the date, time, and location for receipt of the bid or proposal. The analysis and bid preparation process required by suppliers should be considered when stipulating the response time. The purchaser should not make it unduly short so as to eliminate potential suppliers.

Care must be taken as to when a solicitation package is issued. The issue date affects the receipt date and the opening/closing date. If possible, do not issue a solicitation on dates that will place the closing date on a holiday when mail delivery may be affected or the purchaser's office may be closed. Also, if possible, avoid issuing solicitations during the affected suppliers' peak season. This may reduce the number of responses and increase prices. Appropriate planning by the user department and purchasing staff can help the organization avoid these situations. On the other hand, issuing solicitations during off-seasons for the affected suppliers may result in better pricing and other concessions.

Developing the Solicitation Documents

Solicitations have two customers, the purchaser and the supplier. The supplier desires a solicitation that is easy to respond to while the purchaser wants a solicitation that is easy to analyze. To accomplish these goals, a solicitation must be well organized, attractive, readable, respondable, and improvable.

Organization - The solicitation document should be well organized. Appendix 5-A presents an example solicitation proposal based on an actual RFP received by the author. It has been modified and restructured to illustrate the following points:

- The purchaser needs to avoid redundant clauses. An item or issue should only be addressed once in a document. This avoids confusion caused by stating something slightly differently at separate locations in the document.
- Related issues or topics should be grouped together.
- The structure of the solicitation document should include the following:

    Title page - The title page should be organized into logical sections: the solicitation data including time of opening, directions to the delivery location, and a summary of the documents.
    Introduction - The introduction provides an overview of the project or requirement, acceptance criteria, evaluation process, and award process.
    Primary specifications - This is the meat of the solicitation. The detailed information as to the requirements is presented here.
    Ancillary specifications - This section may include items such as invoicing process, discounts, delivery instructions including carrier specification, FOB point, and change order process.

General terms and conditions - The normal terms and conditions are referenced here and the actual document is attached. Anything that needs clarification or is additional for this solicitation is covered here. See Appendices 7-A and 7-B for example terms and conditions.

Response structure and evaluation criteria - The first part of this section specifies to the bidder exactly what information is required and the proper format for the information. The second key part of this section tells the bidder what criteria and process the purchaser will use to evaluate the responses and select the winning response.

Forms - All required forms should be provided in this section. Forms should provide adequate space for responses. Providing word processing templates or spreadsheets can reduce the time spent collecting data but require a large time investment on the front end.

Schedules and other attachments - Additional documents referenced in the solicitation are included in this section. Each should be clearly labeled.

Appearance - Although it seems like a minor issue, the appearance of the solicitation can improve the response rate and quality of the responses. Headers and footers can be used to guide the reader through the document. They can provide information as to the section the reader is in, page number, and the due date. The type size should be no smaller than ten points and the document should make liberal use of paragraph headings. In general, avoid crowding too much information on any one page. Use white space to focus the reader's attention on the important sections of the document.

Readability - The easier the solicitation proposal is to read, the greater the probability the purchaser will receive a bid document that addresses all the issues and the smaller the probability of misunderstandings. Avoid convoluted and obscure legalese.

Each section of the document should be labeled with legal-style numbering. That is, include all the section numbers so that it is clear what section the respondent is addressing (for example, I-C-1-a-iii). When providing lists, provide a section number in addition to the list number. This prevents the purchaser from misinterpreting what section the respondent is addressing.

Response friendly - It is important to structure the response areas of the documents to improve ability to compare responses. The best way to accomplish this is to provide pre-printed forms and provide spreadsheet templates that structure the suppliers' responses. It may be useful to require the respondents to identify in one section any variations or deviations from specifications. This prevents them from being hidden elsewhere in the document. This section should also include the procedures for submission including mailing and delivery addresses and e-mail addresses, and/or fax addresses if e-mail or fax are allowable methodologies for response. If the purchaser provides the forms, make sure the space allotted for the response is adequate.

Improvable - Always look for ways to improve your solicitation documents. One source for alternative examples is the NAPM Web page (www.napm.org), which has a section devoted to bid specifications. This listing identifies items and provides contact information to obtain specifications from the original developer. Additionally, there are a number of contract segments available through the InfoOnline search engine at the NAPM Web page.

Supplier Conferences

Supplier conferences grow in importance as the magnitude and complexity of the project increases. At the pre-bid conference, the cross-functional team meets with all the potential suppliers. Common topics discussed at supplier conferences include blueprints and specifications; SOWs; quotation due dates; terms and conditions; delivery schedules and materials; release procedures; invoicing procedures and documentation (including incentives); requirements if awarded the business (such as reporting, insurance, background checks, security clearances, and permits); and other purchaser and supplier requirements. If changes to the solicitation result from conferences, the purchaser issues a written amendment to the solicitation to all attendees.

Pre-bid meetings are advantageous because they establish a forum for two-way communication between the purchaser's and suppliers' organizations to discuss the details of the solicitation package at the beginning of the bid process. It is important that bid packages are obtained by all attendees well in advance of the meeting so that they will have had adequate time to review the contents. By meeting in an open forum, the purchaser will quickly learn of any discrepancies or errors in the bid package. Any corrections should be made in writing as addendums to the original bid package. This serves to expedite the bid process, as well as ensure that the information received complies with all requirements.

It is the purchaser's option whether to make pre-bid conferences mandatory. The greater the proposal complexity, the newness of the technology, or the less clear the specification, the greater would be the need for pre-bid conferences to ensure the purchaser receives useful and comparable bids. If a pre-bid conference is mandatory and attendance is made a condition for bidding, it is important that the bidders are advised of this in any pre-bid notices that are sent to them. When planning a mandatory pre-bid conference, adequate time must be allowed for the suppliers to receive the material and make plans to attend.

Pre-qualification versus Post-qualification of Suppliers

Some organizations require that all suppliers who want to bid on a proposal must be pre-qualified. That is, suppliers must prove that they are responsive and responsible. This approach requires a large amount of work and time with suppliers that may never be used. Post-qualification investigates only the supplier who receives the order.

Evaluation of the Proposals

The proposals are evaluated using the criteria established before the proposals were developed. The use of standard forms and spreadsheets can significantly streamline the evaluation process; however, the evaluation criteria will be unique for each proposal. Factors that affect the choice of criteria include the product or service being acquired, the type of specification, and the type of solicitation. Chapter 6 will discuss supplier evaluation in more detail.

Tools for Automating the Bid Process

The bid process is fundamentally an exercise in communication. Some organizations are distributing notification of upcoming bids and even distributing the solicitation package via electronic mail. Technology can be used to reduce the cost of bid document development, distribution, and compilation of responses. Potential benefits from automating the process include reduced cycle time, reduction of non-value added activities, increased productivity, increased product quality, and reduced process costs. Potential resources an organization would need to implement an e-mail system include public key encryption programs, database systems for use with the Internet, and an Adobe document writer.

Examples - North Carolina is using electronic mail to notify registered suppliers of posted solicitations for more than 250 state agencies. A supplier has previously filled out an online form indicating its areas of interest. The electronic mail notification indicates a Web address where the supplier can find specification information. By law, supplier proposals cannot be received using encrypted e-mail. The state was averaging more than 10,000 e-mail notifications per week in 1999.[4]

The state of Oregon has been using the Vendor Information Program (VIP) system since 1993. The VIP system allows suppliers to access and download proposals open for bid. The system saved more than $60,000 in reduced paper and postage costs in its first year of operation, $500,000 in lower personnel costs, increased by 8,000 the number of suppliers registered to do business with the state, and generated savings of $12.8 million over the previous year as a result of increased competition.[5]

Bid Ethics

During the course of competitive quoting, problems may arise that require action on behalf of the purchaser. These problems typically include one or more of the following:

- **Time extensions and amendments to solicitation** - If one supplier is granted a time extension to respond to a bid, all suppliers must be notified that they are granted the same extension.

Changes to the original bid must be communicated to all bidding
suppliers in a consistent and timely manner.

- **Late bids (without time extensions)** - The purchaser must make
  clear his or her organization's policy relative to late bids before
  issuing a quotation. The practice of not accepting late bids and
  returning them unopened is common.
- **Offers with errors, irregularities, or omissions** - If a supplier
  identifies a mistake in a bid after submission, it is good practice
  to allow that supplier to cancel or withdraw the bid. Courts allow
  the withdrawal of bids only after determining the following:

  - That the mistake was mechanical or clerical in nature and not
    an error in judgment.
  - That the bidder was not guilty of blame-deserving negligence
    in making the error or in delaying notification to the pur-
    chaser of the error.

If an error, irregularity, or omission is so out of proportion as to indicate a mistake, the purchaser should seek confirmation of the bid
from the bidding supplier before proceeding with the award. If a mistake is confirmed, the bidding supplier should be allowed to cancel or
withdraw the bid without penalty.

- **Conflicts of interest** - Ethical practice requires that no employee
  of an organization who has any authority to purchase goods or
  services or is in a position to influence decisions in any way with
  respect to purchases should be employed by, hold any position
  with, serve as a director of, have a financial interest in, or business relationship with any outside concern that is a supplier of
  goods and services to the purchasing organization.
- **Protests** - If not selected, suppliers are entitled to a reasonable
  explanation. However, take care not to disclose the information
  contained in competitors' bids unless, as in a public purchase,
  such disclosures are required by law. General information provided to the supplier will assist in better meeting the needs of the
  purchaser during the next quotation process. In the public sector,
  if a supplier or prospective supplier disagrees with an action or
  decision of the purchaser, it may file a protest and request an

administrative review of the action or decision.

- **Confidentiality** - As with all purchasing documents, files containing bids should be secured to prevent unauthorized access. Confidential information about one supplier should not be shared with others.
- **Alternate proposals** - Suppliers often propose products or services that are different from those specified by the purchaser. Many of these proposals have merit, and a policy of whether and how to consider these is often implemented by organizations.
- **Debriefing process** - When the award is made and the contract has been signed, some organizations have a policy of advising all bidders of the name of the successful organization. The debriefing process should also include in-house departments. The end-users must be advised as to whom the successful organization is and any necessary arrangements made for introductions of staffs that will be working together. Depending on the project, financial, security, and other internal departments may also need to be debriefed on the process. Any third-party organizations that will be involved in the project should also be advised as soon as possible.

Bid Terms and Conditions

A contract consists of both custom and standard terms and conditions. Standard terms and conditions are those that the organization wants to apply to every contract. Potential issues standard terms and conditions may address include changes to the contract, cancellation, subcontracting, confidentiality, delivery, shipping, indemnity, legal venue, applicable laws, inspection, payment terms, packaging, and warranties. See Appendix 7A at the end of Chapter 7 for common terms and conditions.

Custom terms and conditions are those which are unique to the specific contract or purchase order. Issues custom terms and conditions may address include acceptance testing, service information updates, emergency services, financing, installation, training, initial provisioning, maintenance, spare parts, and renewal. See Appendix 7B at the end of Chapter 7 for custom contract terms and conditions. It is appropriate to include all terms and conditions in all solicitations.

This helps avoid surprises and disagreements later in the award process.

Surety - In general, having the supplier post some form of surety increases the cost of bidding and tends to reduce competition. The use of surety does not guarantee financial recovery. Common forms of surety are as follows:

- **Bid bonds** - Sometimes used by government agencies and in construction bidding, bid bonds bring a third party into the transaction. A bid bond guarantees that if the order is awarded to a specific bidder, it will accept the purchase contract. If the bidder refuses, the purchaser's extra costs associated with using an alternative source are borne by the insurer.
- **Performance bonds** - Often used in international sourcing and construction bidding, the purchaser can, as a condition of doing business, require the supplier to post a performance bond guaranteeing prompt delivery of goods or services that meet specifications. In the case of construction projects, a performance bond guarantees that the work done will be completed on time and according to specification.
- **Payment bonds** - The payment bond protects the purchaser against liens that may be filed by employees or subcontractors against the purchasing organization if the prime supplier does not pay its suppliers or employees.
- **Deposits** - Bid deposits may be requested for certain substantial bids as a device to discourage financially unstable suppliers. Bid deposits generally cover the amount in liquidated damages to which the purchaser would be entitled should the supplier not perform to the terms of the agreement.
- **Letters of credit** - A letter of credit, normally used in international business transactions, is a document that assures the supplier that payment will be made by the bank issuing the letter of credit once the terms of the agreement have been met.

Key Points

1. The request for information (RFI) is used to obtain information about products or services, the request for quote (RFQ) is used to obtain commitments for specified items or services, the request for proposal (RFP) is used to obtain supplier solutions, and the invitation for bid (IFB) is used to give suppliers the opportunity to make their best offer.
2. In order to use competitive bidding the following six criteria should be met, otherwise the best strategy is to use negotiation: (1) sufficient dollar volume, (2) clear specifications, (3) adequate number of suppliers, (4) active suppliers, (5) enough time, (6) tooling or setup costs are relatively low.
3. A well-designed and organized solicitation document will improve the quality of bid responses.
4. The purchaser needs to be aware of and be prepared for potential problems including late bids, time extensions, and bid errors.
5. There are a number of methods of surety to guarantee supplier performance including bid bonds, performance bonds, payment bonds, deposits, and letters of credit.

Questions for Review

1. When is it appropriate to use a RFQ versus an IFB?
2. What are the six criteria for using competitive bidding?
3. When is it appropriate to negotiate?
4. What information should be provided in addition to the specifications or statement of work?
5. What makes a good solicitation proposal?
6. What action should a purchaser take if the supplier submits a bid after the deadline?
7. What forms of surety may be used to guarantee supplier performance?

For Additional Information

Caffrey, B. "E-Mail Based RFP Management," *Purchasing Today®*, August 1999, p.16.

Cafiero, W.G. "Using the Internet for RFQ Management," *Proceedings of the 1997 NAPM International Purchasing Conference*, NAPM, Tempe, AZ, 1997, pp. 442-446.

Connolly, R.E. "Bid Rigging – It Happens: What It Is and What to Look For: An Antitrust Primer for Procurement Professionals," *Proceedings of the 1999 NAPM International Purchasing Conference*, NAPM, Tempe, AZ, 1999, pp.18-23.

Harris, T. "The User-Friendly Bid," *Proceedings of the 1997 NAPM International Purchasing Conference*, NAPM, Tempe, AZ, 1997, pp. 424-429.

Hirst, J.F. "An Invitation for Success," *NAPM Insights*, June 1995, p. 5.

James, C.J., "How Manufacturers Can Use Internet-Based Sourcing and Procurement of Producton Materials to Cut Costs and Speed Product to Market," *Proceedings of the 1999 NAPM International Purchasing Conference*, NAPM, Tempe, AZ, 1999, pp.149-151.

Smeltzer, L.R. and S.P. Siferd. "Theoretical and Perceived Differences Between Purchasing Materials and Purchasing Services," *Second Annual North American Research Symposium Proceedings*, NAPM, Tempe, AZ, 1999, pp. 164-176.

Thompson, G.I. "The Proposal: It's a Process," *Purchasing Today®*, September 1996, p. 6.

Thompson, G.I. "Outsourcing Services — The Steps to Success," *Proceedings of the 1997 NAPM International Purchasing Conference*, NAPM, Tempe, AZ, 1999, pp. 300-305.

Sunkel, J. "RFP-ASAP!," *NAPM Insights*, July 1993, pp. 40-41.

Endnotes

1. James, C. "How Manufacturers Can Use Internet-Based Sourcing and Procurement of Production Materials to Cut Costs and Speed Product to Market," *Proceedings of the 1999 NAPM International Purchasing Conference*, NAPM, Tempe, AZ, 1999, p. 150.
2. Smeltzer, L.R. and S.P. Siferd. "Theoretical and Perceived Differences Between Purchasing Materials and Purchasing Services," *Second Annual North American Research Symposium Proceedings*, NAPM, Tempe, AZ, 1999, pp. 170-171.
3. Thompson, G.I. "Outsourcing Services — The Steps to Success," *Proceedings of the 1997 NAPM International Purchasing Conference*, NAPM, Tempe, AZ, 1999, pp. 302-303.
4. Caffrey, B. "E-Mail Based RFP Management," *Purchasing Today®*, August 1999, p. 16.
5. Sunkel, J. "RFP-ASAP," *NAPM Insights*, July 1993, pp. 40-41.

APPENDIX 5-A

EXAMPLE SOLICITATION DOCUMENT

ARR Company
Request for Proposal
for a
Purchasing, Warehousing, and Distribution
System Study

Contents

133

Important Dates

Mandatory Pre-bid Meeting: Monday, January 7, 2002 at 3 p.m., Supply and Logistics Department conference room, Room 565, located at 1903 NW Broadway, Cornelius, OR 97129

Proposal Due Date: Friday, February 4, 2002 at 3 p.m., **Supply and Logistics Department. ARR Company, 1903 NW Broadway, Cornelius, OR 97129.**

I. Introduction

A. Background

The supply and logistics department of the ARR Company employs approximately 500 individuals involved in purchasing, warehousing, and truck operations. The department handles a volume of approximately $450 million in goods and services annually. The total annual operating budget of the supply and logistics department is $20 million. Approximately $9 million of the budget is the warehouse operations.

B. Scope

The supply and logistics department is seeking a proposal to conduct a confidential study of its current purchasing, warehouse, and distribution practices including administrative organization, purchasing practices, inventory control practices, receiving and storage of material, warehouse sizes and locations, types and quantities of material maintained in inventory, warehouse material handling processes and technology, delivery schedules and methods, overall staffing needs, and other related issues.

Recommendations will be provided on how to improve overall department efficiencies while integrating the latest buying, distribution, warehousing, and technology practices. Recommendations will also include an analysis of future technology trends and changes the ARR Company should make now in anticipation of the future. The proposer is expected to provide all source data, formulas, assumptions, and calculations supporting the proposer's recommendations.

C. General Information

1. Description of Branch Operational Sections

a. Buying section

Approximately 30 purchasers procure a wide variety of supplies, materials, and equipment for delivery to multiple warehouses. Warehouse replenishment is coordinated through the inventory management staff. Because of the organization's size, economies of scale often result in buyers realizing very competitive pricing during the legally mandated competitive bid process. Many master contracts are used for the acquisition of supplies, equipment, and non-professional services.

b. Stores section

The storage section currently operates three commodity-specific warehouses occupying about 386,000 square feet. These warehouses serve approximately 900 sites in a 700 square mile area. The three warehouses order, stock, and ship over 6,500 line items per year.

c. Truck operation section

The truck operation section maintains a fleet of over 200 licensed vehicles to support warehouse activities. The fleet consists of tractor/trailers (some refrigerated), straight trucks, and fork lifts.

2. Current Programs

a. Definition of terms

i. Warehouse No. 1

Stocks meats (frozen and refrigerated entrees and desserts), produce, and staples/groceries (canned/dry foods and paper products).

ii. Warehouse No. 2

Stocks materials, operating supplies, equipment, and furniture.

iii. Warehouse No. 3
Stocks maintenance supplies.

iv. Delivery schedule
- **Warehouse No. 1**
  Meat and produce - All food preparation sites every three days.
  Groceries/Staples - All sites every six days.
- **Warehouse No. 2**
  All sites every nine days.
- **Warehouse No. 3**
  All sites every three days.

D. Effective Contract Period
The ARR Company intends to enter into a contract or multiple contracts with a successful proposer(s) to be effective for approximately 30 days after notification of awards. The completion of the study shall be within 20 working days of the notification of award/notice to proceed. All related study data required by the successful proposer in conducting the study should be provided by the organization on an as-requested basis.

E. Acceptance Criteria
Proposals will be evaluated by an evaluation committee that will focus on criteria including, but not limited to, the items below. The committee will consider each aspect of the proposal giving greatest weights and qualifications, experience, and other indicators of the likelihood of providing high-quality responsive product. That committee will also review the tasks proposed and weigh the relative marriage of a monument in proposals.

a. The proposer's understanding of and quality of approach to the services requested.
b. Experience and professional qualifications of key personnel.
c. Proposer's past performance on contract with other agencies for similar projects.

    d. The extent and quality of other resources and capabilities within the proposer's organization.

    e. Cost effectiveness of services provided. However, the proposal selected may not be the one with lowest fees.

A first "cut" may be made reducing the number of firms based on the written proposal submitted. To further assist in evaluation, name "finalists" may be called upon for an oral interview and/or a presentation.

All proposals submitted in timely manner will be allies and in the company will select a firm (for firms) to which a contract will be awarded.

This company's selection will be based on its evaluation of which proposal(s) will provide the package most beneficial to the company. The proposal(s) selected may not necessarily be those with the lowest fees.

F. Evaluation and Award Process

1. Proposer's Pre-Bid Meeting

A mandatory proposers' pre-bid meetings will be held for those interested in submitting proposals on Monday, January 7, 2002 at 3 p.m.

Location of the meeting will be in the supply and logistics department conference room, Room 565, located at 1903 NW Broadway, Cornelius, OR 97129. Proposals will the accepted for evaluation only from proposers who are represented at this meeting.

At this meeting, company staff will provide additional background information and will also answer questions related to this proposal.

Subsequent to the proposers' meeting, no additional requests for information or clarification will be responded to and proposers should not contact company personnel in regard to this RFP.

2. Time and Place for Submitting Proposals

All proposals must be signed by a person authorized to act on behalf of the firm and be delivered or mailed to **Supply and Logistics Department, ARR Company, 1903 NW Broadway, Cornelius, OR 97129.**

The proposals must be received no later than 3 p.m., February, 2002. Please submit six copies of the proposal. Proposals received after the time and date indicated will be rejected.

II. Primary Specifications

A. General

1. Buying Section
  a. What is the most cost-effective procurement methodology given current resources, structure, and customer needs?
  b. What current uses of purchasing technology or methodology can be utilized to increase efficiency?
  c. Is the allocation of purchasing resources sufficient in the area of establishing master contracts, identifying "piggy backable" contracts, and participating in cooperative pur chasing events?

2. Stores Section
  a. Currently, overhead is being charged separately from the general fund budget. Is this the best system?
  b. Currently, an overnight delivery service exists for an additional fee. Is this the best system?
  c. Currently, traffic management is not used. Should it be?
  d. What items are best suited for warehousing distribution and which ones should not be inventoried?

  e. What is an appropriate trade-off between warehouse service levels and inventory turnover rates for our industry?

  f. What inventoried items would be subject to just-in-time inventory strategies?

  g. What economies can be realized from the implementation of a real-time, bar code-based, radio frequency (RF) communication, warehouse management system in the areas of labor cost/productivity, space utilization, inventory turnover, order picking, control systems, and customer service?

  h. What improvements, if any, in the four basic functions of warehouse operation would be recommended?

3. Truck Operation Section

  a. Determine the optimum type of vehicle(s) for making deliveries throughout the service area.

  b. Determine optimum fleet utilization including the use of after hours loading and/or delivery.

  c. Determine the feasibility of combining the delivery of goods from different warehouses on the same vehicle.

III. Ancillary Specifications

Conflict of Interest and Statement of Ethics

The proposer certifies that it has no existing financial interest that could conflict with performance of the services under this RFP. The proposer agrees to abide by the Statement of Ethics which is part of the RFP in Section 7, Part A.

IV. General Terms and Conditions

V. Reply Presentation and Review

A. Data to Be Submitted with Proposal

1. Title page
2. Table of contents

3. Supplier organization
4. Supplier financial data
5. Supplier insurance coverage
6. Equal employment opportunity program information
7. Proposal
8. Economy of presentations
9. Cost and time summary
10. References
11. Deviations from specifications
12. Additional data
13. Proprietary information
14. Certification of proposal

VI. Forms

A. Certification of proposal

VII. Schedules and Other Attachments

A. Ethics Policy Statement

B. Independent Contractor Checklist

C. Request for Taxpayer Identification Status

CHAPTER 6

THE SUPPLIER EVALUATION PROCESS: IS THIS THE RIGHT SUPPLIER?

Chapter Objectives

- Understand what to look for in the supplier's response to the solicitation request.
- Develop the factors to be evaluated in a site visit.
- Understand what factors affect a supplier's ability to perform.
- Understand and apply the tools of supplier financial analysis to evaluate the supplier's financial condition.
- Identify additional requirements of the supplier's costing system.
- Develop the various aspects of supplier quality capability requirements.
- Identify what information is needed regarding supplier management and organization.
- Understand required information on the supplier's labor status.
- Identify what supplier attributes to measure for evaluating supplier performance.
- Understand the basic models for supplier evaluation.

Introduction

The evaluation of supplier quotations and capabilities to determine the best overall competitive offering for a product or service is one of the primary responsibilities of purchasing. The purchaser's evaluation of the supplier's capabilities may include site visits, analysis of the supplier's ability to perform, financial analysis, analysis of the supplier's costing and quality systems, and analysis of supplier management and labor. Information to assist in the supplier evaluation may come from the supplier evaluation system.

Evaluating the Offer

As quotes are received, purchasers should log them according to the date received, and file them with the original bid package. When all of the quotes have been received against a specific bid or at the bid due date, purchasers should prepare a brief summary of the quotations, noting the salient information in a comparison-type chart or spreadsheet.

Perhaps the most critical aspect in evaluating bids offered by suppliers is to ensure that the bid response meets the specifications and SOW requirements of the initial solicitation package. This is important for two reasons:

- The purchaser needs to ensure that the supplier will meet the specifications and/or SOW requirements defined in the solicitation. If not, the purchaser must be aware of the implications in accepting the bid. Not meeting specifications or submitting an alternate statement of work can have either a positive or negative affect on the purchaser's organization. At best, it can result in an alternate design or service at a lower cost that may be acceptable to the purchaser's organization. At worst, it may cause quality concerns or it may not meet the minimum requirements defined by the purchasing organization. The responsibility of the purchaser is to ensure that suppliers are quoting to specification or that the quoted exceptions are acceptable to the total organization. Organizations often will not consider an alternative proposal unless the supplier has also quoted the item or service requested.
- To fairly evaluate all quotes received, suppliers must quote based on a comparable set of specifications or a comparable SOW. Otherwise, it is extremely difficult to determine which supplier offers the most competitive package.

Most solicitations include a set of contract terms and conditions that the purchaser has developed to match the risks and issues related to the product or service being considered. Suppliers typically respond with alternative language to reduce their risks. Including these contract terms and conditions in the solicitation allows the purchaser to consider contractual issues with the other aspects of the evaluation.

Presale technical service is offered by some organizations as part of the quotation process, particularly when technical products or services are being purchased. Purchasing must ensure that it does not take unfair advantage of suppliers offering presale technical assistance, but at the same time must ensure that it receives all of the assistance to which it is entitled prior to award. Acceptance of more presale service than is customary in the industry may obligate the organization to more than is anticipated.

Technical

Purchasing should actively involve the engineering, manufacturing, quality, materials control, operations, and other using departments in the bid evaluation process. This is a natural extension of involving these departments in the initial definition of specifications or the SOW. Each function or department should have guidelines by which it evaluates supplier proposals and should be aware of fair practice procedures before beginning the evaluation process.

Operational

The feasibility of the product or service being purchased must be thoroughly evaluated. Although the supplier might be technically capable of the work, organizations often conduct an operational analysis to determine economic and functional feasibility. The operational analysis could involve a site visit to assess the supplier's equipment, processes, and labor as well as control systems for production planning and quality.

Capability

Purchasing should review the following aspects of the supplier's ability to meet the requirements of the contract:

- **Past performance** - The past performance of a supplier on similar jobs and its implications for performance on future contracts.

- **Capacity** - The supplier's capacity to take on additional business.
- **Skills** - The skills the supplier possesses to manage the specific business in question.
- **Integrity** - The supplier's integrity and conduct in past relations.
- **Time in business or the market** - How long has the organization been in this line of business and what track record and evidence of sustainability does it have?
- **Certification and licensing** - It may be necessary to confirm a supplier's proposal documents that indicate it has the appropriate certifications and licenses. These could include "rights to use" for software or other intellectual property that is part of the supplier's proposal. The supplier's facility may also have ISO 9000 or other certification that indicates a certain level of quality, technical competence, or other qualification.
- **Financial factors** - A solicitation should request supplier financial data (income statement and balance sheet) to allow evaluation of the supplier's financial condition. This will be discussed in more detail below.

Conducting Supplier Visits

A supplier visit, audit, or evaluation is a technique employed by purchasing to determine if business should be placed with a supplier. This visit gives the purchasing organization a first-hand look at the supplier organization's facilities and will answer for the purchaser the majority of questions about the level of technology at the facility, the education and training of the staff, the employees' attitudes toward their work, and the overall effectiveness of the supplier. If the supplier does not make a sincere effort to show its best side during this visit and does not cooperate fully, one can safely assume that the supplier probably will never do so for the purchaser. Information generated during a supplier visit enables the purchaser to ascertain the supplier's capability to meet forecasted needs for a quality product or service, on time, at a competitive price. Visits also show support for a continuing relationship and help facilitate the joint development of suggestions for process and quality improvements.

Visitation Team

The nature of the visit will determine the composition of the visitation team. A carefully selected cross-functional audit team consisting of the proper mix of individuals from purchasing, quality assurance, operations, accounting, and engineering will provide the expertise necessary to recognize problems at the supplier's location and make suggestions for corrective actions.

Costs versus Benefits of Visits

Although supplier visits may be costly in terms of time and expense, such expenditures are sound investments against future problems. An unaudited supplier with poor facilities, old technology, insufficient capacity, or an underqualified staff may experience increased down time and/or lost production. Such an organization is also likely to have limited assets for future growth. Such factors will affect the supply continuity to the purchaser's organization.

Factors to Appraise on Site Visits

There are numerous factors to investigate on a site visit. The purchaser is concerned whether the supplier has the capabilities to produce quality products on time and the flexibility to meet future requirements. Factors that should be evaluated include the following:

- **Facilities** - Items to observe include age and condition of the equipment, cleanliness of the facility, layout of the facility, amount of material in process, facility capacity, and current level of activity.
- **Housekeeping** - Housekeeping is an indicator of discipline and pride in the workplace. The best way to compare housekeeping is to look at two suppliers making the same product. Housekeeping affects quality and efficiency. There are times when a normally well-kept facility or organization will be unorganized due to a surge in business or an emergency order.
- **Technical capabilities** - What is the supplier's research and development capability? What support is available from customer service? What are engineering's capabilities?
- **Process/material flow** - Efficient process and material flows are required to keep a supplier competitive. Where inefficiencies

exist, suggested improvements could help reduce costs for both parties and make the supplier more competitive.

- **Employee morale** - How do the employees feel about working there? What are their perceptions about management? Morale is most influenced by upper management's treatment of employees. There will always be some "malcontents" in any organization but in the truly good ones the employees feel they are treated fairly and that management cares about them. Morale has a great affect on quality, timeliness, and the efficiency of any operation. It also is reflected in employees' willingness to put in extra effort to serve a customer. The purchaser must be very aware of major management shifts and their affect on the supplier's employees.

- **Process control** - What is the system used for planning and controlling process activity? Can it quickly determine the status and location of orders? What criteria are used for establishing an order's priority? What are the inventory and bill-of-material accuracies? What is the percentage of capacity committed to orders already in hand? For example, is capacity utilization at a rate that allows room for your order within the required leadtime?

- **Quality control** - Is there a quality function? Where does it report in the organization? Are process control systems in place? Who maintains them? Does the organization employ statistical process control tools routinely at all processes?

- **Purchasing** - How is purchasing organized? Is the staffing adequate? How are the relationships with current suppliers? What is the organization's credit rating with its suppliers?

- **Management commitment** - Is the supplier's management interested in the purchaser's business? What is top management's involvement in operations? What is top management's commitment to quality and customer service?

- **Technology** - How current is the supplier's process technology? How is information technology used? Does the supplier have e-commerce capabilities? What is the level of technology used in product/service development and design? Does the supplier have a technology plan?

Approved suppliers should be visited at intervals commensurate with their performance. A superior supplier will not be visited as often as one that frequently ships late and experiences quality problems.

During on-site visits, talks should be centered on process enhancements aimed at lowering the cost of business for both parties. Process improvements can result in reductions in leadtimes, back orders, late shipments, early shipments, over shipments, and rejection rates. The purchaser should impress upon the supplier that process improvements lead to higher quality, that can lead to increased future business and the renewal of contractual commitments.

Supplier's Ability to Perform

Some of the items to be considered when analyzing the supplier's ability to perform include the following:

- **Frequency and volume of orders** - How important is the purchaser's business to the supplier? If the purchaser's business occupies a major portion of the supplier's overall work, the purchaser is more likely to get favorable treatment and higher priority.
- **Length of time to process orders** - How long does it take, on average, for the supplier to process orders? Long order processing leadtimes increase total leadtime that could result in a great deal of follow-up or expediting. What is the variation in the supplier's time to process orders?
- **Delivery** - Does the supplier have sufficient facilities or the capacity to deliver ordered materials or services on a schedule that is acceptable to the purchaser?
- **Quality** - Is there evidence of a total quality management (TQM) philosophy? What mechanisms does the supplier have in place to maintain quality? What is its record with regard to quality? Do many of its products need to be returned? How have other purchasers found the quality of materials produced by this supplier?
- **Product/service expertise** - Is this product or service one in which the supplier has extensive experience or expertise or is it merely a "sideline" activity? What is the level of regular and special service provided by the supplier?

- **Order backlog** - Is the organization's productive capacity over-booked? Is it operating efficiently? Is there a great backlog of orders? Have leadtimes been lengthening or shortening?
- **Supplier's "outsourcing" program** - To what extent does the supplier acquire items already produced from its suppliers, or will the items being purchased be solely produced by them?
- **Cycle time/leadtime** - What is the supplier's current cycle time/leadtime? Can this be improved by giving advanced scheduling notice? Will the prospective supplier agree to a stocking program to provide short-cycle deliveries?
- **Productivity** - Productivity is defined as the relationship between the organization's output and input. Productivity will vary based on the amount of capital investment, systems, and skill level of the workforce. Mathematically it is calculated as follows:

$$\text{Productivity} = \text{Output/Input}$$

  To maintain and enhance competitiveness, it is essential that productivity be continually improved. This can be achieved in three ways: improved efficiency (same output with less input), improved effectiveness (greater output with the same input), and improved proficiency (greater output with less input).

- **Flexibility** - Flexibility is the willingness and ability to make or adjust to changes. This skill is important in a supplier because it enables the working relationship to be dynamic and responsive to marketplace shifts. Flexibility is both an operational and a mental dimension. As an operational dimension, it means that an organization is capable of frequent adjustments. As a mental dimension, it refers to a mindset that is customer-oriented, one that views change as an opportunity. As with any operation, constant, sudden, and frequent changes can lead to inefficiencies. A good purchaser provides a supplier with as much advance notice as possible about coming changes. Flexibility in a supplier is characterized by open mindedness, a strong customer focus, and an empowered culture.

- **References** - A list of other customers the supplier has done business with can serve to verify the quality, delivery, and service the supplier will provide.
- **Electronic capabilities** - Does the supplier have a Web site? Can it handle EDI or e- commerce transactions? Is the supplier conducting e-commerce with other customers? Do they make use of bar coding? The investment in electronic capabilities will facilitate business-to-business transactions, reduce administrative costs, and make each party more efficient. The ability to conduct business electronically is an increasingly important criterion.
- **Breadth of product line** - Does the supplier have the ability to make multiple items or provide a variety of services? The ability to place more business with one supplier facilitates supply base reduction, allows for volume leveraging, offers better prices, and improves transportation efficiencies.
- **Available capacity** - Current operating capacity is the output level at which the organization is currently running. This should be compared to theoretical capacity, the capacity of the process if it was running 100 percent of the time. Theoretical capacity is the optimum output under ideal conditions. Comparing theoretical to current level will provide an idea of the excess capacity available. Most organizations can expand capacity in the short-term through overtime or additional shifts. When this ratio of current operating capacity to theoretical capacity reaches 90 percent or above the organization is fairly close to reaching its practical capacity.
- **Supply base** - What is the extent of the supplier's relationships with its key suppliers? Does it manage its second- and third-tier suppliers? What programs does the supplier have in place for supplier development?

Supplier's Financial Status

One area of concern with a supplier is its financial structure and stability. This information is used not only to evaluate the supplier's health but can also be used to develop an understanding of cost structure, profit margins, and whether help may be required to finance tooling or material inventories. A comprehensive review of the supplier's financial data provides the purchasing manager with good information on where the supplier has been and where it is going.

Sources of Financial Data

Sources of financial data include the supplier, Dun and Bradstreet (D&B) reports, publications such as *Moody's Industrials or Standard and Poor's*, Securities and Exchange Commission 10-K reports, annual reports, and various financial analysts' reports. If the supplier does not have public traded stock or bonds, the purchaser is limited to the information provided by the supplier either directly or indirectly through organizations such as Dun and Bradstreet.

Dun and Bradstreet reports provide credit information about the supplier's payment history, such as whether the payments were made in full, whether they were on time; history about the organization; key financial ratios; and the educational level and experience of key management staff. Because privately held organizations have no public disclosure requirements, reports from these organizations are limited in many cases by the amount of information that an organization is willing to provide. D&B provides reports on over 50 million domestic businesses in both paper and electronic formats.

The Securities Exchange Commission (SEC) requires that all publicly held companies issue a 10-K report annually and a 10-Q report quarterly. These reports provide greater detail on items of interest to purchasers such as earnings, assets, and liabilities than the annual report. (If the data is electronically filed it may be available at www.sec.gov/edgarhp.htm.)

The business section of a public library has information on the industry within which each supplier operates, its ranking within that industry, and the long- and short-term factors affecting that industry. Examples include *Moody's, Standard and Poor's*, and Hoover's online (www.hoovers.com). Exhibit 6.1 presents a list of Web sites with information about organizations.

EXHIBIT 6.1
Internet Sources of Supplier Information

Organization	Web Address	Description
Avenue Technologies	www.avetech.com	News and information about 20,000 public and private organizations.
Disclosure, Inc.	www.disclosure.com	Similar to Standard & Poor's site that often has more up-to-date data.
Dun & Bradstreet Online	www.dnb.com	Provides short reports on over 50 million domestic organizations. Credit reports can be obtained by subscriptions.
Hoover's Online	www.hoovers.com	Provides detailed income statement and balanced sheet information for 2,500 organizations.
Inc. 500 database	www.inc.com/500	Revenue information, profits and loss percentages, and number of employees of privately held organizations.
Securities & Exchange Commission	www.sec.gov	Maintains the Edgar Database.
Standard & Poor's	www.compustat.com	In depth strategic financial information on corporate descriptions plus news
The U.S. Department of Commerce	www.doc.gov	Demographics and industry market data of commerce collected by the government.

Source: Hollingsworth, B. "How to Effectively Rate Your Suppliers," *NAPM InfoEdge*, (4:3), November 1998, p. 8.

Financial Analysis

Excessive debt, large accounts payable, declining sales, and poor cash flow suggest that a supplier has a poor credit history and is not likely to be able to obtain additional loans and therefore may not be able to come up with the resources to meet the purchaser's needs. They also suggest that a supplier is on "shaky ground," and may go into bankruptcy in the near future. The supplier's financial health can be evaluated in terms of liquidity, turnover, profitability, history, and other measures.

Income statements - An income statement shows earnings for a given period, usually one year, and reconciles earnings from sales against cost of goods sold (COGS) and operating expenses to produce net income. Net sales, the first item on the income statement, is calculated by reducing gross sales by the amount of returned goods to produce net sales. Gross profit is computed by subtracting cost to produce the goods from net sales. Gross profit minus total expenses (administrative expenses, sales expense, depreciation, interest, and taxes) equals net income.

The supplier's income statement is useful to identify profit and contribution margins and cost structures. The greater the variation in products produced by the supplier the less valuable is the cost structure information obtained from the income statement in terms of a particular product.

Balance sheets - A balance sheet shows the financial position for an organization at a given point in time. A balance sheet shows what the organization owns (assets) and what it owes (liabilities). Assets are composed of money the organization has, money that it is owed, and property that it owns. Liabilities are comprised of debts, including bonds and notes.

Careful analysis of the balance sheet will tell the purchaser the current state of the organization's financial condition. The balance sheet provides information on the age of the accounts payable (are they financing the organization by not paying the bills in a timely manner?); the age of the accounts receivable (are customers not paying because of quality or delivery problems?); inventory information (age of the inventory and where inventory is in the process — raw material, work-in-process, or finished goods); cash availability, and remaining accounting life of capital equipment (ratio of accumulated depreciation to original value of the equipment). Exhibits 6.2 through 6.5 present an example application of the following ratios.

Liquidity - Two measures used to evaluate the financial health of an organization are the current ratio and quick ratio. The current ratio is the ratio of current assets to current liabilities. Current assets are assets that can be converted to cash within the short-term and typically include cash, marketable securities, accounts receivable, and inventory. Current payables are the financial obligations of the organization payable within the next 12 months and typically include short-term debt, the current portion of long-term debt, and accounts payable. The desired value for the ratio is around two but can vary from industry to industry. If the ratio is too high it may be caused by excess inventories or high accounts receivable. If the ratio is too low the organization may not be able to meet its short-term obligations or finance the necessary materials.

$$\text{Current Ratio} = \frac{[\text{Cash} + \text{Marketable Securities} + \text{Accounts Receivable} + \text{Inventory}]}{[\text{Short-Term Debt} + \text{Current Long-Term Debt} + \text{Accounts Payable}]}$$

The Quick (or Acid Test) Ratio is similar to the current ratio but leaves out inventory from the current assets. A desirable ratio value is greater than one.

$$\text{Quick Ratio} = \frac{[\text{Cash} + \text{Marketable Securities} + \text{Accounts Receivable}]}{[\text{Short-Term Debt} + \text{Accounts Payable}]}$$

Turnover - Another set of financial health indicators deal with the turnover of assets and liabilities. Accounts payable turnover is calculated by dividing the COGS by the value of the accounts payable:

$$\text{Accounts Payable Turnover} = [\text{COGS}]/[\text{Accounts Payable}]$$

If the turnover rate is divided into 365, the result is the number of days accounts payable is outstanding. Turnover shows how long the supplier is using its supplier's money. If the rate is beyond the industry norm, it may indicate the supplier is having trouble obtaining funds. The shortage could be caused by extended accounts receivables or an inability to obtain additional financing. Industry norms can be obtained from *Annual Statement Studies* published by Robert Morris Associates or *Industry Norms & Key Business Ratios* published by Dun & Bradstreet.

The second turnover measure deals with accounts receivable. Accounts receivable turnover is calculated by dividing sales by the accounts receivable:

$$\text{Accounts Receivable Turnover} = [\text{Sales}]/[\text{Accounts Receivable}]$$

Dividing 365 by the number of receivables turns gives the number of days the supplier is waiting to receive its customer's payment. If this number is above the industry norm, it may indicate the supplier is having quality or delivery problems causing delays in payments.

Inventory turnover is calculated by dividing the cost of goods sold by the average inventory value:

$$\text{Inventory Turnover} = [\text{COGS}]/[\text{Average Inventory Value}]$$

Again, dividing 365 by the number of turns provides the average number of days of inventory outstanding.

Cash turnover is calculated by dividing the cost of goods sold by the average cash value:

$$\text{Cash Turnover} = [\text{COGS}]/[\text{Average Cash Value}]$$

Dividing the number of turns into 365 indicates the number of days of cash available to run the organization.

Profitability - Return on investment (ROI) indicates the return the shareholders receive on their investment. It is calculated by dividing the net income after taxes by the shareholders equity from the balance sheet:

$$\text{ROI} = [\text{Net Income After Taxes}]/[\text{Shareholders' Equity}]$$

A second measure of profitability is return on assets (ROA). This is the net income after taxes divided by the total assets of the organization:

$$\text{ROA} = [\text{Net Income After Taxes}]/[\text{Total Assets}]$$

A third measure of profitability is return on sales (ROS). It is calculated by dividing the net income after taxes by the net revenue from the income statement:

ROS = [Net Income After Taxes]/[Net Revenue]

Historical - It is also useful to track the changes in income statement relationships over time. Examples would include sales growth, cost of goods sold to sales ratio, and general administrative expenses to sales ratio. Here the purchaser is looking for changes in the relationships that would indicate rising costs, declining profits, or declining sales.

Other measures - The debt-to-equity ratio indicates the supplier's financing structure. If the ratio is too large it would indicate that the supplier may have difficulty obtaining debt financing even for the short term.

The assets-to-sales ratio indicates the productivity of the supplier's assets. This ratio should be compared with others in the same industry.

Example

Exhibits 6.2 and 6.3 present an example supplier income statement and balance sheet.

EXHIBIT 6.2
Example Income Statement

Year ending December 31
($ amounts in thousands)

	2003	2002	2001
Net sales	$43,140	$38,396	$30,564
COGS	$34,332	$30,417	$24,119
Gross Profit	$ 8,808	$ 7,979	$ 6,445
Gen & admin	$ 4,351	$ 2,854	$ 2,499
Depreciation	$ 1,090	$ 584	$ 378
Interest charges	$ 1,791	$ 882	$ 411
Earnings before taxes	$ 1,576	$ 3,659	$ 3,157
Taxes	$ 788	$ 1,830	$ 1,578
Net Income After Taxes	$ 788	$ 1,829	$ 1,579

EXHIBIT 6.3
Example Balance Sheet

Balance Sheet as of December 31
($ amounts in thousands)

Assets	2003	2002	2001
Cash	$ 594	$ 2,329	$ 1,736
Accts receivable	$21,500	$15,750	$ 5,788
Inventories	$ 5,591	$ 3,914	$ 6,993
Total current assets	$27,685	$21,993	$14,517
Land, building, eqmt	$13,370	$ 8,003	$ 7,365
Less: Accmltd deprcn	$ 2,747	$ 1,687	$ 1,211
Net fixed assets	$10,623	$6,316	$ 6,154
Investments/advances	$ 634	$ 462	$ 232
Other assets	$ 938	$ 1,132	$ 838
Total Assets	$39,880	$29,903	$21,741
Liabilities and Equity			
Accounts Payable	$ 6,239	$ 2,791	$ 4,140
Notes payable-banks	$ 2,000	—	$ 1,000
Accrued taxes, interest	$ 1,508	$ 1,941	$1,901
Current sinking fund	$ 514	$ 383	$ 324
Total current liabilities	$10,261	$ 5,115	$ 7,365
Long-term debt:			
From banks	$12,000	$ 9,000	$ 1,777
Bonds	$ 7,170	$ 4,650	$ 5,163
Total liabilities	$29,431	$18,765	$14,305
Preferred stock	$ 2,254	$ 2,348	$ 2,393
Common stock and surplus	$ 8,195	$ 8,790	$ 5,043
Total Liabilities and Net Worth	$39,880	$29,903	$21,741

Exhibit 6.4 presents the financial analysis for the example supplier data in Exhibits 6.2 and 6.3. The summary results are presented in Exhibit 6.5.

EXHIBIT 6.4
Example Supplier Financial Analysis Calculations

LIQUIDITY

Current ratio

2001:	[$14,517/$7,365]	=	1.97
2002:	[$21,993/$5,115]	=	4.30
2003:	[$27,685/$10,261]	=	2.70

Quick ratio

2001:	[($1,736+$5,788)/($4,140+$1,000+$1,901)] =		1.07
2002:	[($2,329+$15,750)/($2,791+$1,941)]	=	3.82
2003:	[($594+$21,500)/($6,239+$2,000+$1,508)] =		2.27

TURNOVER

Payables

2001:	[$24,119/$4,140]	=	5.83 turns	=	63 days
2002:	[$30,417/$2,791]	=	10.90 turns	=	33 days
2003:	[$34,332/$6,239]	=	5.50 turns	=	66 days

Receivables

2001:	[$30,564/$5,788]	=	5.28 turns	=	69 days
2002:	[$38,396/$15,750]	=	2.44 turns	=	150 days
2003:	[$43,140/$21,500]	=	2.01 turns	=	182 days

Inventory

2001:	[$24,119/$6,993]	=	3.45 turns	=	106 days
2002:	[$30,417/$3,914]	=	7.77 turns	=	47 days
2003:	[$34,332/$5,591]	=	6.14 turns	=	59 days

Cash

2001:	[$30,564/$1,736]	=	17.61 turns	=	21 days
2002:	[$38,396/$2,329]	=	16.49 turns	=	22 days
2003:	[$43,140/$594]	=	72.63 turns	=	5 days

PROFITABILITY

Return on investment

2001:	[$1,579/$7,436][100]	=	21.2%
2002:	[$1,829/$11,138][100]	=	16.4%
2003:	[$788/$10,449][100]	=	7.5%

Return on assets

2001:	[$1,579/$21,741][100]	=	7.3%
2002:	[$1,829/$29,903][100]	=	6.1%
2003:	[$788/$39,880][100]	=	2.0%

Profit to revenue

2001:	[$1,579/$30,564][100]	=	5.2%
2002:	[$1,829/$38,396][100]	=	4.8%
2003:	[$788/$43,140][100]	=	1.8%

OTHER
   Debt/equity
       2001:   [\$14,305/\$7,436]   =   1.92%
       2002:   [\$18,765/\$11,138]   =   1.68%
       2003:   [\$29,431/\$10,449]   =   2.82%
   Assets to sales
       2001:   [\$21,741/\$30,564]   =   0.71%
       2002:   [\$29,903/\$38,396]   =   0.78%
       2003:   [\$39,880/\$43,140]   =   0.92 %

HISTORICAL
   Sales growth
       [(\$38,396/\$30,564)+(\$43,140/\$38,396)]/2 =   19.0%
   COGS/Sales
       2001:   [\$24,119/\$30,564]   =   78.9%
       2002:   [\$30,417/\$38,396]   =   79.2%
       2003:   [\$34,332/\$43,140]   =   79.6%

EXHIBIT 6.5

Example Summary Table of Supplier Financial Analysis

	2001	**2002**	**2003**
Liquidity Ratios			
Current ratio	1.97	4.30	2.70
Quick ratio	1.07	3.82	2.27
Turnover			
Payables	63 days	33 days	66 days
Receivables	69 days	150 days	182 days
Inventory	106 days	47 days	59 days
Cash	21 days	22 days	5 days
Profitability			
ROI	21.2%	16.4%	7.5%
ROA	7.3%	6.1%	2.0%
Profit to revenue	5.2%	4.8%	1.8%
Other			
Debt/Equity	1.92%	1.68%	2.82%
Assets to Sales	0.71%	0.78%	0.92%
Income Statement			
Sales growth	—	25.6%	12.4%
COGS/Sales	78.9%	79.2%	79.6%

At first look, the liquidity ratios appear to be healthy over all three years. Studying the balance sheet data, the increases in years 2002 and 2003 may be of some concern because of the increases in accounts receivable.

Looking at the turnover ratios we see several causes for alarm. The first problem indicator is the sudden decline in the receivables turns. They have increased from 69 days in 2001 to 150 days in 2002 and to 182 days in 2003. This would seem to indicate some severe customer service problems such as quality or late delivery. This has resulted in severe cash flow problems. The supplier has gone from 21 days of cash on hand to only five days currently.

Looking at profitability, there are again some distressing signals. The return on investments has declined by two-thirds, as has the return on assets. One reason for the decline in return on investment and return on sales are sudden increases in general administrative expenses and depreciation. A major investment was made in fixed assets in 2003 and this was financed by $2 million in short-term debt and $3 million in long-term debt, primarily from banks. If the investments have been for process improvements that could be a positive result. The income statement and the balance sheet get double hits with the increase in assets and increase in depreciation causing a lower return on investment and on the assets.

The predominant issue in this example is the sharp increase in receivables in the last two years. The purchaser should investigate what has happened before placing business with the supplier.

Supplier Costs

It is increasingly important for organizations to know whether they are operating within their identified strategic directions. Central to this strategic thrust are measurement systems designed to track an organization's costs. Accounting systems are a major element of this and offer the ability to segregate costs by jobs, tasks, product lines, and customers. Further, from a purchasing standpoint, it is important for the system to treat costs consistently from job to job and customer to customer. The techniques for cost analysis are presented in Chapter 3. Some general aspects to also consider are as follows:

- **Capability of segregating costs by task** - Does the supplier's accounting system have the ability to segregate costs by tasks? This segregation will allow both the purchaser and supplier to focus on reducing high cost tasks.
- **Consistent treatment of cost** - Are costs allocated fairly across all work? What system is used to allocate these costs? Does the supplier use traditional cost accounting allocations or activity-based costing? Activity-based costing is a tool that attempts to more accurately identify and allocate indirect costs to the products they support. Activity-based management is an extension very similar to activity-based costing that attempts to identify what factors drive these indirect costs and then identify methods to reduce them. (See Chapter 3 for more discussion.)
- **Compliance with cost-accounting standards** - Does the organization use generally accepted accounting principles and abide by the standards of internal costing from such organizations as the National Association of Accountants?
- **What steps has the supplier taken, if any, to reduce costs** - A purchaser should analyze such information as well, to determine if the supplier is adding costs to the selling price that could be reduced or eliminated.

Supplier Quality

There are several aspects to analyzing a supplier's quality capability. One desirable piece of information is the process capability indices for the processes used to produce the purchaser's products (see any statistical quality control (SQC) text for a discussion of process capability indices). Testing the product before purchase can be useful but is no guarantee of the quality of the product when delivered to the purchasing organization. Often the samples are produced on a custom basis and will have a higher quality level than the production items. The supplier's quality control organization should be focused on prevention activities such as process improvement, process control, and education as opposed to simply measuring the number of defects. Also important is the supplier's past quality performance.

Close examination of the quality control of a supplier's operation is critical for two reasons:

- The quality of the supplier's product/service directly affects the quality of the purchaser's organization's final product/service.
- Purchasing is responsible for ensuring the quality of supplies and services.

Perhaps the most obvious indicator of a supplier's attention to quality is the existence of a total quality management (TQM) program. TQM is a philosophy that promotes a never-ending quest on the part of all employees to meet or exceed customer expectations by improving processes and quality. Four key indicators highlight the TQM philosophy. They are as follows:

- The level of top management commitment through policies and actions.
- The emphasis on educating and training all employees.
- The evidence of statistical methods to ensure good quality.
- The seeking and using of customer feedback to improve operations and processes.

In addition to the overall TQM philosophy, the quality audit team will examine the supplier's quality-control procedures, record keeping, and compliance with regulations. These details provide proof that the organization embraces an overall commitment to producing a high-quality product or service. The quality member of the audit team should lead this portion of the site visit with a review of incoming, in-process, and outgoing quality inspection procedures, documentation, and gauge calibration logs and procedures.

Assessing quality capabilities of service providers is much more difficult because of the intangibility of services, the inability to guarantee repeatability of a service, and the perception of quality being dependent upon the decision maker. Because a supplier has performed well in the past is no guarantee about the future. The things to look for in a service provider include existing processes, past performance, employee training, quality measurements, and continuous improvement activity. Exhibit 6.6 presents a number of issues to consider in evaluating supplier quality.

EXHIBIT 6.6
Evaluating Supplier Quality

Internal Operations
- Does management provide quality leadership?
- What is the extent of quality commitment?
- Are there identified quality control points in all processes?
- Are employees at all levels able to relate the tasks they perform to meeting customer needs?

Continuing Process Improvement
- Are there specific results attributable to the quality improvement process?
- Are there documented improvements in methods and processes?
- Are future improvements documented and methods established to ensure improvements will be implemented?

Performance Measurement and Tracking
- Can data be collected to support measures such as on-time delivery, shipping discrepancies, invoice accuracy, and line item fill rates?
- Are performance indicators established for all partnering agreements?

Problem Solving Capability
- Is there a preventive action orientation rather than a reactive response to problems?
- Is problem solving performed in a timely and conclusive manner?
- Are employees at all levels involved in identifying and solving problems?

Employee Participation and Involvement
- Is there active participation and involvement by all employees in the quality process?
- Are employees empowered to take action?

Procedure Development
- Are written procedures established for all processes?
- Are procedures consistently followed?

Training
- Is a continuous quality training program in place and operational?

Source: Wehr, W.S. "Selecting World Class Distributors: A Case Study, *Proceedings of the 1992 NAPM International Purchasing Conference*, NAPM, Tempe, AZ, 1992, pp. 327-332.

Acceptance/Rejection History

What do the records indicate about the supplier's performance? Acceptance/rejection history should be readily available and reviewed, along with traceable records. A check should be made to ensure that measuring device calibration dates have not expired.

Testing Capability

What abilities does the organization have to detect correct and incorrect work by both the workers and equipment? A batch-sampling technique or some form of statistical sampling procedure will probably be used instead of 100 percent inspection of the incoming components. Final examination of finished products will probably take place in a secured area awaiting final release. Quality control personnel should complete this task and the inspection procedures should be in writing. Test methods, procedures, and instruments should be the same as those to be used by the purchaser's incoming quality control department to ensure compatibility. All gauges and test devices should be reviewed to ensure calibration dates are current. Shop floor quality checks should be conducted at regular intervals by members of the quality control staff to verify those performed during the process by production floor employees. In a service, capability is assessed by process documentation, identified quality control points in the process, and the ability to collect data to support quality measures.

Indicators of worker capability include the number of hours of SQC/TQM training, worker certifications, and the use of process control charts by the equipment operators. For services, indicators may include implementation of employee training programs and employee involvement in quality improvement.

The equipment capability can be monitored in several ways. The purchaser could review the maintenance history of key elements in the process for frequency of breakdowns and preventive maintenance activity. The presence of process control charts is another way to monitor machine capability.

Process Control

What type of quality detection and correction systems are used? Primary systems in effect today include statistical process control

(SPC) and Six Sigma/C_{pk} Process Bounds. Validation of the production process should be properly documented. If the organization has a program of Statistical Quality Control or Statistical Process Control (SQC/SPC) in place it should be reviewed. When dealing with a service, verify that the supplier's processes are documented. Are there check sheets and other tools in use to ensure the repeatability of the service?

SQC/SPC involves checking products while they are being produced. Samples are periodically taken by line employees and compared to an existing range of tolerance. If a process is out of its tolerance range, production is stopped and corrected. This ensures that no additional out-of-tolerance products are produced. There should be visual evidence of the control charts at individual workstations indicating that checks are being made during production.

The Six Sigma program permits only three defects per million parts and supplier adoption of this program reflects an outstanding commitment to quality. C_{pk} refers to a comparison of the purchaser's specification to the supplier's process capability. Suppliers should have equal or better process capability when compared to the purchaser's requirements.

Organization and Management of Quality Systems

What are the overall organizational systems in place for quality? Is it the traditional "check after an item was made," or is it a proactive system that checks the work as it is being produced?

All inspection procedures should be in writing, and a solid training program with periodic updates should be in place. Purchasers today are applying various types of quality certification to suppliers. These range from being qualified, to preferred, to certified. Many forms and distinctions are in use. Quality certification involves a high degree of integration of the supplier's and purchaser's quality systems which permit the bypassing of incoming inspection at the purchaser's facility.

The International Organization for Standards (ISO) has guidelines on the process necessary to produce quality goods. The major standards in this area are in the ISO 9000 series. If a supplier has attained ISO certification or applied Malcolm Baldridge National

Quality Award standards to its internal operations the need for a complete and comprehensive quality audit is reduced.

Supplier Organization and Management

The supplier's organization and management are important factors to consider in selecting a supplier. Things to look for include the following:

- How well trained are the sales people?
- What is the amount of technical support provided to both the sales force and the customer?
- What are employee attitudes and overall interest in your business?
- What is the history and stability of the organization?
- What are the backgrounds of key personnel?
- What is the ownership involvement of top management?

A purchasing organization should carefully analyze a supplier's management staff and information about its relative turnover, educational background, policies, and future plans. Management is ultimately responsible for the performance of a business and its commitment to retaining industry leadership.

A purchaser needs to analyze the skill levels of the supplier's employees. Are employees well trained? Do they have the experience and competence for meeting the purchaser's needs? How long have they been on the job? Is the workforce stable?

The prior work experience, length of employment with the organization, and educational background of the supplier's personnel are useful indicators of the organization's technical competence and stability. Suppliers are proud to display this talent in front of a prospective purchaser. Clearly technical capability is a factor when the purchaser's organization seeks ideas and input concerning design or operations.

A well-documented training program is further evidence of management's commitment to being an industry leader. The purchaser should inquire about the level and frequency of training throughout the organization. Continuous training implies continuous improvement in skills.

Does the supplier support and reflect diversity in its workforce? Has it been cited for any EEO violations? Violations could hurt employee morale and may cause the purchaser's organization to appear insensitive to these issues.

If the supplier plans to employ subcontractors to perform any major portions of the work, audits should be conducted by the supplier and records reviewed by the purchaser. If possible, it is beneficial to encourage the supplier to use subcontractors who are suppliers to the purchaser's organization.

Supplier Labor Status

Whether the supplier is union, non-union, or a combination of the two is also important to know. If the organization is unionized, the current contract expiration date is very important, as is the current and past labor relations' history.

Unionization provides employees with an organization to collectively represent their concerns to management. Many employees are not represented by a union and address their concerns directly to management. If relations are good between labor and management there is much less need for a union. The Taft-Hartley Act of 1947 set up certain guidelines for unions and management. The Act allowed states to pass "right to work laws" which created the open shop. An open shop is a condition whereby workers do not have to join the union but share in the benefits won by the union through strikes as well as negotiation. This contrasts with a union shop where an agreement exists between organized labor and the management of a unionized organization requiring employees to join the union within 30 days following employment. The union shop has been outlawed in some states due to right-to-work laws. However, the agency shop, which requires nonunion members to pay union dues and fees, has been approved in some of these states.

If a supplier does have a unionized labor force, the purchaser should know the contract expiration date, because this may significantly affect the ability to have materials shipped from the supplier. The purchaser should obtain as much information as possible about recent contract negotiations, including whether there was a strike, how long the strike lasted, whether production continued during the strike with supervisory personnel, whether there was an inventory build-up prior to the strike, whether there was violence or picket lines prohibiting deliveries, whether there was damage to the facility, the results of the negotiation, and what type of back-up plan the organization has in place in case another strike occurs.

Other Factors

Other factors include the use of third-party evaluations, logistics concerns, and environmental performance.

Third-party Evaluations

The purchaser may elect to use a supplier evaluation that has been performed by someone else. Another organization — federal, state, or local government — or an independent evaluation such as ISO 9000 may have already evaluated the supplier. If these third-party evaluations contain criteria satisfactory to the purchasing organization, they may be accepted in lieu of a purchaser's own inspection and evaluation.

Major manufacturers - One option available to the purchaser is to select organizations that have been certified by a major organization such as Ford, GM, Intel, Motorola, or Hewlett Packard. The rationale is, "Why spend the money on an additional evaluation which may add very little additional information and may not be completed with the thoroughness that a larger organization's resources would allow?" The goal is to avoid situations such as one where an organization spent 1,700 man-hours hosting 37 visits from just three major customers over a 15 month period while another went through 40 different certification audits in one year.[1]

Federal, state, or local government qualified bidder lists - Other potential sources for identifying qualified suppliers are government lists of prequalified suppliers. However, many of the suppliers listed may not be relevant to the manufacturing organization.

ISO 9000 - An often touted solution to supplier qualification is the use of suppliers that are ISO 9001, 9002, or 9003 registered. The problem with basing the evaluation on a supplier's ISO 9000 registration is that the ISO standards tell you nothing about the product's suitability to your needs, the supplier's financial health, employee relations and morale, and equipment. All an ISO registration implies is that the supplier's quality system is documented and the supplier follows the documented system.

Logistical Concerns

Unique items may require special planning, transportation requirements, and/or permits. Examples include large reactors or tanks, fabricated steel items, and hazardous materials. What experience has the supplier had with these issues, both good and bad?

Environmental Performance

A new dimension for evaluating suppliers is to review their environmental record. Suppliers are being evaluated in terms of their environmentally friendly practices, such as sources of raw material, scrap and surplus disposal methods, packaging reduction, and reduced fuel consumption. For example, the Herman Miller Company eliminated rosewood from its product designs and only purchases tropical woods from suppliers who can document that they practice responsible forestry.[2] Questions the purchaser should ask include the following:

- Has the supplier had to pay environmental cleanup fines in the past?
- Is the supplier in danger of being closed by the government because of environmental violations?
- What is the supplier's employee exposure and safety record?

Measuring Supplier Performance

Measurements of supplier performance are critical to the selection of the best supplier and to the improvement of a supplier's performance over time. Measurements also tell the supplier what the purchasing organization values (and by exclusion, what it does not). If an issue matters, then it must be measured. Without a measurement, it is impossible to determine if the issue is improving. Subjective judgments can be swayed by specific events and are at best highly unreliable.

What to Measure

Any issue can be measured. Almost all issues fall into one of three categories: cost issues, performance issues, or policy issues. Cost issues include price and all other ancillary costs (for example, transportation); performance issues include any attribute of supplier performance the purchaser's organization cares to measure (for example, on-time delivery); and policy issues include matters of compliance to those policies the purchaser's organization chooses to enforce regarding supply (an example might be disadvantaged business status).

The first step in establishing a supplier rating system is to select the attributes the purchasing organization values enough to measure. The second step is to develop a valid measurement method for each attribute. The third step is to collect the data and determine the level of performance. The fourth step is to use the findings to select a supplier or improve the current supplier's performance.

Because a supplier's status may change over time, these factors need to be reviewed regularly. Some attributes frequently used in supplier performance rating systems include the following:

- **Supplier capabilities** - Does a supplier have the capability to do what is asked of it? Does it have capabilities that the purchaser's organization could use in the future?
- **International, national, and local capabilities** - Does the supplier's geographic distribution of product and services coincide with your needs?
- **Pricing methods** - To measure acceptability of pricing, there must be a basis for comparison. These typically include prior prices (trend), competitive prices, industry standard price indices, or cost-based pricing.
- **Financial strength** - Is the supplier profitable? What is its stability for the long term? Are the supplier's current and quick ratios acceptable? Is the debt to equity ratio appropriate?
- **Inventory locations and methods** - Does the supplier have the right inventory in the right places to service your needs within the

leadtime required? What are the inventory levels? What is the supplier's service level?

- **Delivery performance** - For the delivery of goods, delivery performance is usually measured as percent on time. On time consists of on-time delivery, defect free goods or services, and correct documentation. To establish a delivery performance measurement:

  - Define the "on-time" window (the due date plus or minus a period within which delivery is allowed and considered to be on time).
  - For each receipt, compare the actual receipt date to the due date on the purchase order. If the receipt is within the on-time window, then the delivery was on time.
  - Calculate the percentage of goods or services delivered on time by dividing the number that were on time by the total number received and multiplying by 100 to convert the fraction into a percentage.

Measuring service delivery performance is a bit more subjective because there is no "receipt of goods" transaction. Compare the time the service was scheduled to be performed with the time that it actually was performed, and calculate the measurement the same way as described above.

- **Quality history** - Quality performance is typically measured by the percent defective or reject rate. This measure is calculated as a ratio in the same manner as on-time delivery ratios - by comparing the number that were found to be defective to the total that were received.
- **Service history** – To measure any factor of a supplier's service, first define what constitutes acceptable performance. Second, measure events as they happen. Did each event meet the defined expectations or not? Then calculate service performance as a percentage in the same manner as quality or delivery.
- **Margin performance and inventory turnover** - Is the supplier moving inventory and is it making a sufficient margin to remain profitable? Although any organization can suffer periods of slow

business, if the downturn is prolonged, the signs of increasing inventories and shrinking margins may indicate trouble ahead.
- **Innovation history and performance** – Is the supplier creative? Does it bring suggestions you can use? Is it a leader in new products? These attributes are worthy of measure and of inclusion into your selection criteria.

Example - Case Corporation, in developing a supplier performance measurement program, benchmarked several other companies to determine what factors to use and the weighting each factor should receive. The results are shown in Exhibit 6.7. Case decided on four factors: quality, delivery, value, and partnering with weights of 30, 30, 20, and 20 percent respectively. The next step was to develop measures for each factor. The measures chosen were as follows:

- **Delivery** – On-time delivery percent on total orders and on adequate leadtime orders. The measure was calculated using ship date and on-time was defined as shipping from three days early up to the ship date.
- **Quality** – Number of rejects versus lines inspected and warranty data.
- **Value** – Value was calculated using a quarterly survey that asked the purchaser to look at total acquisition cost. Total acquisition cost includes freight, handling, quality, administrative, and price. Cost reductions such as cycle time reductions, inventory reductions, EDI transactions, and design assistance were also to be considered.
- **Partnering** – Score on a survey that measured accessibility, responsiveness/attitude, engineering/technology, administrative practices, and proactive/innovation. The survey was filled out by the purchaser, expediter, engineering, receiving, accounts payable, and quality.[3]

EXHIBIT 6.7
Supplier Performance Measures Benchmarking Results

| Walker Manufacturing | | AT&T | | S C Johnson's Wax | | GTE | | Cummins Engine | |
Factor	Weights	Factor	Weights	Factor	Weights	Factor	Weights	Factor	Weights
Quality	35%	Quality/ Reliability	8%	Quality	35%	Delivery	25%	Quality	25%
Delivery	35%	Delivery	25%	Delivery	35%	Pricing	10%	Delivery	25%
Price	20%	Business Issues	15%	Price	20%	Customer Service	25%	Price	25%
Support	10%	Qualification	10%	Support	10%	Product Quality	25%	Subjective	25%
		Quality Management	12%						
		Supplier Cooperation	20%						

Evaluation Systems

Supplier evaluation systems perform two primary functions: to maintain ongoing records of supplier performance for use in selecting a supplier for a requirement and to monitor for control purposes to identify and address problems before they become serious. The main criteria used to evaluate supplier performance are quality, on-time delivery, service, and price. There are several models for evaluating supplier performance. They include the categorical, weighted point, and cost-ratio models.

Categorical model - The categorical model is based on the subjective judgments of a supplier's performance over the evaluation period by several individuals from the purchasing organization. Major suppliers are evaluated on a regular basis, such as quarterly, on a number of factors. For each factor judged above average, the evaluator assigns a "+"; for each judged below average a "–"; and for each judged acceptable or neutral a "0." The results are combined and an overall rating is assigned.

The process is relatively simple to administer but does have some problems. First, the model assumes all criteria are of equal importance. Second, the overall rating is determined by reviewing the individual ratings and making a subjective overall assessment. Third, an evaluator's perception may be affected by recent activity. For example, if a supplier has had a perfect quality record for the last six months but experienced problems with its latest delivery, it would probably receive a lower rating than a supplier which had a problem six months ago and has had no problems since. Exhibit 6.8 presents an example categorical evaluation form.

Weighted point model - In the weighted point model, each criterion is quantitatively measured. Weights are established for each criterion and the supplier's score is the total of the weights multiplied by the criterion value. For example, a supplier is evaluated on the following criteria:

Weight	Criterion	Measure
0.50	Quality	One minus the fraction defective
0.30	Cost	Bid price/Total final cost
0.20	Delivery	Order cycle reliability (1-0.1(number of days late))

EXHIBIT 6.8

Sample Supplier Performance Evaluation

SUPPLIER _____ DATE _____

Summary Department Evaluation:	Positive	Neutral	Negative
Contract administration	[ ]	[ ]	[ ]
Internal customer	[ ]	[ ]	[ ]
Accounting	[ ]	[ ]	[ ]
_____	[ ]	[ ]	[ ]

PERFORMANCE FACTORS

Contract Administration:

Performs on schedule	[ ]	[ ]	[ ]
Performs at quoted prices	[ ]	[ ]	[ ]
Representative is available	[ ]	[ ]	[ ]
Prompt and accurate with routine documents	[ ]	[ ]	[ ]
Anticipates our needs	[ ]	[ ]	[ ]
Helps in emergencies	[ ]	[ ]	[ ]
Does not unfairly exploit a single source position	[ ]	[ ]	[ ]
Does not request special consideration	[ ]	[ ]	[ ]
Furnishes specially requested information promptly	[ ]	[ ]	[ ]
Advises of potential problems	[ ]	[ ]	[ ]
Performs without constant follow-up	[ ]	[ ]	[ ]
Fixes problems promptly	[ ]	[ ]	[ ]
Invoices correctly	[ ]	[ ]	[ ]

Internal Customer:

Performs per instructions	[ ]	[ ]	[ ]
Provides quality service	[ ]	[ ]	[ ]
Responds to requests	[ ]	[ ]	[ ]
Has ability for difficult work	[ ]	[ ]	[ ]
Readily accepts responsibility	[ ]	[ ]	[ ]
Provides quick and effective action in emergencies	[ ]	[ ]	[ ]
Furnishes requested data promptly	[ ]	[ ]	[ ]
Replies with corrective action	[ ]	[ ]	[ ]

Accounting:

Invoices correctly	[ ]	[ ]	[ ]
Issues credit memos promptly	[ ]	[ ]	[ ]
Does not ask for special financial consideration	[ ]	[ ]	[ ]

The problems with the weighted point model have to do with the determination of criteria weights and the definition of the measures. The relative weights to be assigned to each criterion are difficult to determine and may change over time and with different decision-makers. The measures also need to be on the same scale and move in the same direction. Using the example above, quality could be measured as the fraction defective, cost as the difference between the bid and actual cost in dollars, and delivery as the number of days late. If one tries adding fraction defective, dollars, and days the answer makes no sense even though the directions of improvement are the same.

Example - Supplier "N", a computer maintenance supplier, has the following performance criteria:

Weight	Criterion	Measure
0.50	Quality	One minus the percent of service calls to service the same problem
0.30	Cost	Bid price/Total final cost
0.20	Delivery	One minus 0.02 times the number of hours the technician arrived beyond the contract's standard response time of three hours.

Supplier N's performance over the last month was as follows:

Quality: The average percent of repeat calls to service the same problem was three percent.
Cost: The bid price was $85 per hour while the actual cost per hour for the last month was $86.69.
Delivery: The delivery performance was a total of 4.5 hours of late arrivals.

The following summarizes the total performance evaluation calculation for Supplier N.

Weight	Factor	Actual Performance	Performance Evaluation
50%	Quality	3% repeat calls	50 x [1.00 - 0.03] = 48.5
30%	Cost	$86.69	30 x [85/86.69] = 29.4
20%	Delivery	4.5 hours late	20 x [1.0-(0.02x4.5)] = 18.2
			Overall Evaluation = 96.1

Cost-ratio model - The cost-ratio model attempts to deal with the units of measure problem by expressing all measures in terms of cost. For example, if the actual fraction defective from a supplier was one percent, the costs associated with identifying and correcting the defective items would be determined and expressed as a percentage of the quoted cost. The process is used for each criterion. The percentages are then multiplied by the quoted price to obtain a performance-adjusted cost.

The difficulty with using the cost-ratio model is that most organizations cannot identify the costs associated with dealing with a particular problem. The model also has a large data requirement and does not specifically consider qualitative factors.

Example - Two current suppliers have been asked to bid on a new service item. Supplier "A" bid $150 and Supplier "B" bid $152. Past experience in dealing with these suppliers has indicated that different additional costs will be incurred during contract performance. This fact is reflected in different cost ratios. Supplier A has had minor quality problems that resulted in a cost ratio of three percent of purchases. Supplier B has constantly delivered excellent quality, resulting in a cost savings of one percent. Supplier A has invoiced incorrectly a few times but has given excellent service otherwise. Supplier B has had a nearly perfect record on both factors.

As shown below, the overall cost ratios amount to + five percent for Supplier A and + two percent for Supplier B. This means that Supplier B, in spite of its higher initial bid price, is likely to perform the contract for less money than Supplier A.

Cost Factor	Supplier A	Supplier B
Quality	+3%	-1%
Invoicing	+4%	+2%
Service	-2%	+1%
Overall Cost Ratio	+5%	+2%
(Quality + Invoicing + Service)		
Original bid price	$150.00	$152.00
Adjustment factor	1.05	1.02
(1+ overall cost ratio)		
Adjusted bid price	$157.50	$155.04
(Original bid price)(Adjustment factor)		

Sharing the Information

When ratings are shared with suppliers, the purchasing organization must insist on supplier confidentiality. Such confidentiality must be a two-way street.

Confidentiality - Rating information should be shared with the supplier whose performance was measured and not with anyone else outside the purchaser's or supplier's organization. Revealing a supplier's performance data to a competitor would very likely result in a significant breech of trust and subsequent damage to the relationship. This does not preclude recognizing top suppliers as part of a supplier certification or recognition program.

One method to provide information to a supplier about how it compares to other suppliers without providing information about another supplier's performance, is to provide the supplier with its score, its rank, and the high and low scores. Exhibit 6.9 provides example quality data for 10 suppliers and their rankings.

EXHIBIT 6.9
Example Supplier Rankings

Supplier	Score	Rank
A	9.22	1
B	8.95	2
C	8.58	4
D	8.52	5
E	7.87	7
F	7.76	8
G	6.92	10
H	8.78	3
I	8.27	6
J	7.24	9
Maximum	9.22	
Minimum	6.92	

Another method for presenting supplier performance is the spider web chart, also called the radar chart in Quattro Pro and Excel. The radar chart allows multiple dimensions to be displayed on one chart. Exhibit 6.10 is an example radar chart. The two suppliers have been evaluated on a scale of one to 10 for five criteria: quality long-term, quality short-term, utilization, management, and technology. The outer circle indicates the desired standard for each dimension while the line inside indicates the supplier's actual performance. The difference can be shaded to indicate to the supplier where it is falling short of the standards. The advantage to this presentation is that multiple criteria can be displayed without having to develop a weighted point system.

EXHIBIT 6.10
Example Radar Chart

Supplier	**P**	**A**
Technology	9.6	9.8
Utilization	8.0	8.2
Management	9.4	9.2
Quality-LT	5.0	9.0
Quality-ST	9.5	9.0

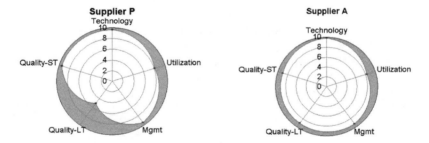

Supplier reaction to ratings - A supplier's reaction to its performance measurements may be affected by the following:

- **The credibility of the numbers** - Suppliers may react negatively if they are recipients of evaluations based on inaccurate data.
- **Attitude of the purchasing organization** - Sometimes poor performance originates inside the purchasing organization. Unclear specifications or fluctuating schedules can cause a supplier to look bad despite its very best efforts. An attitude of judgment and condemnation (rather than problem-solving) can provoke resistance. However, if the purchasing organization presents accurate

data in a problem-solving mode, and the supplier still does not respond, then the supplier's lack of response can be taken as a signal of its unwillingness to work toward improvement.

- **Management attention** - Providing suppliers with regular reports on performance serves to focus the attention of the suppliers' management on the contract. This, in turn, usually enhances the purchasing organization's status as a customer.
- **Use of ratings** - The supplier and the purchaser both can use the ratings as a tool for communication and supporting work on the contract. Objective, accurate evaluations combined with a positive reaction on the part of the supplier can lead to improved performance and can encourage good performance.
- **Problems** - There are a variety of factors that can result in ineffective supplier performance measurement systems. These include the following:
- **Inaccurate data** - If the databases from which the performance numbers are calculated include errors, the resulting measurements will be incorrect and result in zero credibility with internal customers and suppliers.
- **Improper weighting of factors** - Weights assigned to factors must reflect accurately the value the organization places on them.
- **Subjectivity** - Measurements that are subjective can be affected by selective memory of the evaluators and can be skewed by an unusual recent event.

Key Points

1. Upon receipt of the supplier's bid, purchasing should ensure that the proposal meets the requirements of the solicitation as well as conduct the technical, operational, and capability analysis.
2. The purpose of site visits is to evaluate the supplier's facilities, housekeeping, technical capabilities, process flow, employees, production control, quality control, purchasing, and management commitments.
3. The supplier's ability to perform will be affected by frequency and volume of orders, leadtimes, quality, expertise, flexibility, and available capacity.

4. The supplier's financial statements should be evaluated for liquidity, profitability, turnover, historical changes, and other measures.
5. The supplier's costing systems should be capable of segregating costs by task and providing consistent treatment of cost, and comply with cost accounting standards.
6. Purchasing should investigate the supplier's testing capabilities, acceptance/rejection history, and process control.
7. The purchaser should investigate the supplier's union status including labor-management relations and expiration date of contract.
8. Other factors to consider include the use of third-party evaluations and logistics concerns.
9. The major criteria to evaluate supplier performance include quality, delivery, service, and customer relations.
10. Common supplier evaluation systems are the categorical model, weighted point model, and cost-ratio model.
11. Supplier rankings and radar diagrams are useful tools for sharing supplier performance results without disclosing the individual performance of other organizations.

Questions for Review

1. What factors will affect the supplier's ability to meet the requirements of the contract?
2. What areas of the organization should be represented on a site visitation team?
3. What three factors should the visitation team investigate on a site visit?
4. What is the purpose of supplier financial analysis?
5. What are the five categories of ratios for evaluating a supplier's financial condition?
6. What aspects of the supplier quality systems should be investigated?
7. Why investigate the supplier's organizational management structure?
8. What are the three general categories of issues that should be measured in evaluating supplier performance?

9. What are the three standard supplier performance evaluation models?
10. What are two techniques for sharing supplier performance?

For Additional Information

Wood, P. "Adding it Up: Performing Effective Supplier Price and Cost Analysis," *NAPM InfoEdge*, (3:10), June 1998.

Aspuro, M. "Supplier Financial Analysis: By the Numbers," *Proceedings of the 1998 NAPM International Purchasing Conference*, NAPM, Tempe, AZ, 1998, pp. 323-327.

Clayborn, S. "How to Accurately Evaluate Your Supplier's Finances," *NAPM InfoEdge*, (3:2), October 1997.

Estrada, M.U. and M. Harding. "Developing an Effective Source Evaluation and Selection System," *NAPM InfoEdge*, (1:12), June 1996.

Hollingsworth, B. "How to Effectively Rate Your Suppliers," *NAPM InfoEdge*, (4:3), November 1998.

Miller, M.S. "Tips for Measuring Supplier Performance," *Proceedings of the 1997 NAPM International Purchasing Conference*, NAPM, Tempe, AZ, 1997, pp. 365-368.

Stubbings, D.L. "Supplier Evaluation Matrix - Establishing Supplier Objectives and Motivate Improved Performance," *Proceedings of the 1999 NAPM International Purchasing Conference*, NAPM, Tempe, AZ, 1999, pp. 344-349.

Endnotes

1. Hyma, P. and J. D'Alessandro. "Customers Team Up to Build Standards," *Electronic Buyers' News*, January 3, 1994, p. P1.
2. Handfield, R.B. and S.A. Melnyk. "GreenSpeak," *Purchasing Today®*, July 1996, p. 35.
3. Miller, M.S. "Tips for Measuring Supplier Performance," *Proceedings of the 1998 NAPM International Purchasing Conference*, NAPM, Tempe, AZ, 1998, pp. 365-368.

CHAPTER 7

THE LEGAL ISSUES: HOW DO YOU AVOID GOING TO COURT?

Chapter Objectives

- List the benefits of the Uniform Commercial Code (UCC) to the purchaser.
- Describe the differences between actual, implied, and apparent authority of an agent.
- Understand how federal antitrust laws affect the purchaser.
- List the warranties guaranteed by the UCC.
- Understand the purchaser's rights regarding the inspection, acceptance and rejection of goods.
- Describe the legal problems associated with the various forms of electronic commerce.

Introduction

The American Dredging Company purchased 38,000 gallons of fuel oil from Plaza Petroleum. American contended the oil was contaminated and sued for breach of warranty. Plaza responded by pointing out a clause in the terms and conditions that disclaimed warranties and related liabilities. When American indicated it had not seen the clause because the transaction was carried out via telex, Plaza produced the telex which included a statement indicating that Plaza's terms and conditions were applicable and available upon request. The court ruled in favor of Plaza indicating that reference to the terms and conditions in the telex constituted adequate notice.[1] The example above illustrates what can happen to the unwary purchaser who does not understand the legal rights of both the purchaser and supplier in today's business environment. The goal is not to bog down the acquisition process with legalese, but to ensure knowledge and compliance with rules of law covering the purchase transaction. Because one of purchasing's major goals is to ensure continuity of supply, he or she must realize that if it becomes necessary to resort to legal remedies, the purchaser has already failed to achieve this goal. The reader is cautioned to seek professional legal counsel when an issue arises and to not rely on the views and interpretations of the author.

The Legal Environment For Purchasing

The purchaser operates within four legal environments:

(1) The Uniform Commercial Code which governs transactions by and between merchants of goods.
(2) The common law system of the United States which applies to transactions for services.
(3) The local, state, and federal governmental regulations regarding issues such as antitrust, hazardous materials, and intellectual properties.
(4) The international regulations and laws regarding tariffs, hazardous materials, and the laws of the various countries where an organization operates.

Commercial Transactions and the Uniform Commercial Code

The Uniform Commercial Code (UCC) was first created in 1951 to:

- Simplify, clarify, and modernize the laws governing commercial transactions.
- Permit the continued expansion of commercial practices through custom, usage, and agreement of the parties.
- Make uniform the law among the various jurisdictions.

Before the UCC was adopted, each state had its own laws dealing with commercial transactions. This was not a problem when most commercial transactions were local. As trade increased, the differences in laws from state to state became more of an issue.

The UCC deals with sales by and between merchants and does not apply to personal or consumer transactions. It is primarily oriented to the sale (and lease) of goods. Thus, a transaction which is 90 percent goods and 10 percent services will fall under the UCC while the reverse (90 percent service and 10 percent goods) will fall under common law.

Uniform Commercial Code Articles

The Uniform Commercial Code consists of 11 articles. A brief discussion of each is presented below. The articles which are of most concern for the purchaser are Articles 2 and 2A. This chapter will focus on Article 2.

Article 1 - General Provisions - The article discusses the purposes, general definitions, and principles of interpretation of the code. A guiding principle for the purchaser is that remedies are to be liberally administered under the UCC. Other principles of the UCC are:

- The aggrieved party is to be put in as good a position as if the other party had fully performed as specified in the contract.
- Compensatory damages are limited to compensation and do not include consequential, special, or penal damages.
- Damages do not have to be calculated with mathematical accuracy but with the definiteness and accuracy the facts permit.

Article 2 - Sales - Major sections deal with the form, formation, and readjustment of a contract; general obligation and construction of a contract; title, creditors, and good faith purchasing; performance; breach of contract, repudiation, and excuse; and remedies.

Article 2A - Leases - This article's purpose is to address the unique problems of leasing which are not adequately addressed in Articles 2 and 9. Sections include formation and construction of a lease contract; effect of a lease contract; performance of a lease contract; repudiation, substitution, and excuse; and default.

Article 3 - Negotiable Instruments - A negotiable instrument is an unconditional promise or order to pay a fixed amount of money, with or without interest or other charges, described in the promise or order. Examples of negotiable instruments include checks, cashier's checks, teller's checks, traveler's checks, or certificates of deposit. Sections deal with negotiation, transfer, endorsement, and enforcement of instruments; and liabilities of parties, dishonor, discharge, and payment.

Article 4 - Bank Deposits and Collections - The article provides a uniform statement of the principal rules of the bank collection process and defines the rights between parties with respect to bank deposits and collections. Sections cover collection of items by the depository and collecting banks; collection of items by the payor banks; relationship between the payor bank and its customers; and collection of documentary drafts.

Article 4A - Funds Transfers - This new article deals with the series of transactions, beginning with the originator's payment order, made for the purpose of making payment to the beneficiary of the order.

Article 5 - Letters of Credit - A letter of credit is a legal instrument that obligates the issuer, normally a bank, to pay the supplier upon presentation of the documents required under the terms of the letter of credit. The article is intended to provide a framework for the development of the law dealing with letters of credit.

Article 6 - Bulk Transfers or Bulk Sales - This article was created to provide protection for creditors from customers who purchased goods, sold them, and absconded with the proceeds without paying the creditors. The authors of the UCC now believe this article is no longer necessary and recommend its repeal. If states feel a need for regulation, an alternative article entitled Bulk Sales is proposed.

Article 7 - Warehouse Receipts, Bills of Lading, and Other Documents of Title - The article covers the provisions, obligations, negotiation, and transfer of warehouse receipts and bills of lading.

Article 8 - Investment Securities - The article covers the issue, transfer, registration, and entitlements of investment securities such as stocks, bonds, and treasury securities.

Article 9 - Secured Transactions; Sales of Accounts and Chattel Paper - The article sets out a comprehensive system for the regulation of security interests in personal property and fixtures.

Benefits of the UCC to the Purchaser

There are several key benefits of having commercial transactions covered under the UCC in addition to increasing consistency of application and interpretation.

- If the supplier makes an offer in writing, the supplier has to live up to it for the period of time stated in the offer.
- Verbal agreements are legal if confirmed in writing and no objection is made by either party to the writing.
- Conflict between purchaser's and supplier's terms have generally been resolved in favor of the purchaser.
- Warranties are spelled out and the purchaser can rely on the supplier to supply the item needed to do the job.
- In the absence of specific terms or conditions on some issues, the UCC defines the remedies to be applied in many situations.

Law of Agency

One of the key legal concepts the purchaser must understand is the concept of agency. An agent is an individual who is appointed by another person or legal entity, such as a corporation, to act on the entity's behalf in transactions with third parties. In the purchasing context, an agent is given authority to attend to the business of purchasing in accordance with the employer's instructions. Those instructions may be as general as a job description or narrowly delineated such as specifying the classes of products and services as well as dollar value limitations.

What makes the purchaser different than most sales representatives is that sales representatives are not usually authorized agents of their companies. They are authorized to receive orders and to invite customers to negotiate but are not usually empowered to commit their organization or sign contracts. Getting the salesperson's acceptance on an offer does not necessarily mean that the salesperson's organization will accept the offer.

Authority of Agents

An agent's authority can be one of three types: actual, implied, or apparent.

- **Actual authority** - The statement from the employer, oral or written, which tells the purchaser what he or she has the authority to do. This could be a job description or dollar limit of purchase authority.
- **Implied authority** - Besides the express authority received from an employer, the law provides an agent with the legal rights and power to carry out the purposes for that which the agent was appointed. This would include negotiating the contract; arranging transportation, insurance, or storage; and any other actions that are required to accomplish the mission granted in the statement of express authority.
- **Apparent authority** - If an individual acts in such a way as to lead a reasonable outsider to believe that the individual has agency authority, an organization may be bound by the individual's contract, even if it exceeds the individual's express authority because the supplier will not normally be aware of the agent's limits of authority.

Examples - A production purchaser is authorized to commit the purchaser's organization for specific production materials consistent with the approved schedule for up to three months in the future but is not authorized to purchase office equipment. If the purchaser was to phone a local office supply organization and order a typewriter, giving an appropriate purchase order number, the supplier would have no reason to question the purchaser's authority especially because it could call the organization, ask for purchasing, and be able to reach the purchaser. To the supplier the purchaser has apparent authority, even though internally the purchaser has violated authority limitations.

A hospital vice president for administration walks into a computer store and begins negotiating for two personal computers with printers. After an appropriate amount of haggling, an order is written up and signed by the vice president who also leaves a business card indicating his position. When the retailer attempts to make delivery, purchasing is contacted as there is no purchase order or receiving paperwork. The purchasing agent tells receiving to reject the order causing the retailer to threaten a lawsuit. What happens next?

The retailer contacts a lawyer who pays a visit to the purchasing agent and informs the agent that the hospital is in breach of contract and unless prompt action is taken, a suit will be filed which the retailer will win resulting in triple damages being awarded. The vice president appears to the supplier to have apparent authority and the hospital is liable for the purchases.

Duties of an Agent

There are seven primary duties purchasers, as agents, owe their employers. They are loyalty; obedience to the instructions of the employer; performance with reasonable care; to provide an accounting to the employer; to inform the employer; confidentiality; and to bring the necessary skills and training to the agency.

- **Loyalty** - The purchaser must put aside all conflicts of interest and act as the employer would act at all times. The use of suppliers in which the agent has significant financial interest or are owned by a relative would be considered a conflict of interest. The agent's responsibility is to make decisions that are in the best interests of his or her employer.
- **Obedience to the instructions of the employer** - The purchaser's employer has the right to give instructions on how the purchaser's work is to be performed including what is or is not to be done and how it is to be done within legal limits.
- **Perform with reasonable care** - The agent is expected to act as a reasonable, prudent person might act in a similar situation or circumstances. This does not imply the purchaser is free from error.
- **Provide an accounting to the employer** - Under agency law this means acknowledging collections that are made and passing them on to the principal. For purchasing this would include gifts, commissions, rebates, and fees received from suppliers. As an agent, the purchaser also owes the employer an accounting for any employer assets over which the agent has control such as petty cash, an organization car, or inventories.
- **Inform the employer** - Information provided to the agent is considered to have been provided to the employer. Therefore, the agent has an obligation to ensure that information received from

a supplier or any contact is forwarded to the appropriate individuals in the organization. Examples might include information about competitors, an industry, or new product developments.

- **Confidentiality** - The purchaser is to keep the organization's business affairs confidential. The affairs should not become public knowledge because of the purchaser's access to information. Examples might include organization costs, new product developments, or facility expansion plans.
- **Bring the necessary skills and training to the agency** - The purchaser is to bring to the job the relevant skills and abilities required to perform the job. This includes ongoing training.

Legal Liabilities of an Agent

The organization may be responsible for the purchaser's action but may sue the agent for damages. An agent can be held personally liable if he or she:

- Makes a false statement concerning authority with intent to deceive or when the misrepresentation has the natural and probable consequence of misleading.
- Performs without authority a damaging act, even though the purchaser believed he or she had such authority.
- Performs an illegal act even on authority from employer. An example is involvement in activities that constitute antitrust violations such as price fixing.
- Willfully performs an act that results in damage to anyone.
- Performs damaging acts outside scope of authority even though act is performed with the intention of rendering a valuable service.

Preventing Unauthorized Procurement

A problem experienced by many organizations is that of items being ordered by various individuals without the necessary paperwork. The individual may have the budget authority for the item but ignores or bypasses purchasing in the process. Some actions that can be taken to reduce improper purchasing include notifying suppliers not to accept orders except from designated individuals, setting up blanket orders or system contracts with suppliers allowing the user to place orders directly, or refusing to accept delivery of items that do not reference a purchase order.

Governmental Regulations

There are several types of government regulations of which the purchaser must be cognizant. These are antitrust laws, hazardous materials laws and regulations, and intellectual property laws.

Antitrust Laws

Sherman Antitrust Act - The Sherman Antitrust Act prohibits contracts, combinations, and conspiracies in restraint of trade and prohibits monopolization and attempts to monopolize interstate or foreign trade. The key test is whether the facts show a reasonable and understandable business arrangement or an attempt to impair free enterprise. Examples are:

- **Price fixing** - Agreeing with competitors on prices to charge for products or services.
- **Dividing fields of manufacture, markets, or customers** - Agreeing with competitors to not compete in specific regions or markets.
- **Reciprocity** - Buying from a supplier solely because the supplier buys products from the purchaser's organization.

Clayton Act - The Clayton Act deals with trade practices like tie-in arrangements, full-time forcing, and exclusive dealing. The act also deals with mergers that may have adverse affects on competition.

Robinson-Patman Act - The Robinson-Patman Act prohibits price discrimination for goods of like grade and quality where the end result may substantially lessen competition. This also includes discriminations in services and promotions that are connected with the sale of a product. The primary goal of the act is to prohibit discriminatory and preferential pricing. This is not a problem if the goods are made to the purchaser's specifications. Unacceptable price differences include the following:

- Discriminating price between purchasers of like grade and quality where the consequences tend to create a monopoly or injure, destroy, or prevent competition.
- Offering brokerage fees to purchasers except for services actually rendered to the supplier.
- Paying for advertising and similar services unless such payments are made available on proportionally equal terms to all purchasers.

Acceptable price differences include the following:

- Product can be sold to different purchasers at different prices if, and only if, the price difference can be justified by differences in the supplier's cost of production and distribution.
- Quantity discounts must be offered equally to all purchasers and must be traceable to economies of scale.
- Selling at a reduced price is legal to dispose of perishable goods, dispose of seasonal goods, and meet, in good faith, an equally low price of a competitor.

The Robinson-Patman Act is the only antitrust law to specifically list purchasers as well as suppliers as potential violators. Soliciting suppliers to offer different prices to customers who purchase like quantities and qualities of goods is illegal.

The rules on advertising and promotional allowances under Robinson-Patman are strict and difficult to apply. To avoid potential problems, negotiate directly on price not on better advertising and promotional allowances. The lower price must have an affect on competition. Purchasing supplies and components that are converted into other products are probably not an issue under Robinson-Patman because they do not significantly affect an organization's competitiveness.[2]

Hazardous Materials

In today's environmentally conscious world, organization's are spending more time and resources dealing with hazardous and potentially hazardous materials both as inputs and outputs from its processes. There are currently over 95,000 state and federal environmental protection, pollution control, and toxic waste remediation laws and regulations. Currently over 33,000 materials are considered potentially hazardous and the EPA has identified 189 materials which must be eliminated from use by the year 2000. Purchasers must be aware of the issues involved in the purchase and disposal of these materials because they not only acquire the material but also are responsible for arranging for the transportation and ultimately the disposal of the material.

Definitions - A hazardous material is defined as a substance or material that has been determined by the Secretary of Transportation to be capable of posing an unreasonable risk to health, safety, and property when transported in commerce. Examples of hazardous materials include explosives such as welding gases or dynamite, or corrosives such as acids.

A hazardous substance is a material, including mixtures and solutions, that is:

- Listed in the Hazardous Materials Regulations (HMR).
- Is in a quantity in one package which equals or exceeds the reportable quantity (RQ) listed in the HMR.
- When in mixture or solution equals or exceeds certain concentrations explained in the HMR.

A hazardous waste is any material that is subject to the Hazardous Waste Manifest Requirements of the United States Environmental Protection Agency.

Packaging and transportation - The packaging of hazardous materials, substances, and waste is governed by Hazardous Materials Regulations which include standards and requirements for the manufacture, reconditioning, repair, or testing of a package or container for transporting a hazardous substance, material, or waste. All U.S. regulations are to be consistent with United Nations standards.

Material Safety Data Sheets (MSDS) - The Occupational Safety and Health Administration (OSHA) requires Material Safety Data Sheets, that provide information about the physical dangers, safety procedures, and emergency response techniques for all hazardous materials, substances, and wastes, be readily available for affected employees. OSHA also requires that all employees who potentially can have contact with a hazardous material be provided appropriate training about hazardous materials. Often, it is purchasing's responsibility to not only ensure suppliers have supplied the appropriate MSDS, but also arrange for training for the employees regarding their rights, responsibilities, and actions when handling hazardous materials.

Ownership and liability issues - Under The Resource Conservation and Recovery Act (RCRA) a purchaser of waste transport, treatment, storage, or disposal services must identify whether the waste is a hazardous waste and comply with various packaging, labeling, and record keeping requirements. RCRA imposes liability on any person who has contributed to the handling, storage, treatment, transportation, or disposal of any solid or hazardous waste that may present an imminent and substantial endangerment to health or the environment. Thus, a purchaser contracting for hazardous waste treatment, transportation, storage, or disposal could be held liable if these materials are not properly processed. While the hazardous materials are on the organization's premises, the ownership and liability are the responsibility of the organization. After disposal, producers of hazardous waste do not alleviate ownership and liability unless the material is no longer classified as hazardous.

To help reduce an organization's potential liabilities caused by hazardous waste, the following steps are useful:

- Develop and implement a program to reduce or eliminate all waste, especially hazardous waste.
- Investigate alternative disposal methods that destroy or treat hazardous waste.
- Maintain records that meet statute requirements.
- Carefully select hazardous waste contractors for transportation, packaging, treatment, and disposal including bonding and indemnification.

Intellectual Property Rights

Intellectual property rights deal with patents and copyrights. The purchaser needs to ensure that both the organization and the supplier are abiding by the laws governing patents and copyrights and/or that the supplier is providing indemnity for any legal actions for patent or copyright infringement by the supplier.

Patents - A patent is granted to an individual or organization giving the owner the sole right of making, using, and selling patented articles and preventing anyone else from making, using, or selling patented items without permission. A patent is issued only upon application and is based on providing a new or different mechanical, process, composition, article of manufacture, or design. A patent lasts for 20 years if filed after June 8, 1995 (only 14 for a design patent). The purchaser has a responsibility to avoid infringing on a patent through:

- Unauthorized use of a patented article, either directly or in combination with other parts.
- Unauthorized manufacture of a patented article.
- Conspiring purposely or unintentionally with another in any way which contributes to an infringement.
- Purchasing and reselling an infringing device even if purchaser believes the supplier had a license to sell or use the device.

Copyrights - A copyright on a work gives the holder the exclusive right to its reproduction. A copyright lasts for the life of the author plus 70 years. A copyright is automatically secured when a work is fixed in any tangible medium of expression, such as print or on computer disk, but the holder cannot collect unauthorized reproduction charges unless the work is registered and two copies are deposited with the Copyright Office.

Purchasers should take steps to ensure that their organizations do not violate patent or copyright laws by requiring appropriate language be included in the terms and conditions. If the purchaser has doubts or questions regarding compliance by the supplier, a written statement acknowledging compliance should be requested from the supplier.

Key Provisions of the UCC For Purchasing

This section presents several important issues covered by the UCC which are relevant to the purchaser. The areas covered are elements of a contract, written versus oral contracts, terms and conditions, warranties, rights of inspection, rejection and acceptance, and liability issues.

Contract Elements

There are four basic elements required to establish a contract between two parties. These are an agreement between the parties involved, the contract must be for a legal purpose, there must be consideration, and the parties involved must be competent.

Agreement of the parties - For the parties to a contract, the purchaser and supplier, to reach agreement, two separate acts must be completed, an offer by one party and an acceptance of that offer by the other party.

- **Offer** - An offer is a promise by the party making the offer (the offeror) which binds that individual to fulfill the promise if the second party (the offeree) responds with a return promise, act, or forbearance (not performing an act or exercising a right which one has the legal right to do). The offer must be definite and certain, that is the terms of the offer must be communicated to the offeree and the party making the offer must intend to be bound by the offer. The UCC looks at the intent of both parties to be bound by an agreement. If the intent is clear, indefiniteness is not grounds to void the agreement if both parties have intended to make a contract and there is a basis for appropriate remedy.

When an offer is made, the offeree has a reasonable period of time (up to 90 days in commercial transactions) to respond to the offer. The offer remains valid until it is:

- Revoked by the individual making the offer.
- Rejected by the individual receiving the offer.
- The offer becomes illegal (caused by a change in regulation or law making the product illegal).
- The offer expires.
- The offer is accepted.

If the offeree rejects the original offer, the offeree may make a counteroffer. In fact, if the second party's order acknowledgment contains any differences from the original offer it is technically a counteroffer. It is most desirable that the supplier return the acknowledgment copy of the purchase order. Purchasing must be on the lookout for the supplier who uses its own acknowledgement form which may contain terms and conditions different from or in conflict with those of the purchaser.

- **Acceptance** - Acceptance is the intentional indication by the party receiving the offer to be bound by the terms of the offer. Acceptance can be given in any reasonable manner and medium such as:

  - Return of a signed acknowledgment copy of the contract.
  - Prompt promise to ship.
  - Shipment of the goods.
  - Possibly beginning the production of the goods provided the goods could be specifically identified and linked to the order.

Also, the acceptance must:

- Agree to the exact terms of the offer.
- Be within the time specified in the offer.
- Be in the form specified by the offer.

If the terms of acceptance vary from the terms of the offer, a counteroffer may have been made indicating a possible rejection of the original offer. The party receiving the counteroffer has a reasonable period of time to accept or reject the counteroffer. Even if the terms of acceptance are different or additional from the offer, the acceptance is effective unless the original offer specified that assent must be made on additional or different terms.

Additional terms become part of the contract unless:

- The offer expressly limits offer to original terms of offer.
- They materially alter the contract.

- Notification of objection is given within a reasonable time after notice is received.

Counteroffer - A counteroffer occurs when the offeree proposes terms that are materially different from those of the original offer. Such material differences may be in description of the goods, their price, their quality, or warranties. If a counteroffer occurs, all of the conditions required of an original offer apply.

Legal purpose - The contract must be for a legal purpose. Examples of actions that could make a contract invalid are:

- Contracts against public policy.
- License requirements violation.
- Contracts disclaiming liability.
- Agreement in restraint of trade.
- Usurious contracts.
- Gambling contracts.

Consideration - Consideration is the price bargained for and paid for by each party or what thing, tangible or intangible, each party receives or gives up according to the terms of the agreement. Consideration must pass the test of sufficiency. Sufficiency can be established either as a benefit or a detriment.

- **Benefit** - Some benefit must accrue to the one making the promise. The benefit does not have to be tangible but may be some legal right to which the one making the promise was not entitled.
- **Detriment** - A detriment to the promise may be performance of an act which it is not legally bound to perform or not doing something the promisee has a right to do.

The courts are not concerned with value. If you were to sell a used car for $1, the courts would hold that consideration had taken place. The exception to this is contracts that are too one sided (at least the clause involved). The court would call such a term unconscionable and would not enforce the contract. Preexisting conditions or past consideration would not qualify as consideration. Performance of preexisting contractual or statutory duties is not consideration. Also, an act done in the past does not make a promise binding.

Consideration may take the following forms:

- **Performance** - "I agree to do (or not to do) something if or when you agree to do (or not to do) something else." For example, "I agree to sell you these goods and you agree to pay for them."
- **Forbearance** - "I agree not to build more than a one-story building on my lot (and thereby not block your view) even though code and zoning regulations allow me to, in return for your payment of a specified amount or your agreement to mow my lawn every week."

Competent parties - Competency deals with the mental state or capacity of the parties involved. There are three categories of competency: minority (under the age of majority which varies from state to state), insanity, and intoxication.

- **Minority** - Contracts where one party is a minor are voidable by the minor but not by the adult except when the contract is for the necessities of life such as food, clothing, and shelter.
- **Insanity** - The question for insanity is, "Did the party possess the mental state to comprehend the nature of transaction?" If the answer is no, then the contract is only enforceable for the necessities of life.
- **Intoxication** - The test for intoxication is the same as for insanity. However, the contract is voidable whether the intoxication was voluntary or involuntary. When the intoxicated party is made aware of the contract after becoming sober, he or she may either disaffirm or ratify the agreement when sober. If the contract is disaffirmed, the intoxicated party is required to make restitution for expenses incurred prior to the disaffirmation.

Example - Collins and Aikman (C&A), fabric wholesalers, received an unsigned, printed purchase order from Pantsmaker, Inc. for 5,000 yards of a certain fabric, the color unspecified. The form was interpreted by Collins & Aikman as intent to buy 5,000 yards upon approval of samples, color being determined prior to sampling.

Shortly thereafter C&A received an order, again signed only by the typed company name, for 4,200 yards of this fabric in a given color.

It should be noted that each form included that "*the order shall become a contract when signed and returned by buyer and accepted by seller in writing or when buyer has retained it for ten (10) days without objection, or when buyer accepts delivery of any part of the merchandise specified, or otherwise indicates acceptance.*" Again the supplier took no action, awaiting sample approval as agreed verbally in previous transactions. After a period of time without delivery of any fabric, Pantsmaker demanded arbitration for breach of contract. Although Collins & Aikman claimed the order was not a proffered contract until sample approval was received, Pantsmaker maintained that the 4,200 yards were ordered and expected. Collins and Aikman demanded relief from arbitration for a nonexistent contract.

The question here is that of intent. Given the information, intent is subject to factual dispute. The UCC allows that a printed but unsigned form may be read as a signature "if it is clear that it was so intended or adopted." The facts are as follows:

- There was no delivery or acceptance to seal the contract or prove intent.
- The purchaser obviously retained the offer of fabric at the stated price more than 10 days.
- The conversation about sample approval would be admissible evidence to controvert the existence of a contract, if such a conversation can be substantiated.

The court granted relief from arbitration pending a hearing on the validity of the alleged contract.[3]

Written versus Oral Contracts

The UCC states that oral contracts over $500 are not enforceable unless there is written confirmation of their existence. Exceptions may be possible if:

- The goods were made specifically to the purchaser's order and are not readily salable to others.
- Both parties behave as if a contract exists.

• The parties have always done business on an oral basis.

If time requires an oral contract, it is best to submit a confirming purchase order at the first opportunity. A confirmation purchase order is a confirmation of an "already existing contract" made verbally between the parties, often by phone. There is one other exception: when one party takes an action based on an oral promise to its detriment.

Example - Allied Grape Growers said there was an oral contract for delivery of 850 tons of grapes with Bronco Wine Company. The wine company accepted one truckload of grapes, but then rejected the rest. The reason, the court found, was simply because the wine company had over-contracted for grapes, not because of any deficiencies in the grapes supplied by Allied.

Bronco argued that it had to pay for the one truckload it accepted but it owed nothing because there was no written document and the value was over $500. The court held that the elements of promissory estoppel were present as Allied had a contract with another wine company which had agreed to purchase all of Allied's grapes. Promissory estoppel holds that if one party makes a promise, even orally, that party cannot renege on that promise. Allied had to get special permission to sell to Bronco. Thus, Allied had relied to its detriment on the promises made by Bronco.[4]

Letters of Intent

A letter of intent is a form of contract used to confirm agreements between the purchaser and supplier while procurement is being negotiated. The purpose of the letter is to serve as an interim purchase order and provide immediate confirmation of relevant terms of the agreement. Letters of intent can be used to:

• Reserve a place "in line" for standard equipment when a purchase order will require more time.
• Base volume discounts on future business without giving a firm order for the entire quantity.
• Encourage the supplier to stock items of interest to a purchaser.
• Provide a supplier with evidence of a contract to secure bonding.

Types of letters of intent - A letter of intent may be binding or nonbinding depending on the wording in the letter.

- **Binding letter of intent** - Any letter of intent, given as an authorization to begin producing goods or the like, will certainly be regarded as binding. An example could be signing an agreement confirming the terms already agreed to in a negotiation.
- **Nonbinding letter of intent** - For a letter of intent to be nonbinding, it must pass the test of explicit and clear statement to that effect, with the understanding it must be bilateral and not unilateral. That is, both parties must indicate that they understand the letter is not binding to either party. It is good practice to have the letter spell out, in layman's language, whether or not it is intended to be binding.

Terms and Conditions

A contract consists of both custom and standard terms and conditions. Standard terms and conditions are those that the organization desires to apply to every contract. Potential issues standard terms and conditions may deal with include changes to the contract, cancellation, subcontracting, confidentiality, delivery, shipping, indemnity, legal venue, applicable laws, inspection, payment terms, packaging, and warranties. Appendix 7-A presents a list of example standard terms and conditions.

Custom terms and conditions are those which are unique to the specific contract or purchase order. Issues custom terms and conditions may address include acceptance testing, updating service information, emergency services, financing, installation, training, initial provisioning, maintenance, spare parts, and renewal. Appendix 7-B presents a list of some common issues to be considered with relevant questions the term or condition should address.

Warranties

A warranty is a promise made by a supplier and can either be made expressly or in an implied form under the UCC.

Express warranty - An express warranty is a statement of fact made by the supplier either orally or in writing about the characteristics or specifications of the product. Such statements may be in the form of advertisements, catalog descriptions, photos, proposals, samples, and oral claims by the supplier provided they are included as the basis of the contract or form the basis of the purchaser's purchase decision. Purchasers should include expressions regarding warranties in the contract to ensure their inclusion as part of the contract.

Implied warranty - There are three implied warranties given to purchasers under the UCC. They deal with ownership, merchantability, and fitness of the goods for the purpose they are purchased.

- **Title** - Under the UCC it is implied that the supplier has legal ownership and clear title to the goods being sold. The goods involved are not subject to security interests, liens, or any other encumbrance not known to the purchaser at the time of contract formation such as copyright or patent violations.
- **Merchantability** - The concept of merchantability under the UCC implies that the goods should be of fair or average quality, they would pass without objection within the trade, and they must be fit for the general purpose for which such goods are normally used. For example, a hammer should be fit for pounding nails (its intended use) even though the purchaser may also use it for chipping concrete (not its intended use).
- **Fitness for particular purpose** - If a supplier is aware of purposes for which goods are being purchased and that the purchaser is relying on the supplier's expertise to furnish a suitable product, it is implied that the supplier warrants the goods as suitable for that purpose.

Examples - Company A manufactured automatic extendable-retractable steps for motor homes. Company A went to its supplier and described the purpose of the switch to activate the steps. Company A with no expertise in electronics, relied upon its supplier's knowledge and skill. After installation, the new units failed. Company A refused to pay for the units and the supplier sued. Company A won because it had relied on the supplier's knowledge and expertise.[5]

Company X contracted with Supplier Y to furnish and install a dump body on a truck to be provided by Company X. After completion it became impossible for the truck to be used for its intended purpose. Company X had the work redone and sued Supplier Y for the rework costs. Supplier Y established that Company X had been told the body would not work because the truck wheelbase was not long enough. Company X had stated that it had had truck bodies built before and this was what it wanted. The court held for Supplier Y as it was clear that Company X had relied on its own expertise not Supplier Y's.[6]

Failure of essential purpose - If there is a failure of essential purpose of the goods in question, the UCC gives the supplier the right to repair or replace the goods in question within a reasonable time-frame. The UCC also states that if circumstances cause an otherwise fair and reasonable clause to deprive a purchaser of the value of the purchaser's bargain, it has failed in its essential purpose and would be considered unconscionable. For example, suppose that a supplier delivers goods that are defective. Even if the purchaser has the capability to make repairs, the purchaser cannot do this and back charge the supplier without first notifying the supplier and giving it the opportunity to remedy the problem. If the purchaser remedies the problem without first notifying the supplier and giving it the option to make repairs, it may relieve the supplier of responsibility for the repairs or remedial action. If the supplier's delay in remedying the problem caused the purchaser to lose a sale and no longer need the goods, the goods would have failed their essential purpose.

Disclaimer of warranties - It is possible for a supplier to disclaim any oral express warranties and limit express warranties to those stated in the written contract. A supplier may not disclaim warranties which are written such as advertisements, catalogs, and brochures. A supplier may also disclaim the implied warranties of merchantability and fitness for use in any one of three ways:

- By specifically disclaiming them in a conspicuous manner. A disclaimer of merchantability must specifically include the term merchantability. An example statement disclaiming both implied warranties is: "There are no implied warranties of merchantability or fitness for a particular purpose which accompany this sale." The term "conspicuous manner" is often interpreted as being in bold print on the face of the document.

- By the conspicuous use of the terms "as is" or "with all faults" as a general disclaimer on the face of the contract.
- By having the purchaser actually examine the goods before the sale. This binds the purchaser by all defects found or which should have been found.

Rights of Inspection, Acceptance, and Rejection

Inspection - The purchaser has the right to inspect the goods before accepting them but it must be done in a reasonable time period. The definition of a reasonable time period is somewhat dependent on the goods involved. A product such as lettuce would not be treated the same as an aluminum casting.

Acceptance - Acceptance occurs when the purchaser notifies the supplier of acceptance, does not reject the goods after a reasonable time allowed for inspection, or acts in a way consistent with ownership of the goods such as using them or selling them to a third party. Acceptance of part constitutes acceptance of the whole unless the purchaser has notified the supplier to the contrary. After acceptance the purchaser must pay for the goods.

Rejection - The purchaser, upon inspection, has the right to reject the entire shipment, accept the entire shipment, or accept part of the shipment. If the goods are rejected, the purchaser must notify the supplier and hold the goods with reasonable care until the supplier has sufficient time to remove the goods.

The purchaser has the right to withhold payment for nonconforming goods. If the contract calls for payment of any kind before inspection, payment must be made unless the material is clearly nonconforming without inspection. Payment required before inspection does not constitute final acceptance of goods and the purchaser can recover the payments if the goods are later found to be nonconforming.

As stated earlier, the purchaser is obligated to give notice of intention to reject in a timely fashion. If the supplier does not respond to a reject or rework notice within a reasonable amount of time the purchaser may, after expiration of the reasonable time:

- Store the goods and file a claim for storage charges.
- Ship the goods back to the supplier freight collect.

- Resell the products and deduct reasonable sales costs from the proceeds, the balance of which are due to the supplier.
- Deduct the cost of rework from the price of the goods.

The supplier, upon notification does have the right to replace or repair the goods in question in a timely fashion.

If a product is unacceptable, the purchaser should notify the supplier that the he or she considers the supplier in breach of contract. Simply notifying the supplier of the defect may not be considered notification of breach in some courts. Therefore, postpone acceptance as long as there is a problem with the product.

Care for nonconforming goods - The purchaser may elect to accept nonconforming goods as they are, or with reasonable expectation that the supplier will cure the nonconformity. Alternately, the purchaser may reject the goods outright and return them to the supplier at the supplier's expense. At this point the purchaser must decide whether the original purchase order is still in effect or whether the order is terminated. If the original purchase order is still in effect, the goods have been returned for replacement. Although the supplier is technically in breach of contract, it may be in the organization's best interests to work with the current supplier, rather than restart the acquisition process with a new supplier. The purchaser may elect to have the supplier make the necessary adjustments at the purchaser's plant or work out a satisfactory application of the nonconforming materials.

Revocation of acceptance - Even after accepting goods, the purchaser's acceptance can be revoked when the goods fail to conform to a contract to such an extent that the defects substantially impair their value to the purchaser. Such revocation may occur provided the goods were accepted without knowledge of the nonconformity or the purchaser had reason to believe supplier would cure the nonconformity. The purchaser may revoke acceptance of the entire order or just the nonconforming goods. The supplier must be given timely notice and must be given a reasonable amount of time to attempt to correct the problem.

Example - A purchaser regularly imports glove parts into New York for assembly in the Philippines. They are not inspected at the warehouse in New York, but sent to the factory in the Philippines.

During assembly it is noted that some parts, shipped from New York two months ago, are below standard. The supplier refuses to authorize return of the goods due to the delay in inspection.

The issue becomes "is the time until inspection reasonable?" The delay between arrival in New York and discovery of defects in the factory was two months. Is that reasonable? The supplier argues, no it is too long. The judge ruled yes, it is reasonable. The key to the issue is the fact that the purchaser "regularly imports" glove parts in this manner. The supplier must therefore be aware that these items are sent elsewhere for assembly. Perhaps the supplier has even received some minor complaints from the factory before this. Also, given the nature of the garment business, it is not reasonable to expect the purchaser to inspect the gloves 100 percent in a New York warehouse prior to transport to the factory. A small sampling of parts would not be sufficient to ensure that all the gloves are acceptable.[7]

Breach of Contract

If at any time the purchaser or the supplier does not live up to the terms of the contract, they are technically in breach of the contract. The supplier can breach the contract by failing to deliver as agreed upon or by delivering nonconforming goods. The purchaser may breach by wrongful rejection, wrongful revocation of acceptance, canceling the contract, or by failing to pay on time. It is important that if one party breaches the contract, the other party must provide notice that a breach has taken place. This does not mean everyone is headed for court, but it is important in turning on the clock for determining damages. The purchaser's goal is to resolve the problem as expeditiously as possible to ensure continuity of supply.

In contracts for services, which are not covered by the UCC, a breach occurs when there is a total or partial failure to perform or there is a flaw in the service. If the breach is material (the supplier has not substantially performed) the purchasing organization is excused from performing its obligations under the contract. If the breach is immaterial (the supplier has substantially performed) the purchasing organization is entitled to compensation but still must perform its obligations. For example, a contractor knowingly installed the wrong brand of pipe but one of comparable grade. The purchaser is entitled to any reduction in value because the contractor had substantially performed because the deviation was minor.[8]

Liability Issues

Limitations of supplier liability - The intent of the UCC is not to penalize the one who defaults on a contract but to make the aggrieved party whole again. Therefore, the party who breaches the contract would be liable for direct damages as well as incidental or consequential damages resulting from the breach. The burden of proof of damages rests with the injured party. Thus, if the supplier defaults, the purchaser must be able to document any damages. Under the UCC, the supplier is allowed to limit liability for incidental and consequential damages.

To ensure proper and timely inspection and acceptance or rejection, carefully defined procedures should be written for receiving, tracking late shipments, inspection, rejection, and supplier notification.

Consequential damages - Consequential damages normally include lost profits and other damages resulting as a "consequence" of the supplier's inability to perform. They are permitted because they are foreseeable consequence which a reasonable purchaser and supplier would expect.

Incidental damages - These are expenses reasonably incurred in the inspection, receipt, transportation, and care of goods rightfully rejected. They also may include any expenses or commissions in connection with purchases required from alternative suppliers as a result of the breach and other reasonable expenses incidental to the delay or other breach.

Liquidated damages - A liquidated damages clause is only used to predetermine damages in case of a future breach of contract when both parties agree that damages will be difficult to calculate. The amount specified must be a reasonable estimate. Liquidated damages are applied in place of actual damages and must be agreed to prior to contract signing.

A liquidated damages clause can be used for situations such as service response times and downtime on equipment, late deliveries, and failure to deliver certain critical materials. The clause can be used for partial breaches as well as a breach of the entire agreement.

Liquidated damages, like other types of damage awards, are for restitution, not penalty.

Only use a liquidated damages clause if both parties agree it will be very difficult to calculate actual damages. The clause must be negotiated as part of the original contract, not after the breach has occurred. The amount of the liquidated damages should be a reasonable estimate of the damages that could be incurred. The clause cannot be punitive. If in doubt, obtain legal counsel before signing the contract.[9]

Hold harmless and indemnity clauses - The purpose of "hold harmless" or "indemnity" clauses are to protect the purchaser from loss or damage. Indemnity is the legal exemption from penalties of liability incurred by one's actions and normally pertains to financial or monetary loss. Hold harmless normally applies to consequential damages or economic injury while defend means an obligation to defend the other party from any legal action and incur the cost of such action. One common application is to protect the purchaser from liabilities incurred from patent or copyright infringements by the supplier.

Types of Contracts

There are three classes or types of contracts: fixed-price contracts, cost reimbursable, and indefinite delivery contracts. The choice of which type of contract to use is dependent on the time available; the certainty of information regarding price, delivery time, and product or service specifications; and the relative strengths of the purchaser and supplier.

Fixed-price Contracts

Fixed-price contracts are based on the premise that the price agreed to in the contract is the price that will be paid. There are several types of fixed-price contracts.

Firm fixed-price - A firm fixed-price contract is probably the most common form of contract. The purchaser agrees to pay the supplier a fixed price for the specified goods or services. Any risks that the costs of the specified goods or services will exceed the fixed price are borne by the supplier.

Fixed-price with adjustment - When a contract is for an extended period of time (typically one or more years) the supplier and purchaser may agree to either a process for considering price changes or a formula and price indicator to be used for adjusting prices.

For example, the price on a particular item may be tied to changes in the Producer Price Index (PPI) such that the price for the next period is based on the changes in the PPI over the previous period. In today's continuous improvement environment, in many industries it is not appropriate to consider escalation clauses. Rather, the contract may state that the initial price is the highest the purchaser expects to pay over the life of the contract. Many auto industry contracts are of this type with the onus placed on the supplier to develop and pass on to the purchaser productivity improvement driven cost reductions.

Fixed-price with redetermination - Similar to a fixed-price with adjustment clause, a redetermination clause is used when there is a high degree of uncertainty about the costs involved in a contract. The invocation of the clause may be based on the completion of a number of units, a time period, or an agreed-upon variance in costs. For example, if uncertainty exists, a price may be agreed upon and production begun. After a specified number of units have been produced, costs are examined and a firm fixed-price is established for the remainder of the production run. The redetermination may be either up or down.

Fixed-price with incentive - The purpose of a fixed-price with incentive contract is to reward the supplier for bringing in a contract under specified criteria such as cost or leadtime by developing a mechanism to share the cost reductions between purchaser and supplier. This is best used on long leadtime projects with high costs.

Cost Reimbursable Contracts

Cost reimbursable contracts reimburse the supplier for actual allowable costs incurred plus an additional amount as profit or an administrative fee, which can be calculated a variety of ways. One of the difficult issues in cost-based contracts is defining what constitutes reimbursable costs. For example, if a supplier includes a profit contribution in its overhead rate in addition to direct labor and materials, then the supplier would make a profit on each dollar of cost charged in addition to any negotiated fees. There are a number of cost-based contract types.

Cost plus a fixed percentage of cost - In this contract the supplier is paid based on legitimate costs incurred plus a percentage of the costs incurred. This is an undesirable form as the supplier has no incentive to control or reduce costs.

Cost plus a sliding percentage of cost - Only slightly better than a fixed percentage of cost, the sliding percentage fee reduces the fee as the costs increase and could even be scaled such that the supplier is reimbursed only for costs above a specified level.

Cost plus fixed fee - The supplier receives a fixed amount irrespective of the costs incurred. The supplier still has no incentive to control costs.

Cost plus with incentive fee - The use of an incentive fee which rewards the supplier for performing below a mutually agreed-upon target cost can provide the supplier with a motivation to reduce costs. The incentive may be scaled such that if costs exceed the target by more than a specified margin, the fee is lost but the supplier's costs are still covered.

Cost plus with a not to exceed clause - This form puts an upper bound on the contract to ensure the purchaser that the costs will not exceed a specific amount. This is useful when a fixed amount of funds are available and the purchaser cannot commit to more than the funds available. As the supplier's costs approach the not-to-exceed price, the supplier's profit declines toward zero.

Indefinite Delivery Contracts

Indefinite delivery contracts are employed when the purchaser is not sure of the production schedule or timing of a service activity, the quantity of material required, or the frequency of service required.

Indefinite delivery/indefinite quantity - Indefinite quantity contracts provide that during a given period of time, the purchaser will place requirements with a specific supplier. Quantities and delivery dates are unknown, but minimum and maximum quantities are usually given.

Time and material contracts - Time and material contracts generally provide payment for labor and overhead at a given rate per hour plus the sales price of parts, supplies, and materials. For example, most automobiles are repaired under time and material contracts.

Legal Issues in Electronic Commerce

Types of Electronic Commerce

There are three predominant forms of electronic commerce today, electronic data interchange (EDI), fax, and the Internet/World Wide Web. Electronic data interchange is the computer-to-computer transmission of business documents. A number of different business documents have been defined including purchase orders, order acknowledgements, invoicing, transportation paperwork, notice of shipment, and payment to name just a few. For a complete list see www.harbinger.com/resource/X12/.

Fax transmission is the transmission of documents by scanning the source document, sending the digital representation of the scan by telephone, and recreating the original document at the destination. Fax provides the ability to send both text and pictures in a relatively short time for the cost of a long-distance phone call.

The latest form of electronic commerce involves using the Internet to identify and select suppliers and to place orders electronically. There is an ongoing concern about security on the Internet at this point in time. There presently exist problems in verifying the identity of the other party and in transmitting confidential data such as purchase order or credit card numbers in a secure manner. Solutions are being developed now, thus some of these difficulties may soon be resolved.

Problem Areas

None of the problem areas discussed below is necessarily fatal to establishing a contract. Rather they are meant to be issues that the purchaser and supplier need to resolve in advance to avoid problems in the future. Many of these issues are common to all three forms of electronic communication and will be discussed generically.

Power to recall - Once in the mail, a message cannot be recalled but in some electronic messaging systems a message can be recalled after reaching the addressee's mailbox. What constitutes receipt would need to be defined in advance or the system would need to be designed so that a message could not be recalled. This is especially important in contract formation relative to making and accepting offers.

Time stamping - Time stamps issued by a system may be used to identify when the transaction took place. The parties involved in the transaction need to specify whether to use the time the transaction was created, transmitted, received, or read.

Return receipt - There is no uniform method to acknowledge receipt electronically. The purchaser and supplier should establish a procedure for acknowledging receipt of a document.

Writing and signing - What constitutes a signature? In an EDI or Internet transaction there is no signature to authenticate. Authorization could be accomplished through the use of a code. There is also a security concern even when an authorization code is used. It may be desirable to use an encryption scheme that would have to be agreed on by both parties.

Interpretation of terms - Interpretation of terms is a potential problem in any contract. Electronic transactions add to the problem by including computer readable codes as well. Thus, the parties must define how each code is to be interpreted. Also, if there is a discrepancy between order and acknowledgement, a procedure needs to be defined to resolve it.

Logistics - In EDI, the route the communication will take should be specified. That is, what, if any, third-party providers will be used, who will pay for the network service charges, how often and when will mailboxes be checked for messages, and how much advanced notice is required to change networks?

Record keeping and control - Questions which will need to be addressed in advance include:

- What happens if a party fails to detect an electronic transmission error?
- To what extent is each party liable for costs incurred due to the error?
- What happens if fraud results from inadequate security?
- What procedures are in effect to monitor transactions?

Authenticity - Did the message originate from indicated source? Is it unaltered? The ability to intercept and potentially modify electronic messages is a major issue today. Organizations need to develop procedures that address this issue. Faxes are not exempt either. For example, someone could use a signature from another document, paste it on a desired document, photocopy it, and then fax it. This has been tried. An attempt was made to make a $1.2 million wire transfer by pasting an authorized signature onto another form and faxing it to the bank involved. One solution to the problem is to notarize each page but that would slow the process and add unnecessary costs. On the Internet, simply because a party has an e-mail or World Wide Web address that appears to be the intended party, there is no guarantee of authenticity.

Reliability - No electronic transmission system is error free. Although many systems have built-in error detection and correction mechanisms, information can be lost. Faxes are notorious for losing words, paragraphs, last lines, or pages in transmission. Also, the medium may create a problem with faxes as an image can fade on thermal papers over time causing them to become unreadable. Using a plain paper fax machine or photocopying the thermal copies upon receipt can resolve this.

Terms and conditions - Many purchasers have faxed purchase orders to suppliers and only sent the front side of the document. If the terms and conditions are not faxed or referenced on the face of the purchase order, they will not apply unless they have been sent to the supplier in advance. In either case, it is still good practice to refer to the terms and conditions as being part of the contract on the face of the purchase order.

Security, especially payment - Security may be dealt with through a variety of means such as encryption of data and the regular changing of authorization codes.

Key Points

1. The Uniform Commercial Code (UCC) is primarily oriented toward the sale and lease of goods.
2. The purchaser, as an agent of the organization, is authorized to acquire goods and services for the organization.

3. Most sales representatives are not agents and cannot commit their organizations to a contract.

4. The purchaser must be cognizant of federal antitrust laws and cannot solicit suppliers to offer different prices to customers who purchase like quantities and qualities of goods.

5. Purchasers must ensure that hazardous materials are packaged, transported, and disposed of according to federal regulations.

6. There are four basic elements required to establish a contract between two parties: an agreement between the parties involved, legal purpose, consideration, and competent parties.

7. In general, oral contracts over $500 are not enforceable unless there is written confirmation of their existence.

8. Under the Uniform Commercial Code there are three implied warranties given to purchasers: ownership, merchantability, and fitness for use.

9. It is possible for a supplier to disclaim any oral express warranties and limit express warranties to those stated in the written contract.

10. The purchaser, upon inspection, has the right to reject the entire shipment, accept the entire shipment, or accept part of the shipment.

11. The intent of the UCC is not to penalize the one who defaults on a contract but to make the aggrieved party whole again.

12. The burden of proof of damages rests with the injured party, thus the purchaser needs to have procedures in place to document any damages incurred when a supplier is in breach.

13. Fixed-price contracts are generally preferred over cost-based contracts.

14. The use of the various forms of electronic commerce, EDI, fax, and the Internet, require a large number of issues to be addressed in advance to avoid problems at a later date.

For Additional Information

The American Law Institute and National Conference of Commissioners on Uniform State Laws. *Uniform Commercial Code*, Thirteenth Edition West Publishing, St. Paul, MN, 1994.

Dobler, D.W. and D.N. Burt. *Purchasing and Supply Management: Text and Cases*, Sixth Edition The McGraw-Hill Companies, Inc., New York, 1996.

Fearon, H.E., D.W. Dobler, and K.W. Killen, eds. *The Purchasing Handbook*, Fifth Edition, McGraw-Hill, Inc., New York, 1993.

Leenders, M.R and H.E. Fearon. *Purchasing and Materials Management*, Tenth Edition Irwin, Homewood, IL, 1993.

Purchasing, published by Cahners Publishing Co., has a regular column on legal issues in purchasing.

Purchasing Today®, published by the National Association for Purchasing Management has a regular monthly column entitled "Legal Briefs."

Ritterskamp, Jr., J. and D. King. *The Purchasing Manager's Desk Book of Purchasing Law*, Third Edition.

Ritterskamp, Jr., J. *Ritterskamp Views the Law - A Collection of Legal Articles for Today's Purchasing Manager*.

Scott, S. "You Be the Judge: Test Your UCC Knowledge," *Proceedings of the 1999 NAPM International Purchasing Conference*, NAPM, Tempe, AZ, 1999, pp. 413-417.

The Uniform Commercial Code is accessible on the Internet at www.law.cornell.edu/ucc/ucc.table.html.

West's Business Law, Interactive CD-ROM Edition, West Publishing Company.

Endnotes

1. Murray, J.E. "Murray's Law: Notable Decisions," *Purchasing*, July 15, 1993, pp. 30-31.

2. Hankcock, W.A. "Purchaser Liability Under Robinson-Patman," *NAPM Insights*, September 1991, p. 8.

3. Scott, S. "You Be the Judge: Test Your UCC Knowledge," Proceedings of the 1999 *NAPM International Purchasing Conference*, NAPM, Tempe, AZ, 1999, pp. 415-416.

4. Hancock, W.A. "Partial Performance in Oral Agreements," *NAPM Insights*, August 1990, p. 8.

5. Dubroff, S. "Fitness for a Particular Purpose," *NAPM Insights*, June 1991, p. 8.

6. Dubroff, p. 8.

7. Scott, p.414.
8. Carrara, M.J. "Are You Being Served?" *Purchasing Today®*, February 1998, p. 16.
9. Woods, D.L. "Liquidated Damages," *NAPM Insights*, April 1991, p. 8.

APPENDIX 7-A

EXAMPLE STANDARD TERMS AND CONDITIONS

This appendix provides example terms and conditions on a wide variety of topics. Some topics may have more than one example so that you may choose the version that works best for your organization or create your own. It is recommended that you have any changes in your standard terms and conditions reviewed by your organization's legal counsel before being published. Each clause should be titled to make its content clear to the reader. Your organization's name can be inserted wherever [COMPANY] appears, your state where [STATE] appears, and your city where [CITY] appears.

Advertising

Advertising - Supplier shall not, without first obtaining the written consent of [COMPANY], in any manner advertise, publish, or otherwise disclose the fact that Supplier has furnished, or contracted to furnish to [COMPANY] the materials and/or services ordered hereunder.

Amendments and Changes

Amendments - If the articles ordered are to be manufactured in accordance with drawings and specifications furnished by [COMPANY], [COMPANY] may make changes in such drawings and specifications. Any difference in Supplier's costs or increase in time required for delivery by the Supplier, resulting from such changes, shall be equitably amended in writing. No change in the articles ordered, or in the terms and conditions of our orders proposed by the Supplier, shall have effect unless the order is amended in writing.

Changes - The only changes to this Purchase Order by which Purchaser will be bound are express, written changes, signed by an authorized Purchaser representative. In no event shall Purchaser's silence be construed as acceptance of proposed changes in or additions to this contract.

Cancellation - [COMPANY] may cancel any undelivered portion of orders at any time, by written notice to the Supplier. In the event of such cancellation and if Supplier is not in default, [COMPANY] shall pay to the Supplier, such costs incurred by the Supplier pursuant to this order, prior to such cancellation as shall be unrecoverable in the normal course of business.

Default - [COMPANY] may cancel all or any part of the undelivered portion of an order, if the Supplier does not make deliveries of acceptable quality within the time specified on the order, or if the Supplier otherwise breaches any of the terms or conditions specified thereon. Supplier will not however, be liable for delay in delivery due to causes beyond the Supplier's control and without Supplier's fault or negligence, provided the Supplier promptly notifies [COMPANY] in writing of any such delay or expected delay, as soon as such delay becomes, or should have become apparent.

Cancellation - Purchaser reserves the right to cancel any or all of the order prior to date of shipment and any items back ordered. On items not as ordered and items on back order, Purchaser will charge Supplier with all or excess transportation and cartage. Any added costs incurred by Supplier not following Purchaser's detailed shipping and routing instructions will be charged to Supplier.

Changes - [COMPANY] may at any time, without invalidating the contract and without notice to Contractor's sureties, if any, order any changes in the work. [COMPANY] will issue written orders to Contractor for any such changes provided that, in the event of an emergency which [COMPANY] determines endangers life or property, [COMPANY] will issue oral orders to Contractor for any work required by reason of such emergency. Such orders will be confirmed in writing as soon as practicable. Such orders, whether written or oral, may be accompanied by drawings and data as are necessary to show the extent and nature of such change.

Assignment

Substitutions - Do not substitute without Purchaser's written consent.

Subcontracting - Supplier shall not subcontract or delegate its obligations under this order without the written consent of [COMPANY]. Parts and materials normally purchased by Supplier or required by this order shall not be construed as sub-contracts or delegations. In addition, Supplier shall not re-export, and except for purchases or parts and materials normally purchased by Supplier, shall not divert to others any [COMPANY] specifications, drawings or other data, or any product of such data.

Confidentiality

Confidentiality - Supplier shall not disclose to any person outside of its employ, or use for any purpose other than to fulfill its obligations under this order, any information received from [COMPANY] pursuant to this order, which has been disclosed to Supplier by [COMPANY] in confidence, except such information which is otherwise publicly available or is publicly disclosed by [COMPANY] subsequent to Supplier's receipt of such information or is rightfully received by Supplier from a third party. Upon termination of this order, Supplier shall return to [COMPANY] upon request all drawings, blueprints, descriptions, or other material received from [COMPANY] and all materials containing said confidential information. Also, Supplier shall not disclose to [COMPANY] any information which Supplier deems to be confidential, and it is understood that any information received by [COMPANY], including all manuals, drawings and documents, will not be of a confidential nature or restrict, in any manner, the use of such information by [COMPANY]. Supplier agrees that any legend or other notice on any information supplied by Supplier, which is inconsistent with the provisions of this article, does not create any obligation on the part of [COMPANY].

Proprietary tooling - [COMPANY] owned tools or tooling held by Supplier are to be used only for making parts for [COMPANY]. Tools of any kind held by Supplier for making [COMPANY]'s parts must be repaired and renewed by Supplier at Supplier's expense.

Proprietary parts - All parts and components bailed by [COM-PANY] to Supplier for incorporation in work being performed for [COMPANY] shall be used solely for such purposes.

Delivery

Order release - Ship per Purchaser's written release only; Purchaser reserves right to return material not released or material overshipped, at Supplier's expense.

Late delivery - Purchaser will not be responsible for merchandise shipped after final date specified in this order. Shipment of goods constitutes acceptance of "Conditions of Order" as specified unless Purchaser has confirmed a change.

Early delivery - Shipment by Supplier before the date indicated on the Purchase Order subjects the goods to return by Purchaser at the expense of Supplier. If Purchaser retains goods shipped before the date indicated, any additional storage or freight expenses incurred because of early receipt will be deducted from Supplier's invoice amount.

Performance and delivery - Time is of the essence. Purchaser may cancel the unreceived portion of this purchase order at any time if delivery of the goods is not timely. If Supplier can fulfill its delivery obligation only by shipping by premium routing, the premium charges shall be at Supplier's expense and, if shipment if F.O.B. point of shipment, Supplier shall reimburse Purchaser for the premium paid.

Late delivery - In the event of Supplier's failure to deliver as and when specified, [COMPANY] reserves the right to cancel this order or any part thereof without prejudice to its other rights, and Supplier, agrees that [COMPANY] may return part or all of any shipment so made and may charge Supplier with any loss or expense sustained as a result of such failure to deliver.

Definitions

Acceptance - Supplier's written acceptance, or the commencement of Supplier performance shall constitute acceptance. Acceptance of the order constitutes agreement to all terms, conditions, and instructions thereon.

Acceptance - This Purchase Order which incorporates any prior specification, samples, or descriptions of the goods and all express and implied warranties, becomes the entire and exclusive agreement between Purchaser and Supplier when acknowledged by Supplier in writing or if earlier when Supplier commences performance. This offer to purchase is expressly conditioned on Supplier's acceptance of these terms and conditions. By accepting this Purchase Order or by shipping goods in response to it, Supplier agrees that Purchaser is not to be bound by any term or condition of Supplier in any written acknowledgment, invoice, or otherwise which is inconsistent with or in addition to the terms and conditions herein and that any such inconsistent or additional terms are understood to be rejected by Purchaser.

Acceptance - [COMPANY] expressly limits acceptance to the terms set forth on the face and reverse side of this purchase order and any attachments hereto.

Enforcement of terms - [COMPANY] may at any time insist upon strict compliance with these terms and conditions not withstanding any previous custom, practice, or course of dealing to the contrary.

Equal Employment Opportunity

EEO - Purchase orders issued by [COMPANY] are subject to Presidential Executive Order No. 11246 and section VII of the Civil Rights Act of 1964. The Supplier is required to comply with the regulations and orders authorized thereby.

EEO - There are incorporated in this order the provisions of Executive Order 11246 (as amended) of the President of the United States on Equal Employment Opportunity and the rules and regulations issued pursuant thereto with which the Supplier represents that he will comply, unless exempt.

Entire Agreement

Entire agreement - This purchase order, including the terms and conditions on the face and reverse side hereof and any attachments hereto, contains the complete and final agreement between [COMPANY] and Supplier. Reference to Supplier's bids or proposals, if noted on this order, shall not affect terms and conditions hereof, unless specifically provided to the contrary herein, and no other agreement or quotation is any way modifying any of said terms and conditions will be binding upon [COMPANY] unless made in writing and signed by [COMPANY]'s authorized representative.

FOB-Shipping Freight

Express charges - If shipment by express becomes necessary in order to fulfill the Supplier's delivery obligation, Supplier shall pay express charges and freight charges.

F.O.B. - Ship F.O.B. Destination unless otherwise specified.

Routing - On F.O.B. origin shipments when shipping point will be other than shown hereon, contact Purchaser's Traffic Department for correct routing instructions. Any excess charges due to Supplier's failure to do so will be charged to Supplier.

Routing - As indicated in transportation guidelines on face of this order.

F.O.B. - Unless otherwise specified, ship collect, F.O.B. origin.

Prepaid transportation (when specified) - Charges must be supported by a paid freight bill or equivalent.

Cartage - No charge allowed unless authorized by [COMPANY].

Premium transportation - No charge allowed unless authorized by [COMPANY].

Consolidation - Unless otherwise instructed, consolidate all daily shipments to one destination on one bill of lading.

Force Majeure

Force majeure - Purchaser excuses Supplier from nonperformance or delays in delivery caused by acts of God or force majeure but Supplier agrees it is not excused by unexpected difficulty or commercial impracticality of any degree.

Gifts

Gifts/gratuities - Supplier shall not make or offer gifts or gratuities of any type to [COMPANY] employees or members of their families. Such gifts or offerings may be construed as Supplier's attempt to improperly influence our relationship.

Indemnification

Indemnification - Supplier agrees to indemnify, defend, and hold harmless [COMPANY], its trustees, officers, agents, and employees, of, from, and against any and all claims and demands which may arise in any way out of the furnishing of goods or services hereunder including with limitation, claims and demands arising from injury to or death of personnel of [COMPANY] or for damage to the property of [COMPANY], except those arising by reason of the negligent or willful act of [COMPANY], its officers, agents, or employees.

Indemnification - Supplier agrees to defend, indemnify, and hold Purchaser harmless of and from any claims, loss, damage, or expense arising out of any defect or nonconformity in Supplier's goods or presence of Supplier's agents or employees on Purchaser's premises, including, without limitation, payment of direct, special, incidental and consequential damages, and expenses of defending claims, including attorneys' fees at trial or on appeal. This duty to defend, indemnify, and hold harmless extends to any law suit which may arise out of defects or non-conformity of Supplier's goods or a claim of defect or nonconformity or claims arising out of the presence of Supplier's agents or employees on Purchaser's premises, whether such law suit may be based upon contract, warranty, strict liability in tort, negligence, or other legal theory, and also extends not only to "third-party claims" but also to any direct loss suffered by Purchaser.

Workers' compensation - If Supplier does not have Workers' Compensation or Employers' Liability Insurance, Supplier shall indemnify [COMPANY] against all damages sustained by [COMPANY] resulting from Suppliers' failure to have such insurance.

Insurance

Insurance - Purchaser covers Marine Insurance under our open Marine Policy on all F.O.B. Origin shipments only.

Insurance - No charge allowed unless authorized by [COMPANY].

Inspection

Inspection, rejection, revocation of acceptance - The acceptance of articles supplied per our orders is subject to inspection and approval by [COMPANY] after delivery. Articles rejected by [COMPANY] may be returned to the Supplier at Supplier's expense. No replacement of articles shall be made by the Supplier unless specified by [COMPANY].

Inspection, rejection, revocation of acceptance - Purchaser shall have the right to inspect the goods and reject any nonconforming goods. This right of inspection, whether exercised or not, shall not affect Purchaser's right to revoke acceptance or pursue other remedies if defects are discovered at a later date notwithstanding that any defect or nonconformity could have been discovered upon inspection. Purchaser may return nonconforming goods to Supplier at Supplier's risk and expense, including transportation and handling costs.

Inspection, rejection, revocation of acceptance - Material is subject to [COMPANY]'s inspection and approval within a reasonable time after delivery. If specifications are not met, material may be returned at Supplier's expense and risk for all damages incidental to the rejection. Payment shall not constitute an acceptance of the material nor impair [COMPANY]'s right to inspect or any of its remedies.

Inspection, rejection, revocation of acceptance - In the event materials do not comply with all specifications, the Purchaser shall have the option to reject and return part, or all of such merchandise. The Supplier agrees to pay or reimburse the Purchaser for invoice cost, delivery cost, labor and other expenses incurred in sorting, inspecting and packing said merchandise for return.

Laws

Governing law - The rights and liabilities regarding [COMPANY] purchase contracts shall be governed in all respects by [STATE] law. Venue in any law suit arising out of any purchase order shall lie exclusively in state and federal courts in the state of [STATE].

Hazardous materials - All products covered by this Purchase Order which contain hazardous substances are to be labeled in compliance with the Federal Hazardous Substance Labeling Act.

U.L. approval - All electric appliances and/or component parts and/or wiring on this order must be listed by the Underwriters Laboratories, Inc. in compliance with the electrical code of the city of [CITY], [STATE]. Unapproved merchandise shipped will be returned at the expense of the Supplier.

Federal Flammable Fabrics Act - Any merchandise covered by this Purchase Order containing fabrics which are subject to the provisions of the Federal Flammable Fabrics Act must conform to the provisions of such laws.

Bedding and furniture laws - Any merchandise covered by this Purchase Order which is subject to the provisions of the [STATE] Bedding and Furniture Laws must conform to the provisions of such laws.

Federal law compliance - By acceptance of this order Supplier guarantees that the article covered by the invoice are not adulterated or misbranded within the meaning of the Federal Food, Drug and Cosmetic Act and that all advertising claims, labels and circulars relating to the product do not violate any provision of the Federal Trade Commission Act or other applicable law and that the price charged and allowance and services furnished, if any, in connection with this sale are not discriminatory and were made available on substantially proportionate terms to other customers of the Supplier and that the prices charged for the items furnished are the lowest lawful prices available from the Supplier. Supplier further warrants that the goods are not produced in violation of any provision of the Fair Wage and Labor Law and that the sale, shipping and billing complies with all provisions of law and with promulgations of governmental authority.

Textile Fiber Products Identification Act - In accepting this order, Supplier agrees that he will furnish a guarantee rendered in good faith that any textile fiber products specified therein are properly branded and invoiced in accordance with the Textile Fiber Products Identification Act or any other Federal statutes applicable to the products covered by this order.

Remedies - No remedy provided in this Purchase Order shall be deemed exclusive of any other remedy allowed by law.

[STATE] Law - The rights and liabilities of the parties under this Purchase Order shall be governed in all respects by [STATE] Law.

Venue - Venue in any lawsuit arising out of this purchase order shall lie exclusively in state and federal courts in the State of [STATE].

Retail price maintenance - Notwithstanding any other retail price maintenance agreements, the Purchaser makes no representations of maintaining any specific retail price.

[STATE] Law - The agreement arising pursuant to this order shall be governed by the laws of the State of [STATE]. No rights, remedies and warranties available under this contract or by operation or law are waived or modified unless expressly waived or modified by [COMPANY] in writing.

Federal law compliance - Supplier shall at all times comply with all applicable Federal, State and local laws, rules and regulations.

Fair Labor Standards Act - Supplier warrants that in the performance of this order Supplier has complied with all of the provisions of the Fair Labor Standards Act of 1938 of the United States as amended.

Notice/Request

Notice - Inform Purchaser immediately, if problems are encountered with raw materials, jigs, fixtures, etc. furnished by [COMPANY]. Return all jigs, tools, gauges, unused materials, etc. with completed order and indicate on delivery ticket or packing slip.

Price

Price - If price is not stated on this order, Supplier shall invoice at lowest prevailing market price.

Price - Supplier agrees that Purchaser shall receive benefit of any reduction in price of items included herein which is effective on date of delivery.

Patent Indemnification — US/Foreign

Patent indemnification - Supplier agrees to indemnify and hold Purchaser, its agents and employees harmless from any claim or finding and from any loss, including attorneys fees arising therefrom, that any of the goods sold by Supplier to Purchaser violates any patent, copyright, trade secret, or other proprietary rights of any third person.

Patent indemnification - Supplier agrees to indemnify and hold Purchaser, its agents and employees harmless from any claim or finding and from any loss, including attorney's fees arising therefrom, that any of the goods sold by Supplier to Purchaser violates any patent, copyright, trade secret, or other proprietary rights of any third person.

Patent indemnification - Supplier will settle or defend, at Supplier's expense (and pay any damages, costs, or fines resulting from), all proceedings or claims against [COMPANY], its subsidiaries and affiliates and their respective customers, for infringement, or alleged infringement, by the goods furnished under this order, or any part of use thereof of patents (including utility models and registered designs) now or hereafter granted in the United States or in any country where Supplier, its subsidiaries or affiliates, heretofore has furnished similar goods. Supplier will at [COMPANY]'s request, identify the countries in which Supplier, its subsidiaries or affiliates, heretofore has furnished similar goods.

Packaging

Packaging - No charge will be allowed for boxing, packing, or crating unless agreed upon in writing at the time of purchase.

Damage - Damage to any material not packaged to insure proper protection, will be charged to the Supplier or returned at Supplier's expense, for replacement.

Payment Terms

Discount period - If merchandise does not arrive within the specified discount period, Purchaser reserves the right on initial orders placed with a new account to make payment within 10 days after receipt of merchandise.

Discount period - Calculations will be from the date an acceptable invoice is received by [COMPANY]. Any other arrangements agreed upon must appear on this order and on the invoice.

Quantity

Partial shipments - Make partial shipments only upon authorization.

Shipping Instructions

Packing list - A packing list must accompany each shipment, giving description of the material, quantity and purchase order number. [COMPANY] count shall be accepted as final on all shipments not accompanied by a packing list.

Identification - Packages must bear [COMPANY]'s order number.

Identification - Mark all cartons and Bill of Lading with COMPLETE shipping address. Have Supplier's name on the outside of all packages. All shipments must be packed, marked and described on Bill of Lading as to obtain the lowest applicable rate, except when otherwise specified by Purchaser.

Taxes

Taxes - Unless otherwise agreed in writing, the contract price includes all applicable Federal, State, and Local Taxes, Tariffs, Import Duties, Commissions, or other charges.

Taxes - Unless otherwise directed, Supplier shall pay all sales and use taxes imposed by law upon or on account of this order. Where appropriate, [COMPANY] will reimburse Supplier for this expense.

Warranty

Warranties - Supplier warrants that the articles supplied against our orders will be sufficient for the purpose intended and will conform to the specifications, drawing, or samples furnished or adapted by [COMPANY] and will be merchantable, of good quality and free from defects in material and workmanship. Any added costs incurred by Supplier not following Purchaser's instructions will be charged to Supplier.

Warranties - Manufacturer or Supplier guarantees that merchandise ordered and shipped is free of defect. Defective merchandise will be returned at the expense of the shipper.

Warranties - Supplier warrants to Purchaser that the goods are of merchantable quality and are free from defects in design, materials, workmanship and title, are fit for purposes for which goods of that type are ordinarily used as well as for any purposes Supplier has specified or advertised and that the goods conform in every respect to the specifications of the Purchase Order and any applicable sample or description given to the Purchaser. In addition, Supplier incorporates by reference and passes on to Purchaser the benefits of all warranties given to Supplier by persons from whom Supplier purchased any of the goods.

Attorneys' fees - In any proceeding brought to enforce this Purchase Order the prevailing party will be entitled to recover reasonable expenses of litigation including attorneys' fees, at trial and on any appeal or petition for review.

Appendix 7-B
Custom Terms and Conditions

This Appendix provides a list of potential custom terms and conditions you may want to consider. Under each heading are issues which should be addressed in the clause.

Acceptance Test
Specify how the goods will be tested. Delineate the standards the goods will have to meet including load conditions, length of time the goods must perform at the desired level. For example, in purchasing a computer system it is common practice to require a specific response time at a particular load level on the system.

Changes/Service Bulletins/Modifications
Will the supplier provide notification of any changes or modifications being made to the equipment being provided? At what cost? Will the supplier supply service bulletins as they become available? What time frame?

Emergency Services
If product fails while under warranty, what services will the supplier provide? What is the required response time? Will replacement equipment be provided and under what conditions? What will the services be if the product is out of warranty?

Finance
If supplier is financing, what is the payment schedule? Interest rate? Can the supplier sell the contract to a third party? What is the hold back percentage until acceptance?

Field Service
What will the supplier provide? What is the frequency of visits? What is the scope of services provided?

Installation/Setup

Who will be responsible for installation and setup? What activities are covered?

Initial Provisioning

When purchasing new equipment, the manufacturer often recommends the appropriate spare parts and operating supplies which should be on hand. This clause delineates what is required and who has the responsibility to assure the proper items are on hand. Will the supplier buy-back excess materials? Over what timeframe?

Maintenance

Who will provide maintenance, preventive and emergency? If the purchaser performs the maintenance, what records are required?

Option To Renew

What are the conditions for renewal?

Spare Parts Inventory

What parts should be maintained? Who should maintain the parts? Where should the parts be maintained? What is the required response time to obtain parts?

Technical Publications/Manuals

What technical publications and manuals will be provided at the outset? Will revisions be supplied? For how long? Does the purchaser have the right to use technical data? What are the Supplier's obligations to continue systems, technical, and warranty support?

Training

Who will provide both initial and ongoing training? What will be covered? Timing? Who will pay?

Term

How long is the contract valid?

Termination

What is the process to terminate the contract at a future date? What are grounds for termination of the contract?

Value Analysis

Does the supplier participate in finding ways to reduce both its and the firm's costs?

Chapter 8

Managing the Contract: You Want to Change What and Want It When?

Chapter Objectives

- Define the objectives of contract administration.
- Understand the contract administration process and the various activities involved.
- Define the difference between expediting and follow-up.
- Identify common problems that cause organizations to expedite.
- Understand why expediting efforts fail and ways to improve expediting results.
- Document the types of contract problems the purchaser may encounter and potential ways to deal with them.

Introduction

The purchasing process is not complete once the order is placed with the supplier. The purchaser has the responsibility to ensure the product or service is delivered when needed and meets the specifications or SOW. To accomplish this, the purchaser must monitor the progress of the order through delivery, performance, and acceptance. If the needed delivery date changes or the supplier will be late, the purchaser must take an active role to minimize the ramifications of not meeting the desired delivery dates. This chapter will examine the contract administration, expediting, and follow-up processes, and the options available to the supplier and purchaser if the other fails to perform or conflicts arise.

Contract Administration

Contract administration involves all actions by the supplier or purchaser relating to a contract from the time the contract is awarded through contract closeout. Contract administration's objectives are to:

- Ensure that the supplier's progress and performance are in compliance with the contract.
- Ensure that the purchasing organization fulfills its part of the contract.
- Resolve any problems that arise during the contract life.
- Maintain accurate records and documentation.

After the contract is formed, the first decision to be made is to determine who is going to administer the contract. Extremely complex contracts, very specialized purchases, or highly technical contracts may require the assistance of the internal customer using the product or service or a third-party administrator to ensure supplier/contractor compliance. Professional contract administrators are often used by governmental agencies and large organizations.

If the contract administration is delegated to the user, the purchaser should develop an outline of the contract for the user. The purchaser and contract administrator then need to identify the critical components and issues in the contract including the following:

- Performance standards and the definition of acceptable performance.
- Tactical requirements and specifications.
- Delivery dates.
- Report due dates.
- Payment schedules.
- Consequences of failure to meet the delivery dates.
- Appropriate monitoring techniques.
- Determining how contract changes will be handled and by whom.

The purchaser and contract administrator should also schedule regular meetings to review progress and discuss any issues that have come to light since their last meeting.

The contract administrator should be trained in how to create an appropriate relationship with the supplier, how to work with key staff, and the potential problems that may arise during the life of the contract. In these cases, individuals may be aware of the technical aspects of the contract, but may require training regarding the legal and purchasing aspects. These individuals must be given basic instructions in the following areas:

- Understanding the contract, a requirement if the administrator is to comprehend the entire scope of the undertaking.
- Developing a mutually beneficial, professional relationship with the supplier.
- Understanding the basic requirements of the contract.
- Recognizing potential problems.
- Actions they can take.
- Actions they must not take.
- Areas of authority and responsibility.

Next, the contract administrator needs to setup a post-award conference with the supplier and the members of the purchasing organization who will be involved with the contract. This conference provides an opportunity to review the contract and define expectations. As a part of the post award conference, the supplier should receive an orientation to the purchaser's organization. The orientation serves to familiarize the supplier with the organization's relevant policies and procedures regarding invoicing and payment processes, ethics policies, and reporting processes.

Contract Compliance

Contract compliance is the primary responsibility of purchasing. For a successful contract compliance program, the end-user and contract administrator must understand not only the contract, but also organization operating policies and procedures. The purchasing department has first-line responsibility to get this information to the administrators. Well-established, bilateral communication lines will assist in developing outstanding contract administrators for the organization and the purchasing department. Contract compliance involves having a plan of action in place should the supplier fail to perform or should the purchasing activity have a change of requirements.

Contract compliance monitoring involves several techniques and procedures for determining in a timely manner if satisfactory delivery or contract completion will occur. The contract is monitored to determine if it is being performed in accordance with the requirements and if problems are developing that need to be addressed. The purchaser's aim in compliance monitoring includes reviewing the following areas:

- Will the supplier perform on schedule?
- Will the cost be within the estimate?
- Are resources being applied at originally predicted levels?
- Will the quality of the end products be consistent with the specifications?
- Are progress payments warranted?
- Will new components need to be incorporated in major equipment?
- Will the contractor's own progress monitoring system be adequate?
- Are all contractual provisions (including those not relating to the work itself) being followed?
- Is the purchasing organization receiving all goods and services contracted for at the price, time, place, and quality contracted?
- Are requested changes properly documented and fairly resolved?

The contract administrator also monitors other activities including documenting progress toward specified project milestones, cost control, reporting requirements, and documenting supplier problems and the actions taken to correct them.

Project Management

One tool the contract administrator can use in managing a contract is project management. There are a number of project management software packages available such as Microsoft Project, Corel Time Line, and Primavera (see www.infogoal.com/pmc/pmcswr.htm for a listing of project management software). These packages use project information on the tasks involved, the relationships between tasks, and the time and resource requirements for each task to develop a critical path for the project. The critical path identifies the activities that, if delayed, will delay the completion of the entire project. If the program is used properly, that is task completion estimates are regularly updated, the result is a plan that indicates to the contract administrator where the current problems are and future problems that are likely to appear.

The use of project management techniques can help the contract administrator by improving communications, reducing cycle time, helping to identify problems before the project is adversely affected, and improving interdepartmental relationships. On the downside, project management may not succeed if the project manager is not given enough authority or resources to complete the project.

In 1996, Northeast Utilities used project management on the implementation of a new purchasing, materials management, and accounts payable system. Besides getting the software operational, approximately 3,000 people would need to be taught how to request materials and services; approve requests; create and issue purchase orders; receive, store, and issue materials; and pay for services and materials received. The use of project management techniques allowed the implementation team to determine whether the project was ahead or behind schedule, if additional resources were required, and competitive issues.[1]

Controlling Contract Work

The statement of work (SOW) describes what is expected of the supplier, by whom, when, and, possibly, how it is to be done (see Chapter 2 for a discussion of SOWs). For large, multiyear, complex projects, one part of the SOW deals with controlling the supplier's work. Some types of contracts, such as indefinite delivery contracts, time and material/labor hour contracts, and cost reimbursement contracts, defer the ordering and work authorization processes until after the award (see Chapter 7 for a discussion of the various contract types). In those circumstances, ordering becomes a post-award or contract administration matter.

Work ordering under an indefinite delivery type or time and materials/labor hour contract generally follows a similar pattern. For an indefinite delivery contract, the customer activity initiates a standard work order form describing the desired items along with the unit price. The desired quantity is multiplied by the unit price to arrive at a total. This work order is generally routed to a purchaser for approval and distributed to the supplier, the customer activity, and the finance office.

Cost reimbursement contract work control procedures are often considerably more complex than controls for other types of contracts. These procedures are used in large cost reimbursement contracts extending over several years. Many cost reimbursement contracts require the establishment and maintenance of a process of annual work plans, work authorizations, and notices to proceed (NTPs) as a means to assist in cost and schedule control.

Upon purchaser receipt of preliminary funding guidance, the supplier can be informed of the expected levels of funding for the ensuing (budget) and subsequent fiscal years, milestones based on the current master program schedule, and relevant scope information. This guidance enables the supplier to prepare an annual work plan (AWP).

The AWP is central to the total process in that it provides the initial definition of tasks to be performed in the budget year and a schedule for accomplishment. The AWP provides for a balance of funding guidance and program schedule requirements. During the AWP review, the supplier resource projections are approved and the tasks to be undertaken are scheduled.

The specific elements of an AWP generally include goals and assumptions; work authorization review results; and a schedule, staffing plan, and cost estimate for the budget year. The AWP should be updated at the middle of each fiscal year.

Work authorizations generally cover a variety of duties. These include work breakdown structure designations for the work, information regarding the duration of the work authorization, the baseline cost estimate for the work, and references to the existing AWP and NTPs to be issued subsequent to the work authorizations. Tasks to be accomplished during a certain period or phase of contract performance will be described in NTP documentation and issued to the supplier prior to the supplier's undertaking any work. The NTP normally includes a statement of work, the key schedule milestones for task accomplishment, and the total amount of funds allotted to the tasks.

Upon receipt of the NTP, the supplier will begin work and start cost and scheduling reporting for the tasks concerned.

Documentation Requirements

Each contract will have its own documentation requirements. It is the contract administrator's responsibility to determine what they are and ensure that they are met. Example documentation includes work orders, invoicing, work plans, performance measurements, supplier insurance forms, bond requirements, verification of tax payments, and verification of material payments by the supplier. The procedure can be formal with written checklists or can be handwritten notes in the contract file. The point is to document all actions and verify all requirements.

Progress reports - In some instances, the supplier is required by the contract to submit a phased project schedule for review and approval. A phased project schedule shows the time required to perform the project planning, designing, purchasing, tooling, installation, manufacturing or service performance, and delivery.

The purchaser may include a requirement for project progress information in the RFP and the resulting contract. The ensuing reports frequently show the supplier's actual and forecasted deliveries as compared to the contract schedule, delay factors, if any, and the status of incomplete pre-production work such as design and engineering, tooling, and construction of prototypes. The reports should also contain narrative sections in which the supplier explains any difficulties and the action(s) proposed or taken to overcome them.

Project progress reports do not alleviate the requirement to conduct visits to the supplier's facility or the work site on crucial contracts. The right to conduct such visits must be established in the RFP and resulting contract. On critical contracts, where the cost is justified, it may be desirable to establish a resident site monitor at the supplier facility to oversee the quality and timeliness of the work being performed.

When it is determined that an active system of monitoring the supplier's progress is appropriate, the first step in ensuring timely delivery is to evaluate the supplier's proposed delivery schedule for attainability. In their planning and control activities, many suppliers use a variety of graphic methods including Gantt charts and

PERT/CPM diagrams to portray the proposed schedule and to monitor progress. These are useful management tools that can also be reviewed and evaluated by the contract administrator. (See any text on project management for a discussion of PERT/CPM diagrams and Gantt charts.)

Financial Responsibility

From the award of a contract to final close out, the supplier's primary concern is to receive payment in as timely a manner as possible for work done. The different types of contracts used by the purchaser create different financial relationships between the purchaser and the supplier. The supplier with a firm fixed-price contract has a strong incentive to perform in the most economical way, because every penny saved below the contract price is additional profit. Under most labor hour, time and materials, and cost reimbursement contracts, however, the supplier has little incentive to perform in the most economical way. Under these types of contracts, the supplier is generally entitled to compensation for either a fixed amount per hour or the costs incurred in doing the work, provided that the expenses are not unreasonable. The work description in these cost-plus type contracts is usually broad because it is difficult to predict just what the contractor will be required to do. This gives the supplier wide contractual authorization, which can permit the supplier to perform (and charge for) effort along lines other than those specifically desired by the purchaser. Under these latter types of contracts, the purchaser needs to monitor and guide the supplier's efforts to prevent waste of funds and to ensure the organization gets the products and/or services needed within the amount budgeted.

Change Orders

Ideally, a contract contains all the provisions necessary for completion of the work and discharge of both parties' obligations. Modifications of the agreement are not contemplated when the contract is signed. In practice, however, few contracts are completed without some type of modification. Some are simply administrative changes that do not affect the substance of the contract. Others involve substantial changes to the price, quantity, quality, delivery, or other terms originally agreed to by the purchaser and the supplier.

Because the purchaser's authority under any given contract is defined by the contract's clauses, it is necessary that those clauses contain provisions that allow flexibility to alter the contract after award. It is also necessary that there be provisions requiring the parties to equitably alter the delivery schedule or the price to be paid in correspondence with other changes in the contract's terms. Consequently, contract provisions must give the purchaser the authority to make changes. These provisions should also give the supplier or the purchaser "relief" if the other party does something not contemplated, or fails to do something contemplated, by the original agreement. The provisions should also allow "equitable adjustment" of performance time or price when changes are made. See Appendix 7-A under "Amendments and Changes" for example terms and conditions.

Contract Closeout

The term contract closeout refers to the actions taken by both parties in a contract upon completion of their respective obligations. These actions, at a minimum for a purchase order, include verification that all work has been duly performed, accepted, properly invoiced, and fully paid for. Larger, more complex projects may include supplier delivery of all warranty documents and termination of bond agreements as appropriate. In most complex contracts, a checklist for close out items is recommended with appropriate parties' signatures or initials signifying the work or action is complete.

Expediting and Follow-Up

What is the difference between expediting and follow-up? Follow-up is the normal process of ensuring that the supplier is performing as expected. One of the objectives of follow-up is to ensure that open orders, especially long leadtime orders, receive periodic review. The longer the leadtime, the more likely it is that if the purchaser does nothing during the interim, the order will arrive late. Periodic review assures the purchasing organization that if supplier difficulties arise, the purchaser learns of them in time to take appropriate actions that will ensure delivery as close to the original schedule as possible

Expediting is the process of contacting a supplier or carrier with the goal of speeding up the delivery date on an order because the purchasing organization's need has changed or the supplier will not be delivering on time. After an order has been placed, there are many situations that might cause the purchaser to need to change delivery timing. Expediting may include periodic supplier contact to assess progress of the order to effect early delivery, or even to delay delivery as business conditions and schedules change.

Expediting adds no value to a product - it only adds cost. It should be the objective of all purchasing organizations to decrease the need for expediting, and thus its costs, by selecting suppliers who are reliable and responsive. In addition, internal planning and forecasting should be emphasized to minimize expediting requirements.

There are many reasons for expediting and follow-up activities and many means by which they can be accomplished. Methods range from postcard requests to suppliers for order status, to electronic communication. The most common method is by telephone. Depending on the severity of the problem, supplier site visits and meetings with senior executives may be necessary.

Common Problems

Common problems the purchaser will face include late orders, back orders, dealing with sole source suppliers, and changes in delivery date.

Overdue orders - There are many reasons why suppliers fail to meet promised delivery schedules. Regardless of the cause, expediting activity focuses on problem resolution. With planned follow-up actions, the purchasing organization can identify a problem order quickly and work with the supplier to put the order back on the original delivery schedule. It is worth noting that experienced expediters acknowledge that often suppliers' problems are created, at least in part, by the purchasing organization. Rather than focusing blame, the key issue in the late order situation is to resolve the difficulty and receive delivery at the earliest possible time. After the order has been received, purchasers should work with the supplier to identify and remove the cause of the delay.

Back orders - When a supplier delivers only part of an order by the due date, the remaining undelivered portion is said to be "back ordered." In this situation, expediting is necessary to determine the reason for the back order and schedule the delivery of the balance of the order.

Sole source supplier - A sole source supplier presents some unique problems. If the supplier is late, back ordered, or there is a need to rush the order, the purchaser may have little leverage to effect change. It is important for the purchaser to have a strong relationship with the supplier to facilitate cooperation.

Rush orders - Whenever an order is placed inside a supplier's normal leadtime, it is defined as "RUSH." It is likely to require negotiation with the supplier to determine if it is possible to meet the time requirement. In some cases, alternate suppliers may need to be contacted to find one able to meet the rush requirements.

Tracing - If the order has shipped, the purchaser may wish to trace its in-transit progress. It becomes important that the carrier has the ability to monitor the progress of the order through delivery. It is also important that the supplier be able to identify where the order is within its system.

Changes in production schedule - When changes take place in a production schedule, the purchaser must work with both the supplier and the operation function to identify a delivery schedule that is feasible for both. It is important for the purchaser to have good relations with the supplier when schedule changes are not the fault of the supplier.

Results from Expediting

There are a variety of outcomes possible from attempting to change a delivery date. Some of them are as follows:

- The supplier may speed up delivery achieving the desired outcome, or the supplier may only be able to make a partial improvement in the delivery date.
- The process will probably increase freight costs through the use of a faster form of transportation, or because discounts are lost on smaller shipments.
- Expediting may incur higher costs for goods and services either from the use of overtime, the use of more expensive outside sup-

pliers, or in the form of less time spent in acquiring goods as speed overrides all other factors.

• Over use of expediting may devalue the concept of a rush order to the point the supplier no longer believes the purchaser.

In some cases, the purchaser will not be able to change the delivery date. At that point the purchaser can cancel the order and go without, reorder from a new supplier, or wait it out. Seldom will the purchaser be able to cancel the order and go without, especially for production materials. This option is only viable for optional goods and services. Reordering from a new supplier may make the delivery even later versus waiting for the first supplier to fill the order. Waiting it out may be the only course of action if the material or service can only be provided by a sole source.

Costs of Expediting

Expediting and follow-up are non-value added activities. In addition, they may increase the costs of a transaction, sometimes significantly. One category of expediting costs is back order cost. Examples include clerical costs of tracking completion of the purchase order, increased accounting costs, and extra receiving costs. Another category of expediting costs is excess freight cost such as the need to use a faster form of transportation like truck or airfreight. Increased costs occur from loss of discounts by having to use less than truckload (LTL) or less than carload (LCL) rather than truckload or carload, and the need for extra services from the carrier. A third category of costs is increased product cost caused by selecting suppliers for proximity rather than least total cost and/or the required use of overtime by the supplier or by the purchaser's facility because material did not arrive on time. Collectively, orders requiring expediting of any kind are invariably more expensive than routine transactions. For this reason, it is essential that these situations be minimized.

Why Expediting Efforts Fail

Expediting is not always successful for a variety of reasons. Some causes are as follows:

- **Poor supplier selection** - The key to reducing expediting caused by supplier performance is in the selection of suppliers at the beginning. Focusing on price and/or quality and not looking at past delivery performance may eventually result in a greater probability of expediting.

- **System doesn't start soon enough** - Many times there is inadequate follow-up or early warnings built into the process. Contacting the supplier one week before scheduled delivery may be too late to effect a change in the delivery.

- **No formal method for tracking supplier performance** - Many organizations lack a formal system for monitoring supplier performance. If the purchaser does not measure performance and report it back to the supplier, why should the supplier perceive it as important to the purchaser?

- **Lack of communication or understanding** - The communication process may breakdown within the organization, between the purchasing organization and the supplier, throughout the supply chain, or between the organization or supplier and the carrier.

Improving Expediting Results

There are several things the purchaser can do to reduce the need for expediting and improve the results when necessary. The best place to start is supplier selection. The purchaser should carefully evaluate the supplier's production control system, tracing ability, prior performance, variation in delivery times, frequency of leadtime quote changes, and reliability of the process.

Improving communication is a vital tool for both reducing expediting activity and improving the results. Improved communication starts internally with engineering, production, marketing, receiving, and quality. Early knowledge of demand increases, product changes, production schedule changes, and quality problems may allow the purchaser to make alternative arrangements. Written policies and procedures also facilitate communication by allowing priorities to be established and avoiding known internal conflicts, stock outs, and late delivery.

An important attribute for the purchaser is persistence. Information is the heart of expediting. The purchaser must first identify what caused the need to change the delivery date. Was it internal, the supplier, or the carrier? A set of example questions for the purchaser is provided in Exhibit 8.1.

EXHIBIT 8.1
Example Expediter Questions

Who?	- Who said to halt production? - Who changed the priority? - Who else can I talk to?
What?	- What is the requirement? - What caused the problem?
When?	- When did production start? - When will it ship?
Where?	- Where is it being built? - From where did it ship? Where is it going?
Why?	- Why weren't requirements met? - Why didn't it ship as instructed?
How?	- How will you meet the schedule? - How can we change our requirements? - How can we change our quantities? - How can we change our specifications?

Another skill that is an asset to a purchaser is that of skilled negotiator. As in any negotiation, the expediter needs to have objectives and alternatives defined before talking to the supplier. The primary objective is to ensure continuity of supply. The purchaser needs to know what is critical and necessary and what is non-critical, and be willing to de-expedite other items or orders.

Sometimes the purchasing organization can use its size to help a supplier. For example, a small supplier was going to be late on an order for a large electronics company due to problems with a supplier. The electronics company approached the second-tier supplier and after negotiating on behalf of its supplier, was able to get its order moved up in priority so its supplier could deliver on time.

Secondary suppliers may provide a solution to an expediting problem as well. If there is a secondary supplier, the purchaser must have established guidelines as to when to use the alternate supplier. Decision rules could be based on factors such as the length of delay, the quantity required, and availability of the product.

Contract Problems

The types of problems that a purchaser will normally encounter can be classified into the following categories: quality, delivery and transportation, termination, payment, and dispute resolution.

Quality Problems

A common issue with suppliers can be quality problems. These can be caused by a number of factors such as specification misunderstandings, differences in acceptance testing procedures, defective materials, and process variation. The purchaser's first responsibility, when a quality problem appears, is to determine the cause of the defects. Simply replacing the defective parts will not prevent the problem from recurring. The contract should define the quality standards as well as the testing methods to determine quality. Quality tools that may be useful in measuring and improving quality include process control charts, run charts, histograms, Pareto charts, cause and effect diagrams, and process capability measures. Once the cause of the quality problem is determined, the purchaser can then make arrangements for the necessary materials to be delivered. If the supplier is certified or on a reduced inspection plan, there may be increased inspection for a period of time that will increase incoming material costs and slow down the material acceptance process.

In service contracts, it is even more important that the quality measures are well defined. Services by their very nature are intangible and subject to the perception of the decision maker. Quality assessment can benefit from the use of check sheets to standardize the factors considered in evaluating quality.

Delivery and Transportation Problems

Concerns relating to delivery and risk of loss include:

- **Intransit loss** - The purchaser would expect that suppliers would readily replace goods lost intransit where the supplier bears the risk of loss. However, in the case of problems such as shortages, it may be in the supplier's best interest not to do so. Accordingly, it is good practice to include in the contract a specific timeframe the supplier has to replace goods lost in transit.

- **Piecemeal deliveries** - An important item to include in a contract is a definition of what constitutes a complete order. An order should not be considered complete until the purchaser receives everything needed to test or use the goods or equipment.

- **Use of purchaser specified carrier** - It is common practice in today's environment for purchasers and their traffic departments to negotiate freight rates with one or two carriers to obtain significant discounts on transportation rates. Accordingly, sound practice dictates purchaser specification of the carrier and a systematic procedure of warning and charge back when freight charges are higher due to supplier failure to follow instructions.

- **Ambiguity in F.O.B. point** - Purchasers should remove any ambiguity in F.O.B. points by clearly designating exactly where the risk of loss will transfer. Suppose a contract for delivery at the purchaser's plant in Portland, Oregon, was written F.O.B. Portland and that the loss occurred just inside the city limits. A case could be made that the destination point was reached and that the purchaser had risk of loss, though the goods never actually reached the purchaser. Similarly, if a supplier has goods shipped from some other point, F.O.B. origin contracts may involve shipping costs much higher than from the supplier's address to which the contract is made. For example, the purchaser is on the West coast, the supplier is headquartered in the Midwest and the goods are shipped from the East coast.

- **Over/under shipments** - The purchasing organization should have a policy regarding the treatment of overage or underage on shipments. Receiving a greater quantity than ordered can generate extra costs whether it is kept or returned to the supplier. If the excess material is kept, there will be storage costs, tracking costs, and possibly the costs involved in disposing of the material at a later date. If the excess goods are returned to the supplier, there will be extra handling and tracking costs.
  If less than the required quantity is received, the purchaser must first decide whether to accept the order and back order the

remainder, accept the order and close the order, or reject the order completely. If the order is accepted, the purchaser will need to contact the supplier to determine when or if the missing material will be received. If the order is to be closed, the supplier must be notified not to ship the missing material. If the order is rejected completely, the purchaser needs to ascertain how the missing materials will be replaced.

- **Freight claims** - It is the receiving department's responsibility to inspect incoming material for possible freight damage. Possible indications of freight damage include damaged shipping containers, shock indicator labels on the packaging, scratches, dents, and similar damage to the goods. If the goods were purchased F.O.B. origin, then it is the purchasing manager's responsibility to notify the carrier to begin the settlement process. If the goods were purchased F.O.B. destination, then the purchasing manager will need to notify the supplier that the goods are being rejected due to freight damage. The supplier will then work with the carrier to settle the damage claim.

Termination

Termination occurs when either the purchaser or supplier, exercising a power created by agreement or law, ends a contract for reasons other than breach. Upon termination, all executory obligations are discharged, but rights or obligations based on prior performance or breach survive. Cancellation differs from termination in that it implies cause and does not excuse the "causing" party from damages resulting from its failure to perform.

Terminating for convenience - The UCC does not provide a right to cancel for convenience. Therefore, any such right must result from agreement between the parties and is usually contained in a termination for convenience clause. Still, the UCC requires that all such actions be fair and taken in good faith. For example, terminations for convenience usually involve payment for executed performance, and may include profits for the whole contract.

Note that the federal government, in accordance with regulations, can terminate a contract for its convenience at any time, with or without cause. Furthermore, in government contracts, suppliers cannot realize profits on that portion of the contract not performed.

Terminating for default - This typically results in a cancellation, as the implication is that of breach. If, after a contract is formed, either party fails or refuses to perform as agreed and it is not excused from performance by law, that party is considered to have breached the contract (see Chapter 7 for a discussion of purchaser and supplier rights and obligations when a breach occurs).

Payment

Prompt payment to suppliers is a key factor in an effective purchaser/supplier relationship. However, the timeliness of payments must be considered in relation to an organization's cash flow requirements. Most organizations try to balance their receivable and payable days outstanding to ensure sufficient cash flow to operate.

An effective method for providing suppliers with interim compensation during a long-term contract is to offer progress or milestone payments. To minimize the risk associated with offering such payments, the purchaser should tie them to tangible events that are easily verifiable, such as completion of the foundation of a building or purchase, receipt, and payment for major equipment. Mutually acceptable criteria should be established in writing at the onset of the contract, in order to avoid any confusion as to what event triggers payment to the supplier. The contract may stipulate that satisfactory completion of the entire task is required, or else the purchaser may recoup funds already expended. At times, third-party inspectors can be used to verify specific progress.

Not linking payments to discernible events presents a significant risk to the purchaser. The supplier may be receiving payments, but may not be proceeding in a manner that executes the contract on a timely basis. To protect against nonperformance by the supplier, the purchaser may schedule regular site visits to monitor progress. The purchaser should also document the organization's expectations at various stages in the production or delivery of the service and communicate those in advance to the supplier. A well-written statement of work is the most effective tool for ensuring supplier completion of the work.

Dispute Resolution

There are a number of options available (often stipulated in the contract) to the purchaser to settle disputes with the supplier without going to court. Alternative approaches include arbitration, mediation, conciliation, summary jury trial, and the mini-trial. These are summarized below and compared in Exhibit 8.2.[2]

- **Arbitration** - In arbitration, the parties present their cases to one or more arbitrators who, after hearing the evidence, decide how the case should be settled. The decision is binding on the parties and is enforceable through the courts. Unlike litigation, arbitration cases are private. They can also be less costly, be handled more quickly than other methods, and do not involve evidentiary rules, discovery, or appeals.
- **Mediation** - Mediation involves a neutral third person who encourages and facilitates the resolution of a dispute between two or more parties. The objective of this informal and nonadversarial process is to aid the parties in reaching a mutually agreeable solution. The process procedures are determined by the parties involved and can include private meetings with the mediator, exchanging documents, and expert testimony. Even if mediation does not solve the dispute, it can be a cost-effective way to understand the other side's position.
- **Conciliation** - A conciliator makes a nonbinding recommendation or finding related to the facts or legal issues involved and usually suggests an appropriate resolution to the conflict.
- **Summary jury trial** - A summary jury trial is a nonbinding process where attorneys for both sides briefly present their cases to a jury that gives an advisory decision. Both parties retain their rights to a full trial.
- **Mini-trial** - A mini-trial is a formalized settlement process where attorneys make short opening statements to senior management executives with full settlement authority. The executives then discuss a settlement. The process is voluntary and private.

EXHIBIT 8.2

Comparison of Alternative Dispute Resolution Techniques

	Arbitration	Mediation	Conciliation	Summary Jury Trial	Mini-Trial
Binding on all parties ?	Yes	No	No	No	No
Legally enforceable?	Yes	No	No	No	No
Results private?	Yes	Yes	Yes	No	Yes
Formal or informal process?	Formal	Informal	Informal	Formal	Formal
Adversarial?	Yes	No	No	Yes	Yes
Who presides over the process?	Third party	Third party	Third party	Jurors	Senior Management Panel and Third party
When to use?	Desire a rapid and binding resolution	Desire to promote joint problem-solving and maintain positive supplier relations	To determine if the factual or legal issues in dispute are in your favor	Provide an advance assessment of what a jury might do	Useful in cases dealing with patent infringement, government contracts, product liability, antitrust, and construction cases

Key Points

1. The goals of contract administration include ensuring the purchaser and supplier fulfill the contract requirements, resolve any problems that may arise, and maintain accurate documentation.
2. Activities the contract administrator may be involved in include post award conferences, supplier orientation, controlling contract work, monitoring contract compliance, fulfilling documentation

requirements, auditing supplier financial requirements, dealing with change orders, and closing the contract.

3. The purchasing manager may become involved in expediting changes in delivery dates as well as following up and monitoring supplier progress toward on-time delivery.

4. Common expediting issues include overdue orders, back orders, sole source suppliers, rush orders, and changes in production schedules.

5. Causes of failures of expediting activities include poor supplier selection, late intervention, lack of tracking, and poor communication.

6. Opportunities for improving expediting results include supplier selection, improving internal and external communication, negotiating, and use of secondary suppliers.

7. Problems the purchaser may encounter include quality, delivery and transportation, termination, payments, and disputes.

Questions for Review

1. What are the objectives of contract administration?
2. What are the various activities involved in contract administration?
3. What is the difference between expediting and follow-up?
4. Why do organizations expedite?
5. Why do expediting efforts fail?
6. What can purchasing do to reduce the need for expediting and improve expediting results?
7. What are common types of contract problems the purchaser may encounter?
9. What alternatives does the purchaser have for resolving disputes?

For Additional Information

Anderson, R. and M. Aspuro. "Effective Contract Administration," *NAPM InfoEdge*, (2:10), June 1997

Bigelow, R. "Project: Purchasing," *Purchasing Today®*, December 1998, p. 32.

Blitman, B.A. "Under the Umbrella of Alternative Dispute Resolution," *Purchasing Today®*, February 1996, pp. 16-17.

Crowder, M.A. "Project Management," *NAPM InfoEdge*, (4:2), October 1998

Endnotes

1. Bigelow, R. "Project: Purchasing," *Purchasing Today®*, December 1998, p. 32.
2. Blitman, B.A. "Under the Umbrella of Alternative Dispute Resolution," *Purchasing Today®*, February 1996, pp. 16-17.

CHAPTER 9

THE FUTURE OF THE PURCHASING PROCESS: WHERE DO WE GO FROM HERE?

Chapter Objectives

- Identify environmental trends that will affect the purchasing process.
- Identify trends in electronic commerce and the effects on the purchasing process.
- Identify developing trends in supply management and determine how they will change the purchasing process.
- Identify purchasing's involvement and role in cross-functional teams and the role of teams in the purchasing process.

Introduction

"The most significant trend that will affect the world for decades to come is the willingness of the populace to expect, accept, and even demand, change."[1] In May 1998, NAPM and the Center for Advanced Purchasing Studies released a study entitled The Future of Purchasing and Supply: A Five- and Ten-Year Forecast. In that study, 18 initiatives of concern to purchasing executives were identified. The relationship of these initiatives to the purchasing process can be sorted into four categories as shown in Exhibit 9.1 (Exhibit 9.1 also shows where each of the initiatives interacts with the purchasing process).

The purpose of this chapter is to explore some of the anticipated changes in the purchasing process. This chapter will examine the changing environment of purchasing, the future of technology, supply management issues, and purchasing strategy development.

EXHIBIT 9.1
Forecast Initiatives and the Purchasing Process

	Requisition Process	Identify Potential Sources	Develop Solicitation Proposal	Evaluate Proposals	Evaluate Suppliers	Develop Contract	Manage Contract
Purchasing Environment							
1. Tactical purchasing	X	X			X		
2. Process uncoupling	X	X			X		
3. Third-party purchasing		X			X		
4. Competitive bidding/negotiations			X		X		
Technology							
1. Electronic commerce	X	X			X		
2. Demand-pull purchasing	X	X			X		
Supply Management							
1. Strategic sourcing	X	X	X	X	X		
2. Supply chain partner selection and contribution	X	X	X	X	X		X
3. Relationship management		X	X			X	X
4. Global supplier development		X	X			X	X
5. Virtual supply chain	X	X	X		X		
6. Source development		X	X	X	X	X	
7. Strategic supplier alliances			X		X	X	X
8. Complexity management							X
Purchasing Strategy Development							
1. Strategic cost management	X	X	X	X	X	X	X
2. Performance measurement	X		X	X	X		X
3. Negotiation strategy		X	X	X	X	X	

The Changing Environment

New orientations, skills, and roles will be required in purchasing. Tomorrow's purchasers will need a broad-based business and strategic perspective. Purchasing spends from 40 to 60 percent of an organization's dollars.[2] If the organization does not have talented people with a complete understanding of purchasing in those positions, it is missing an opportunity to improve its bottomline. Southern Natural Gas, based in Birmingham, Alabama, has created the title of alliance manager. The alliance manager is responsible for managing the relationship with the alliance partners including agreement terms, performance measures, and contract changes.[3]

The automation of the tactical purchasing processes coupled with increased use of consortia and third-party purchasing will potentially cause reductions in purchasing staffs. The remaining staff will spend more time managing supplier relationships, evaluating suppliers, and developing new suppliers. Bosch Automation Technology in Racine, Wisconsin, contracted with a supplier to provide an integrated supply service for all non-production items. The supplier owns the inventory and provides the inventory control software as well. Cost savings are estimated in the 20 percent range and Bosch was able to eliminate 70 MRO suppliers.[4]

In the public procurement area, competitive bidding will still be the normal mode of operation. With the continued consolidation of the supply base, negotiation will remain an important part of the purchasing process.

With an increasing focus on time-to-market, many of the product development tasks will need to run in parallel. Thus, purchasing will simultaneously be involved in the design process, the sourcing process, and the acquisition of goods and services for the same product or service.

The area of "green" purchasing will continue to grow in importance. Purchasers must be conscious of the hazardous and regulated materials used by their organizations. They will need to understand how all materials are disposed of, and how all material and components affect the environment in both their manufacture and application. Purchasing can make major contributions to cost reduction by finding new materials and components that cost less to use, make the product or service more cost effective, and lower the costs of recycling or disposal.

How will these potential changes affect the purchasing process?

- The trends in green purchasing will affect the development of specifications that are earth- friendly. The identification of suppliers that use recycled materials will also become important to purchasers. Purchasing will need to work closely with engineering and suppliers to facilitate this process.
- The automation of tactical purchasing will put more importance on the development of alliances and on supplier evaluation and selection. Purchasing's responsibility will be to establish the contracts and systems users will need to access.
- Purchasers will need to develop and improve their communication and facilitation skills as they become more involved with teams and the many phases of the purchasing process.

Technology

The future of electronic commerce lies in the Internet. Not only will this technology continue to be used for order tracking, funds transfer, receipt acknowledgment, and small purchases, but it will also grow with the use of intranets and extranets to cover a majority of purchasing's transactions.

Internally, the use of intranets will grow as more organizations use technology for online catalogs, user ordering, contract information, specifications, and supplier information. Users will be able to access custom catalogs for their organization, select the desired products, and generate a requisition that is processed automatically.

Externally, security will continue to be of concern. The Internet will see increased audio and video activity allowing face-to-face meetings without leaving the office. Suppliers will be able to access production plans online or will receive orders through Electronic Data Interchange (EDI), the computer-to-computer exchange of data in a standardized format, using the Internet rather than the traditional value-added networks (VANs). This will allow even small organizations to use EDI in a cost-effective manner.[5]

Another feature of electronic commerce will be the increased use of electronic auctions. Auctions will allow purchasers to find supply capacity at the lowest possible prices while identifying suppliers with excess capacity or surplus inventory. Example online auctions are TradeOut.com (www.tradeout.com), Biddersnet (www.biddersnet.com), and FreeMarkets (www.freemarkets.com).

An example of what the future may hold can be found in recent announcements by Ford and General Motors (GM). Ford and GM announced they are developing Internet-based trading exchanges to source all of their inputs. In Ford's case that amounts to $80 billion per year and $300 billion throughout the extended supply chain. For GM, the total amounts to $500 billion. There is even talk of extending the process all the way to the consumer.[6]

Globalization will be integrated with information technology as electronic commerce knows no borders. Electronic commerce allows the purchaser to identify, evaluate, select, and place an order without regard to time zones.

What effect will these technology changes have on the purchasing process?

- The automation of MRO purchasing will relieve purchasers and user departments from paperwork, allowing them to spend more time working with suppliers to improve processes. The downside is a possible reduction in purchasing employment.
- The development of an Internet-based EDI system that will allow smaller organizations to have access to EDI. This will facilitate the sharing of information across the supply chain, which will improve the access to information about supplier and product capabilities.

Supply Management

Supply chain partner selection processes are becoming more important and integrated. Purchasers are not only looking at the typical issues of quality, past delivery performance, financial stability, and process competencies; they are starting to develop an understanding of the supplier's market, market share, trends in the industry, and the strategic plans and research investments.

Cisco Systems used strategically selected supplier relationships to begin a build-to-order program using extranets that suppliers use to monitor and fulfill customer orders. This cooperative relationship with suppliers, combined with a high percentage of production out-sourcing, has allowed Cisco to reduce costs, quadruple output with-out investing in additional facilities, and reduce new product intro-duction times by two-thirds.[7]

The goal of the strategic sourcing process is to select a limited number of alliances that will help create market advantage. Some of the philosophies that organizations will want to consider as they seek to identify potential alliances include commonality of purpose, abili-ty of processes to interface seamlessly across organizations, willing-ness to communicate, and willingness to interact at multiple levels of the organizations.

Increased global trade will necessitate the development of global alliances, increase countertrade activity, and fuel the need for cross-cultural skills. This trend will work counter to the desire to reduce the supply base. It will also work against the objective of reducing both new product time to market and general product leadtime by stretch-ing out the supply line geographically.

What effect will these supply management changes have on the purchasing process?

- The identification and development of supplier alliances will reduce the time spent on identifying sources and will increase the time spent evaluating and managing supplier relationships. The development of an alliance takes a great deal of time and effort that can be wasted if the wrong supplier is chosen.
- The concept of managing a supply chain will make the selection of suppliers more complex as the purchaser will need to evaluate the potential supplier's suppliers.

Purchasing Strategy Development

Cost and cost reduction will continue to be a key component of an organization's strategy. Cost reduction will still be a major empha-sis for purchasing, but the trend will be to look at the total cost to the organization and even potentially to the entire supply chain. A greater number of organizations will adopt activity-based costing in order to better understand both the organization's and the supplier's costs.

In order for purchasing to become more strategic, the performance measures used to evaluate purchasing and suppliers must reflect the organization's mission and strategies. The current tactical oriented measures are inadequate and often lead the purchaser to make the wrong decisions.

What effect will these supply management changes have on the purchasing process?

- In order to encourage purchasers to think strategically, the criteria used to evaluate their performance must be changed. You get what you measure; therefore, purchasers must be evaluated on their contribution to the organization's mission and objectives. This will cause changes in their interactions with suppliers, their choice of suppliers, and their analysis of alternative supplier proposals.
- In order to help organizations remain cost competitive, purchasing will need to use total cost of ownership in the selection and evaluation of suppliers and proposals.

Key Points

1. The skills of the purchaser will need to move toward understanding the strategic issues in purchasing.
2. Purchasing performance measures will need to move away from a tactical to a strategic orientation.
3. There will be an increased focus on the development of specifications and in the selection of suppliers that are environmentally friendly.
4. Electronic commerce and technology will reduce the cost of MRO purchases through process automation.
5. Increased use of EDI will facilitate the transfer of information up and down the supply chain.
6. Strategic sourcing and the formal development of supply policies will become necessary to remain competitive.
7. Increased globalization of business will cause purchasing to develop longer supply lines.

8. Purchasers will need to improve their facilitation and communication skills.

Questions for Review

1. What steps in the purchasing process will be affected by green purchasing?
2. What changes will need to be made in purchasing performance measures?
3. How will electronic commerce change MRO purchasing?
4. What value will Internet-based EDI add to the purchasing process?
5. What philosophies should a purchaser look for in selecting a supplier to participate in a strategic alliance?

For Additional Information

Carter, P.L., J.R. Carter, R.M. Monczka, T.H. Slaight, and A.J. Swan. *The Future of Purchasing and Supply: A Five- and Ten-Year Forecast*, Center for Advanced Purchasing Studies, Tempe, AZ, 1998.

Carter, P.L. "The Future of Purchasing and Supply: Electronic Commerce in the New Millennium," *Purchasing Today®*, August 1999, p. 33.

Chambers, G., S. Alfson, B. Holcomb, R. Earle, J. Holec, Y. Burke, A. Brown, M.J. Centron, and J.F. Coates. "Where Do We go from Here?," *Purchasing Today®*, February 1997, pp. 46-48.

Duffy, R.J. "The Future of Purchasing and Supply: A Five- and Ten-Year Forecast — The Reactions," *Purchasing Today®*, May 1998, pp. 40-44.

Duffy, R.J. "The Future of Purchasing and Supply: Supply Chain Partner Selection in Contribution," *Purchasing Today®*, November 1999, p. 41.

Moyer, M.J. "21st Century Macro Trends: Impact on Purchasing/Material," *Proceedings of the 1994 NAPM International Purchasing Conference*, NAPM, Tempe, AZ, 1994, pp. 1-4.

Pye, C. "Internet-Based EDI: Another Option for Electronic Communication?," *Purchasing Today®*, December 1997, pp. 38-40.

Slaight, T.H. "The Future of Purchasing and Supply: Strategic Sourcing," *Purchasing Today®*, October 1999, p. 43.

Endnotes

1. Duffy, R.J. "The Future of Purchasing and Supply: A Five- and Ten-Year Forecast — The Results," *Purchasing Today®*, May 1998, p. 32.
2. See Industry Purchasing Performance Benchmarks at the Center for Advanced Purchasing Studies Web site, www.capsresearch.org.
3. Duffy, R.J. "The Future of Purchasing and Supply: A Five- and Ten-Year Forecast — The Reactions," *Purchasing Today®*, May 1998, p. 40.
4. Duffy, May 1998, p. 44.
5. Pye, C. "Internet-Based EDI: Another Option for Electronic Communication?," *Purchasing Today®*, December 1997, pp. 38-40.
6. Tait, N., L. Kehoe, and T. Burt. "US Car Monoliths Muscle in on the Internet Revolution," *Financial Times*, November 8, 1999, p. 22.
7. Slaight, T.H. "The Future of Purchasing and Supply: Strategic Sourcing," *Purchasing Today®*, October 1999, p. 43.

AUTHOR INDEX

SUBJECT INDEX

liability issues, 208-209
rights of inspection, acceptance, rejection, 205-207
terms and conditions (*See* Terms and conditions)
UCC, 120, 184-187
unauthorized purchasing, 17-18, 190-191
warranties, 183, 202-205, 231
written *versus* oral contracts, 200-201
Legal purpose, 198
Letter of intent, 201-202
Letters of credit, 87, 128, 186
Level-of-effort SOW, 33
Leverage purchases, 73
Leveraged buying, 89
Liability, 208-209
Life-cycle costing, 52-55
Life-of-product contract, 81
Liquidated damages, 208-209
Liquidity, 152-153, 157-158
Logistics, 213
LogLink, 107
Long term contracting, 7

M

Maintenance, repair, and operating supplies (MRO), 21
Malcolm Baldridge National Quality Award, 164-165
Manufacturer *versus* distributor, 84
Manufacturers Information Net, 108
Market grades, 26
MASSnet Packaging Mall, 108
Material and method-of-manufacturing specifications, 26
Material cost analysis, 61
Material costs, 44
Material Handling Industry of America, 106
Material Safety Data Sheet (MSDS), 20, 193-194
Materials budget, 21
McRAE's Blue Book, 96
Mediation, 255-256
Merchantability, 203

Metal Suppliers Online, 108
Metal Treating Institute, 106
Microsoft Corporation, 14-15, 240
Milestone payments, 254
Mini-trial, 255-256
Minority Business and Professional Yellow Pages, 108
Minority-owned business enterprise (MBE), 19-20, 85, 98
Monopolistic competition, 62
Monopoly, 62
Monopsony, 63
Moody's Industrials, 150
Motorola, 167
MRO budget, 21
MRP, 16
Multiple sourcing, 83-84

N

National Association of Accountants, 160
National Association of Purchasing Management (NAPM), 29, 97, 259
National Conference of Commissioners on Uniform State Laws, 215
National Contract Management Association (NCMA), 97
National contracts, 15
National Institute of Governmental Purchasing (NIGP), 97
Negotiation, 116-117
Nell Register, 108
Netsource Asia, 109
New price estimate, 61-62
New Vector Group, 89
Nonconforming goods, care of, 206
Northeast Utilities, 241
Notices to proceed (NTPs), 242-243
NYNEX, 89, 97

O

Obsolete/outdated specifications, 30
Occupational Safety and Health Administration (OSHA), 193
Offer, 196-197
Oil-Link, 108
Oligopolistic, 62-63

W

Walker Manufacturing, 172
Warranties, 183, 202-205, 231
Weighted point model of supplier evaluation, 173, 175
Witco Corporation, 90
Women-owned business enterprises (WBE), 19-20, 85

Workers' Compensation, 225-226
World Access NetworkDirect, 110
World Wide Web (WWW). *See* Internet

Membership Application
National Association of Purchasing Management, Inc.

Members are encouraged to join a local affiliated association. To obtain information on the affiliated association closest to you and dues information, please call NAPM Customer Service at 800/888-6276 or 480/752-6276, extension 401. Applications can also be submitted via the Internet at www.napm.org.

Please check the appropriate box:

❏ New Member ❏ Past Member NAPM ID Number (if known)

❏ I am replacing the following current member in my organization (If replacing a current member, send completed application to the affiliate.)

Member Name _____ NAPM ID# _____

Dr. Mr. Mrs. Ms. Miss _____ _____ _____ _____
(please circle) First Name MI Last Name

Title (required) _____ Organization (required) _____

Please check the preferred mailing address:

❏ BUSINESS ❏ HOME

City	State	ZIP Code	City	State	ZIP Code
Country		Postal Code	Country		Postal Code
E-Mail			E-Mail		

( ) _____ ( ) _____ ( ) _____
Business Phone Number** Fax Number** Home Phone Number **

**For international numbers, please include country and city codes.

Date of Birth (optional): ____/____/____

Industry Code (choose a 3-digit code from the list provided on page two of this application): _____ _____ _____

Number of employees at your location (please check one): ❏ under 100 ❏ 100-249 ❏ 250-499 ❏ 500-999 ❏ 1000+

Education (check highest level completed): ❏ High School ❏ Associate's ❏ Bachelor's ❏ Master's ❏ Other_____

❏ Student (estimated graduation date): _____

Are you a C.P.M.? ❏ Yes ❏ No Are you an A.P.P.? ❏ Yes ❏ No

Do you hold other professional designations? If so, please list:_____

Would you like to serve on a committee? ❏ Yes ❏ No

Are you involved in sales? If so, explain: _____

MEMBERSHIP TYPE: Please select one of the options below. See back for option details.

Option I	Option II
❏ **Regular Membership** – Includes National and local affiliate benefits. I choose to become a member through (please provide affiliate name):	❏ **Direct National Membership** – Includes National benefits only. Does not include affiliate benefits.
	NAPM Dues: $ 270.00
For dues information and District/Affiliate code, contact NAPM Customer Service at 800/888-6276 or 480/752-6276, extension 401.	Administrative Fee: $ 0.00
	TOTAL: $ 270.00
District/Affiliate Code (Code provided by NAPM): ___ / ___ ___ ___	**Method of payment (U.S. Funds Only):**
Annual NAPM/Affiliate Dues: $ _____	❏ Personal Check ❏ Organization Check
Administrative Fee: $ 20.00	❏ VISA ❏ MasterCard ❏ American Express ❏ Diners Club
Affiliate Initiation Fee: $ _____	Charge Card# _____
Other: $ _____	Exp. Date _____/_____ Amount to be Charged $ _____
TOTAL: $ _____	Cardholder Signature _____

NAPM members receive *Purchasing Today*® magazine as a $12 portion and *NAPM InfoEdge* as a $12 portion of the national membership fee.

I agree to abide by the *NAPM Bylaws, Principles and Standards of Purchasing Practice*, and *Statement of Antitrust Policy*, as stated on the back of this application. A copy of the *NAPM Bylaws* may be obtained by writing or calling NAPM Customer Service at the address and telephone number listed below.

_____ _____
Signature Date

RETURN TO:	APPROVALS FOR AFFILIATE/NAPM USE ONLY	
	NAPM _____ Date _____	51
	Affiliate _____ Date _____	SMKS1
	Other _____ Date _____	

NAPM Use Only

Amount $_____ Approval #_____ Date Entered _____ Initials _____

NAPM, P.O. Box 22160, Tempe, AZ 85285-2160 • 800/888-6276 or 480/752-6276, extension 401 • Fax 480/752-2299

STANDARD INDUSTRY CODES (SIC) — If you have responsibility for more than one industry, please use only the one three-digit code representing the major activity of the company, division, or plant for which you work. (Write the three-digit code on the reverse side of this form in the appropriate space.)

AGRICULTURE, FORESTRY, AND FISHERIES
- 010 Agricultural production - crops
- 020 Agricultural production - livestock
- 070 Agricultural services
- 080 Forestry
- 090 Fishing, hunting, trapping

MINING
- 100 Metal mining
- 120 Bituminous coal/lignite mining
- 130 Oil and gas extraction
- 140 Nonmetallic minerals, except fuels

CONTRACT CONSTRUCTION
- 150 General building contractors
- 160 Heavy construction contractors
- 170 Special trade contractors

MANUFACTURING
- 200 Food and kindred products
- 210 Tobacco manufacturers
- 220 Textile mill products
- 230 Apparel/other textile products
- 240 Lumber and wood products
- 250 Furniture and fixtures
- 260 Paper and allied products
- 270 Printing and publishing
- 280 Chemicals and allied products
- 290 Petroleum and coal products
- 300 Rubber and miscellaneous plastic products
- 310 Leather and leather products
- 320 Stone, clay, and glass products
- 330 Primary metal industries
- 340 Fabricated metal products
- 350 Machinery, except electrical

- 360 Electric/electronic equipment
- 370 Transportation equipment
- 380 Instruments and related products
- 390 Miscellaneous manufacturing industries

TRANSPORTATION, COMMUNICATION, AND UTILITY SERVICES
- 400 Railroad transportation
- 410 Local/interurban mass transit
- 420 Trucking and warehousing
- 430 U.S. Postal Service
- 440 Water transportation
- 450 Transportation by air
- 460 Pipelines, except natural gas
- 470 Transportation services
- 480 Communication
- 490 Electric, gas, and sanitary services

WHOLESALE AND RETAIL TRADE
- 500 Wholesale trade - durable goods
- 510 Wholesale trade - nondurable goods
- 520 Building materials/garden supplies
- 530 General merchandise stores
- 540 Food stores
- 550 Automotive dealers/service stations
- 560 Apparel and accessory stores
- 570 Furniture/home furnishings stores
- 580 Eating and drinking places
- 590 Miscellaneous retail

FINANCE, INSURANCE, AND REAL ESTATE
- 600 Banking
- 610 Credit agencies, except banks
- 620 Security commodity brokers/services
- 630 Insurance carriers

- 640 Insurance agents, brokers/services
- 650 Real estate
- 670 Holding/other investment offices

SERVICES
- 700 Hotel/other lodging places
- 720 Personal services
- 730 Business services
- 750 Auto repair, services/garages
- 760 Miscellaneous repair services
- 780 Motion pictures
- 790 Amusement/recreation services
- 800 Health services
- 810 Legal services
- 820 Educational services
- 830 Social services
- 840 Museums/botanical, zoological gardens
- 860 Membership organizations
- 870 Engineering/accounting/related services
- 880 Private households
- 890 Miscellaneous services

GOVERNMENT
- 910 Executive, legislative/general
- 920 Justice, public order, and safety
- 930 Finance, taxation, and monetary policy
- 940 Administration of human resources
- 950 Environmental quality/housing
- 960 Administration of economic programs
- 970 National security/international affairs

NONCLASSIFIABLE
- 999 Nonclassifiable establishments